WATERWAYS OF EAST SHROPSHIRE

THROUGH TIME

Neil Clarke

AMBERLEY

Acknowledgements

I would like to thank the following for their help in providing photographs, information and advice in the preparation of this book: Geoff Barrett, Bridgnorth Museum, Diana Clarke, Steve Dewhirst, Roger Edmundson, Ray Farlow, Allan Frost, David de Haan, Lady Harriet Hamilton, Geoff Harrison, Ironbridge Gorge Museum Trust, Kelvin Lake (I. A. Recordings), Peter Lead, Alan Lees, The National Trust (Dudmaston Hall), David Pannett, Malcolm Peel, John Powell, Dennis Price, Shrewsbury & Newport Canals Trust, Shropshire Archives, Joanne Smith, Kevin Skidmore, Barrie Trinder, Andy Tidy, John and Ida White, and the Howard Williams collection. A number of the photographs are from my own collection, taken over the last half-century.

Every attempt has been made to trace copyright where appropriate, and apologies are extended to anyone who may have inadvertently been omitted from these acknowledgements.

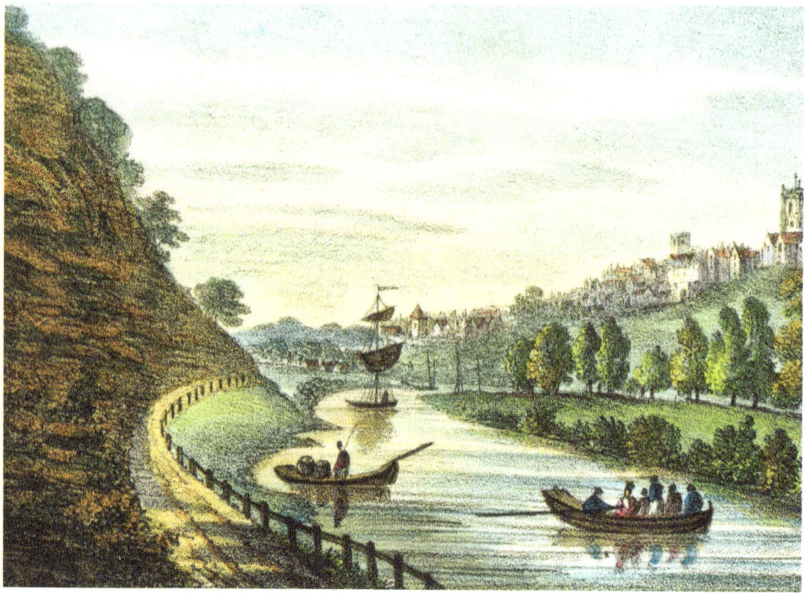

Vessels on the River Severn above Bridgnorth, around 1800.

First published 2015

Amberley Publishing
The Hill, Stroud, Gloucestershire, GL5 4EP
www.amberley-books.com

ISBN 978 1 4456 4488 2 (print)
ISBN 978 1 4456 4508 7 (ebook)

British Library Cataloguing in Publication Data.
A catalogue record for this book is available from the British Library.

Typesetting by Amberley Publishing.
Printed in Great Britain.

Contents

Acknowledgements 2

Introduction 4

Part I

1 The River Severn 5

Part II

2 The Canal Network 46

3 The First Canal 47

4 William Reynolds' Private Canals 53

5 The Shropshire Canal 61

6 The Shrewsbury Canal 76

7 The Last Canal 90

Introduction

At the heart of East Shropshire lie the historic Ironbridge Gorge and the 'new town' of Telford. The abundance of fertile land in the surrounding area has supported farming activity that stimulated the growth of the market towns of Wellington, Newport, Shifnal, Bridgnorth and Much Wenlock.

Bisecting the area, the Severn was for centuries East Shropshire's main transport artery, linking it to other parts of the country. Together with the innovative canal system that developed in the area during the late eighteenth and early nineteenth centuries, the river was essential to the growth of the coal, iron and clay industries on the Coalbrookdale Coalfield, which put East Shropshire in the forefront of the Industrial Revolution.

Today, in addition to any part they play in supplying water or providing drainage, the waterways of East Shropshire – the River Severn and the few remaining sections of canal – are used mainly for recreational activities. This is a far cry from their role in the past, and reflects the decline of these navigations following the arrival of standard gauge railways in the middle of the nineteenth century. It was not until the following century that a modest use was found for the area's waterways and an interest taken in their history. In addition to the licensed fishing along stretches of the river, boat hire became available at Bridgnorth and seasonal boat trips at Ironbridge. Telford Development Corporation, in partnership with the Ironbridge Gorge Museum Trust (IGMT), restored river and canal features in the Ironbridge Gorge area. Further, the Shrewsbury & Newport Canals Trust has been set up with the aim of reopening some 24 miles of canal between Norbury Junction and Shrewsbury.

This book covers pictorially the many aspects of East Shropshire's waterways history, from earlier times to present day restoration schemes, and at the time of the centenary of the First World War, it is of particular relevance to point out the area's two waterway bridges which also act as war memorials.

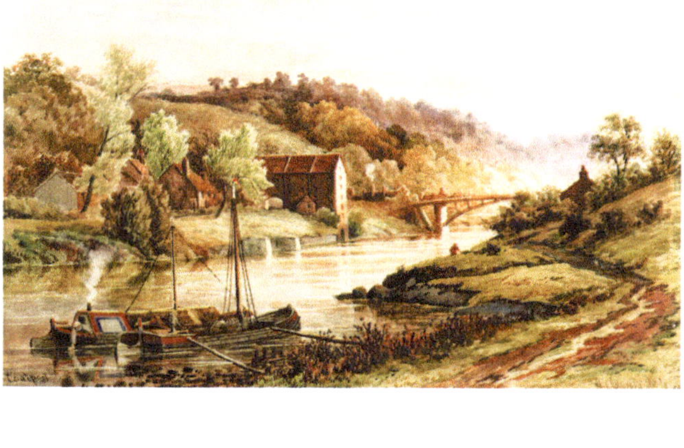

The place where the waterways of East Shropshire met – Coalport. This watercolour by H. Clements is dated 1884 but it portrays an earlier period, when coal was transhipped from tub boats on the canal (on the level of the large warehouse) to barges and trows on the river. It is the only illustration known of a canal narrow boat this far up the River Severn.

Part I

1

The River Severn

Physical features

At 220 miles, Britain's longest river, the Severn, rises in the Cambrian Mountains of mid-Wales and reaches the sea in the Bristol Channel. Originally, its headwaters flowed northward to the Dee Estuary; but, with the damming effect of an ice-age glacier and the eventual outflow of the resulting lake of melt water, the river's course took a southward turn through what is now Shropshire, beyond which it joined another river flowing south to the sea. The outcome of all this in the present Shropshire landscape is a meandering river where the melt-water lake was originally formed, a gorge that is the result of the overflow of melt water and subsequent erosion and a more open valley beyond that. These three aspects of the character of the river can clearly be seen in East Shropshire in the 18 or so miles between Atcham and Bridgnorth.

(Note – References to the river's left bank and right bank are as going downstream towards its estuary.)

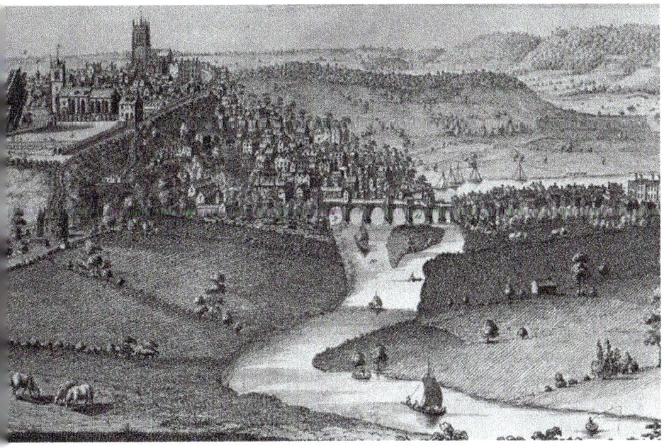

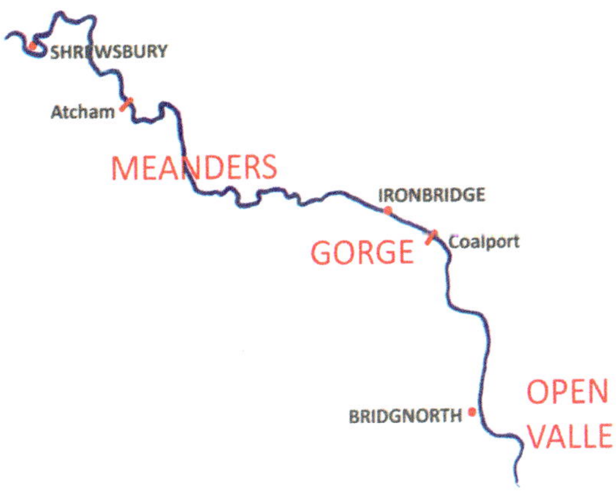

Left: This early eighteenth-century view of the River Severn at Bridgnorth encapsulates many of the features described in the following sections of Part 1.

Right: Map showing the main features of the River Severn in East Shropshire.

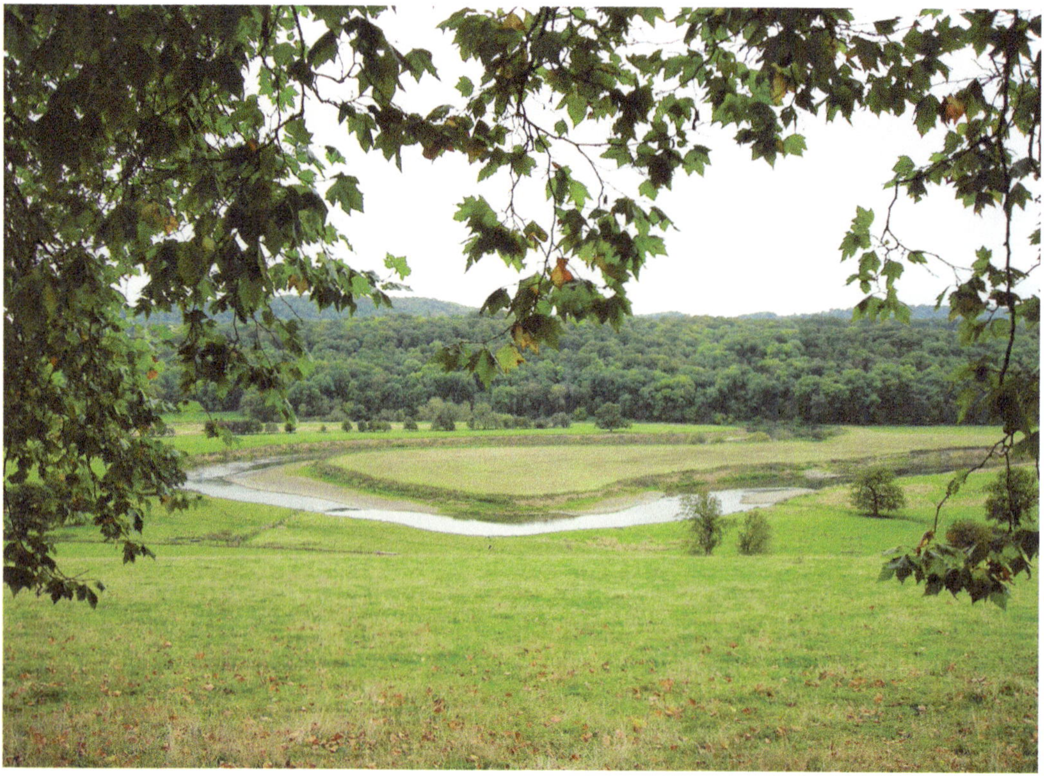

Meanders

What is considered to be a classic example of meander formation, albeit in the middle course of a river, is the S-bend on the Severn near Leighton (above). The lower view (1971) shows the meandering river as it approaches Buildwas and the Ironbridge Gorge, with Ironbridge power station on the right bank.

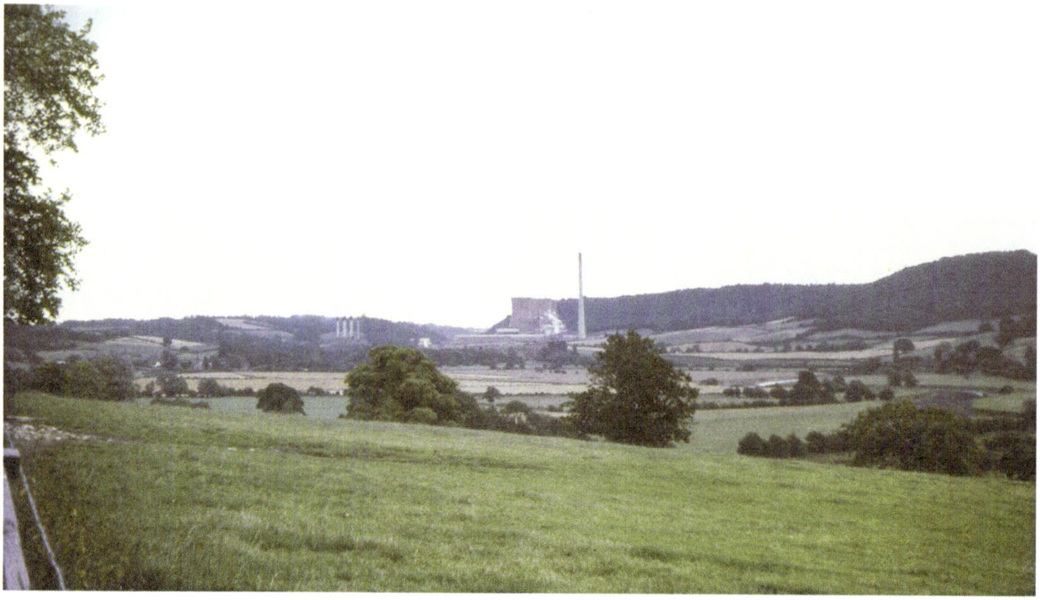

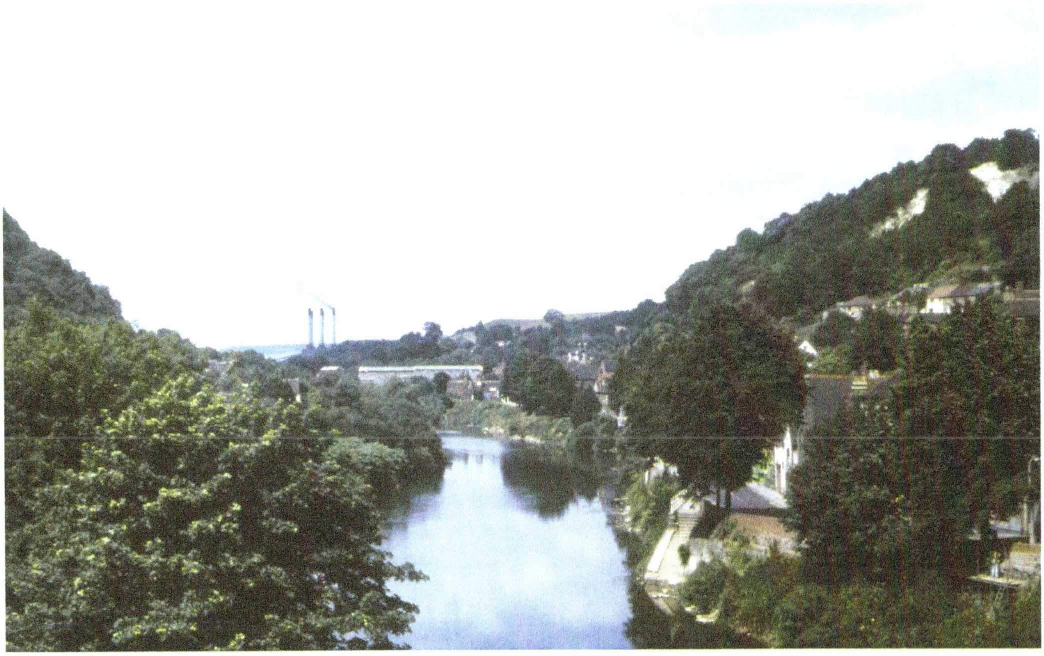

Gorge

Above: The glacial overflow channel, and subsequent erosion of the limestone ridge, formed the Ironbridge Gorge. Looking upstream, the view from the Iron Bridge shows Benthall Edge and Lincoln 'lime-kiln' Hill.

Below: The view from the bridge looking downstream shows the river approaching the Free Bridge and rapids at Jackfield. The hut on the bank of the river, partly hidden by bushes, is where the Rogers family made their coracles.

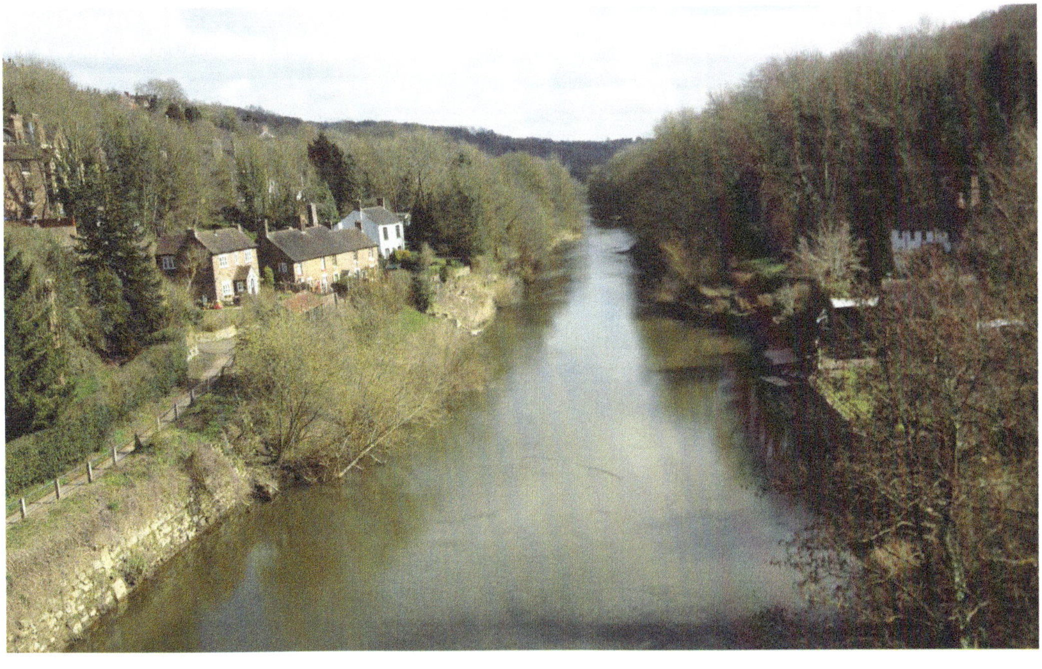

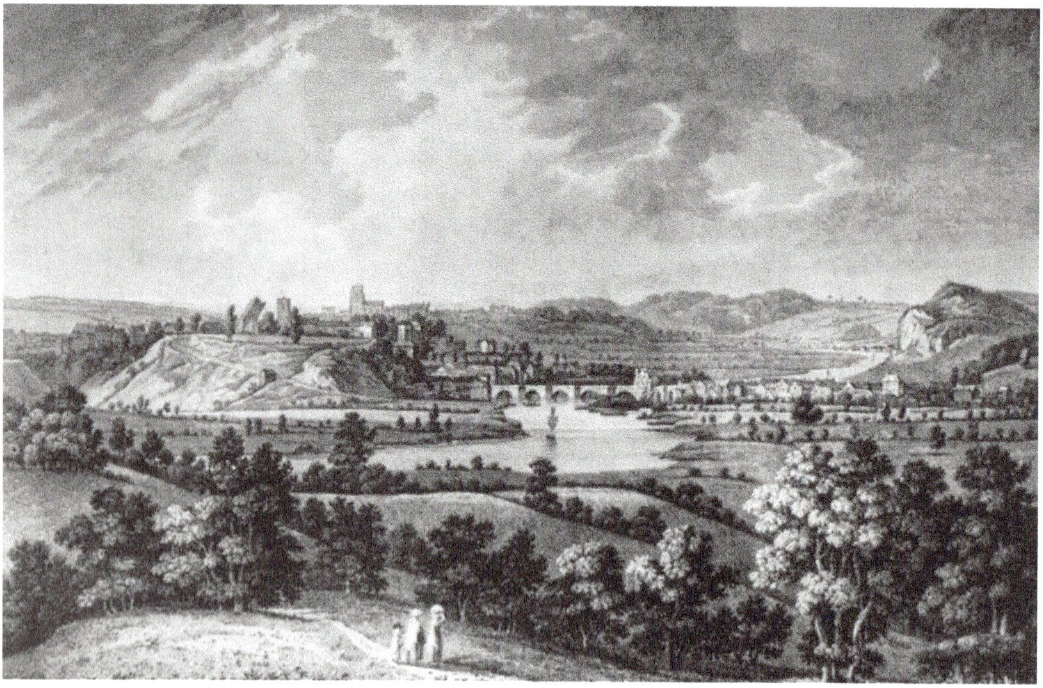

Open Valley

Above: As the river reaches Bridgnorth, its valley begins to open out. The painting by Joseph Farrington (1788), showing the town from the south-east, looks upstream towards the gorge. *Below*: The view downstream of Bridgnorth is from Castle Walk, a promenade said by Charles I in 1642 to be 'the finest in his dominions'.

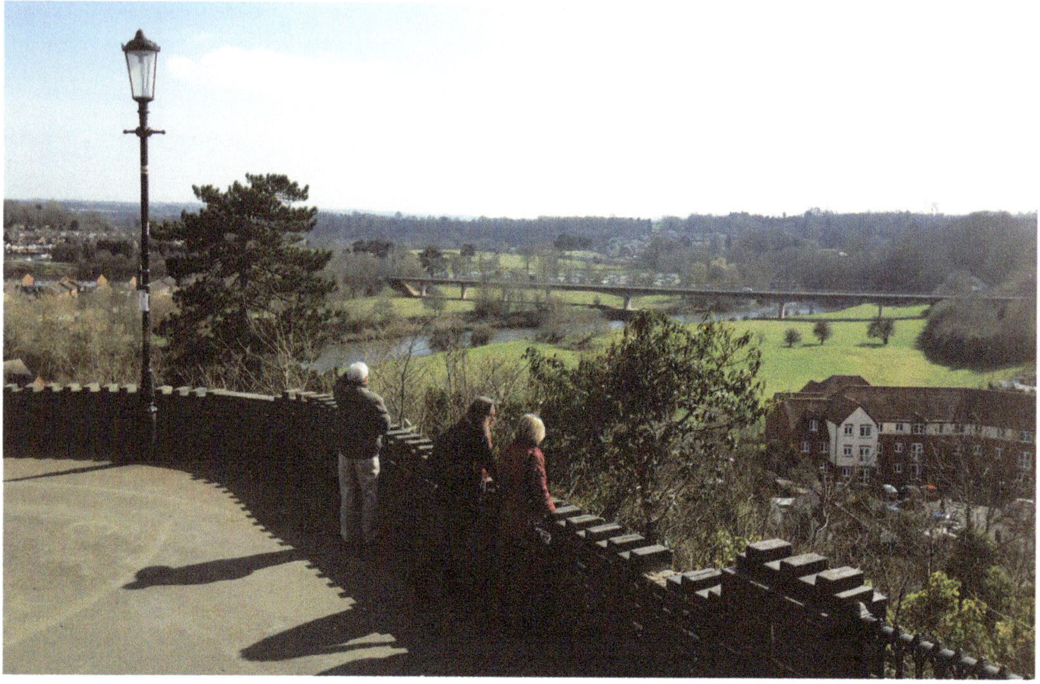

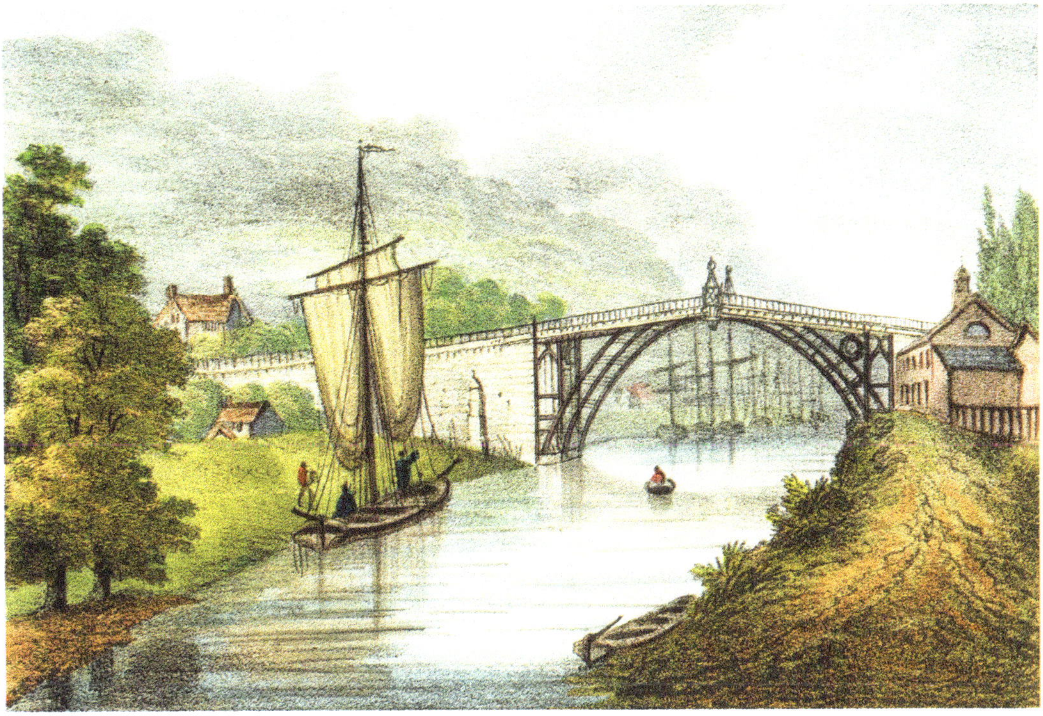

Samuel Ireland's depiction of the Iron Bridge in the 1790s shows a number of vessels upstream of the bridge, possibly awaiting a 'fresh' (high water following rain in the Welsh hills) to carry them downstream.

Navigation and Trade

The valley of the Severn has been a routeway for thousands of years and the river itself was an important transport artery until the end of the nineteenth century. The Roman city of Wroxeter was built on the left bank of the river and although there is little evidence of a wharf there, it would be surprising if the Romans had not used the link by river with their colonia at Gloucester. During the Viking raids on this country, the Danish armies that reached Bridgnorth in the years AD 895 and 910 might well have either sailed up the Severn or been supplied there by boat. The foundation and growth of Bridgnorth from the twelfth century onwards was dependent on its position on the river, as was the Cistercian abbey established at Buildwas in 1135. In the thirteenth century, the monks of the abbey secured the right to load the wool they produced on their estates on to barges at Cressage. From the medieval period the Severn was navigable as far upstream as Pool Quay, near Welshpool, in Montgomeryshire, some 160 miles from its estuary. During this period the river's role as a major transport artery, at a time when usable roads were few and far between, had been enhanced by laws freeing the 'King's High Stream of Severn' from tolls.

Increased use of the river from Elizabethan times onwards stimulated and sustained the growth of the coal, iron and clay industries of East Shropshire, which reached their peak during the Industrial Revolution. An account of barge traffic on the Severn in the middle of the eighteenth century indicates a concentration of vessels and owners in the Ironbridge Gorge, where numerous wharves and several boat-building yards were operating at the beginning of the following century. It was only after the opening of the Severn Valley Railway in 1862 that traffic on the river began to decline.

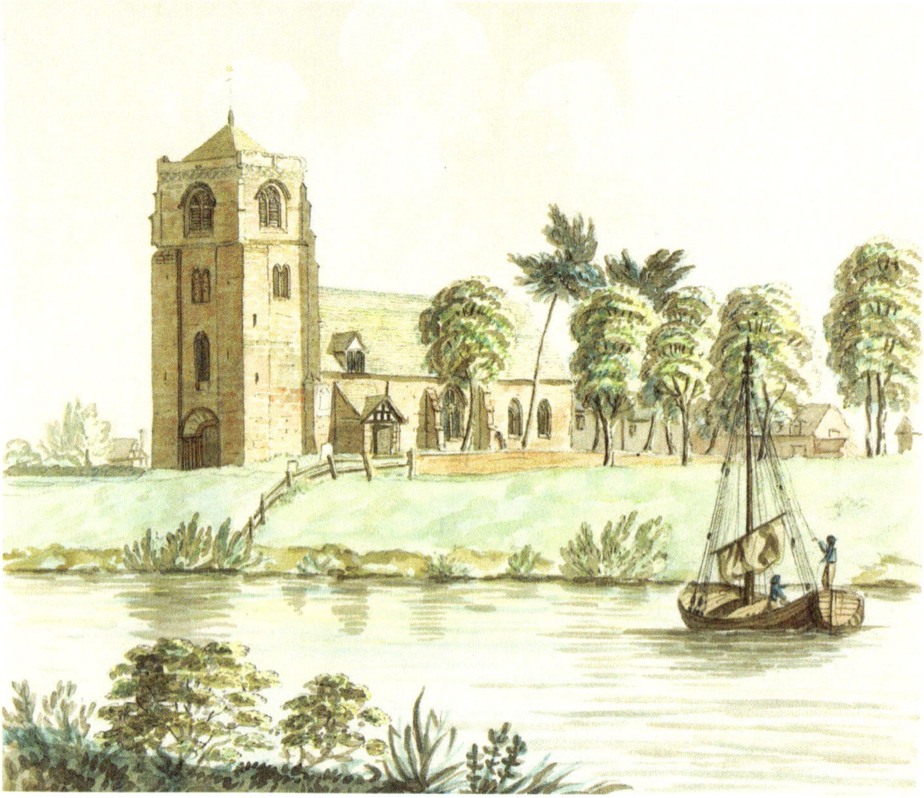

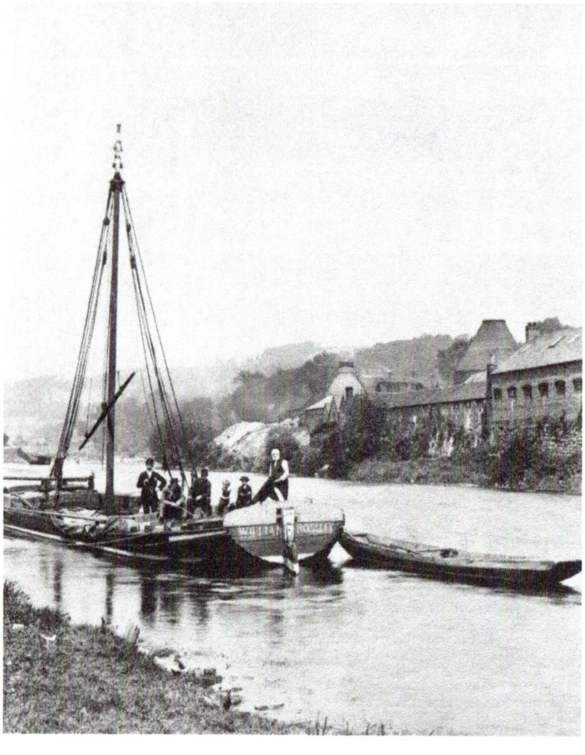

Barges and Trows

The smaller vessels on the Upper Severn (variously called trows, barges and frigates) usually went no further downstream than Gloucester, but the larger ones (trows) could safely navigate the dangerous waters of the estuary. The vessels were of similar construction, clinker-built (i.e. overlapping planking), with D-shaped sterns and masts that could be lowered to pass under bridges. Examples are that depicted in the Revd Edward Williams' painting of Atcham church in 1788 (above), and the *William*, moored opposite Coalport China Works in about 1881 (below).

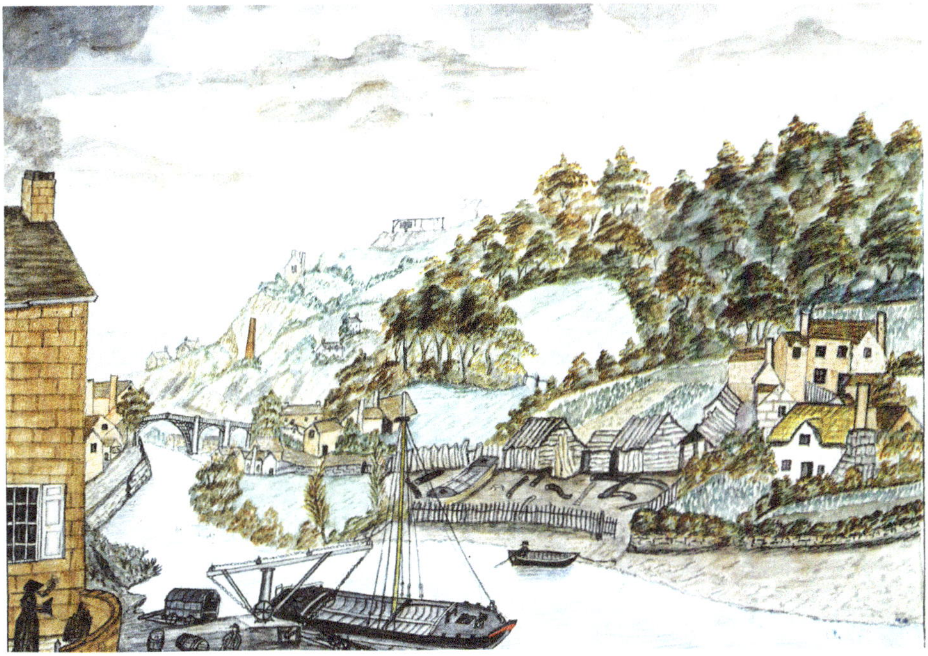

Boat Building

During the eighteenth century, barges were constructed at the Bower Yard (Benthall), at several sites in Jackfield (Broseley), at the Rovings (Barrow) and in three yards in Bridgnorth. By 1851, only two barge builders remained: Edward Gother at Benthall and William Oakes in Bridgnorth. The early nineteenth-century painting (above) includes a vessel under construction at Bower Yard; and the late 1850s photograph (below) shows boats moored at the boat-building premises of Edward Gother, which had finally closed by 1871.

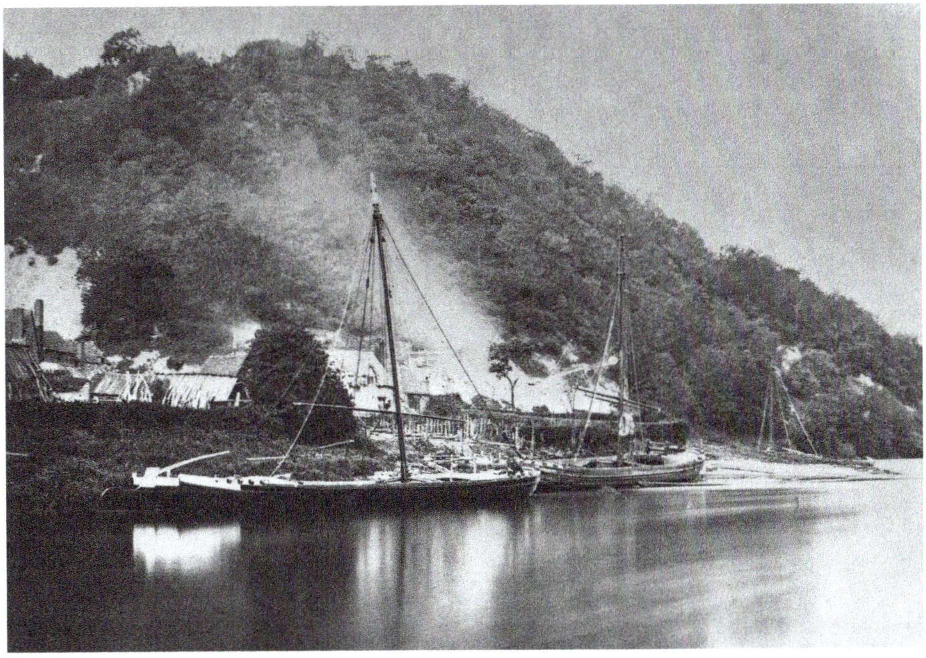

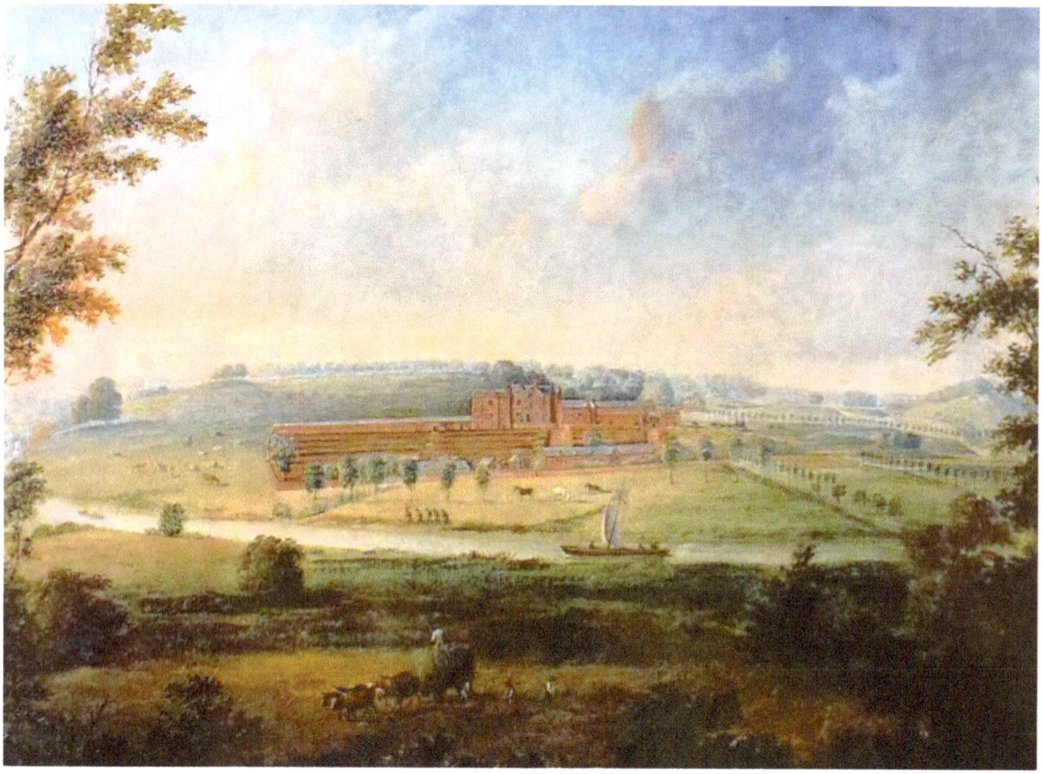

Bow Haulers

Vessels travelling downstream went with the current, using their sails when winds were favourable. Craft also used sails going upstream, when they could, but most needed gangs of men, known as bow haulers, to pull the vessel over particularly difficult stretches of the river. The illustrations show barges being hauled upriver, at Apley (above) and under the Iron Bridge (below), with the hauling line attached to the mast. When a towpath was completed in the early nineteenth century, most vessels were pulled upstream by horses.

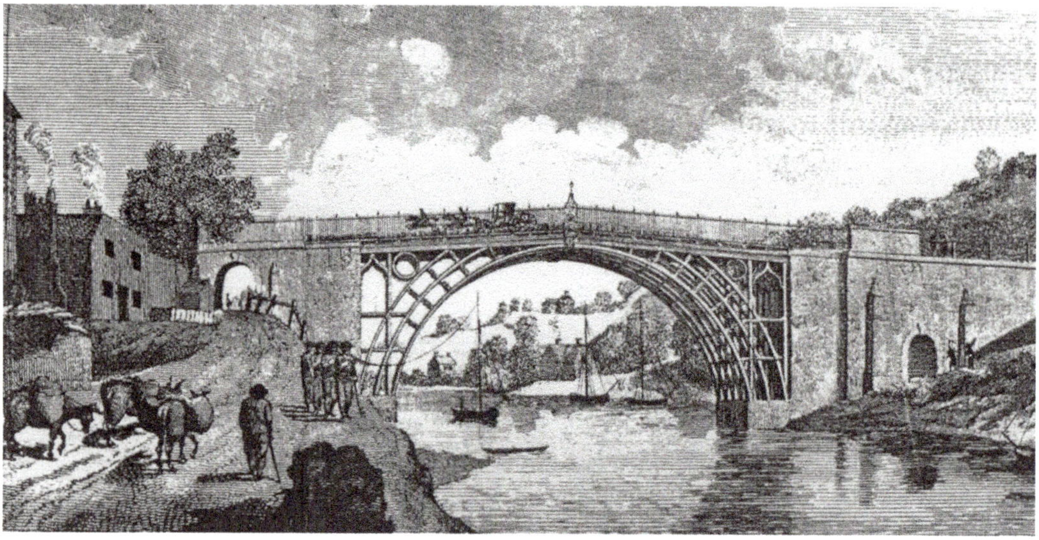

Improvements

Various attempts were made during the eighteenth century to improve navigation, including dredging, and proposals to make the river navigable at all seasons by the construction of weirs and locks as far upstream as Coalbrookdale were also made. Two successful schemes were the realignment of the mouth of the River Tern at Atcham (above) which, by means of a lock, enabled vessels to reach Tern and Upton forges, and the construction of a horse towpath between Bewdley and Coalbrookdale by 1800 and Shrewsbury by 1809. The bridge (below) carried the towpath over the confluence of the Coal Brook at Coalbrookdale.

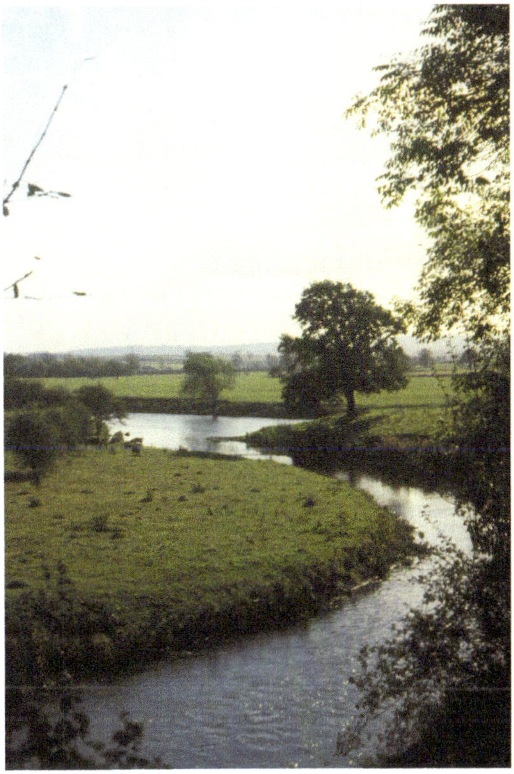

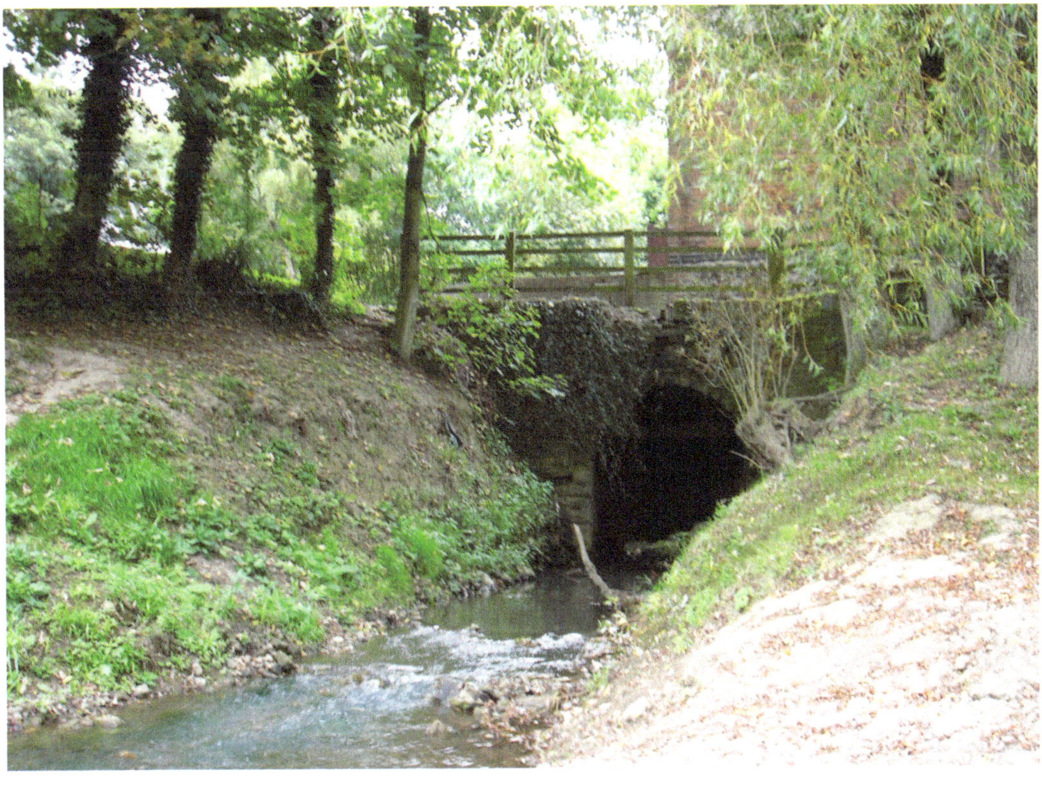

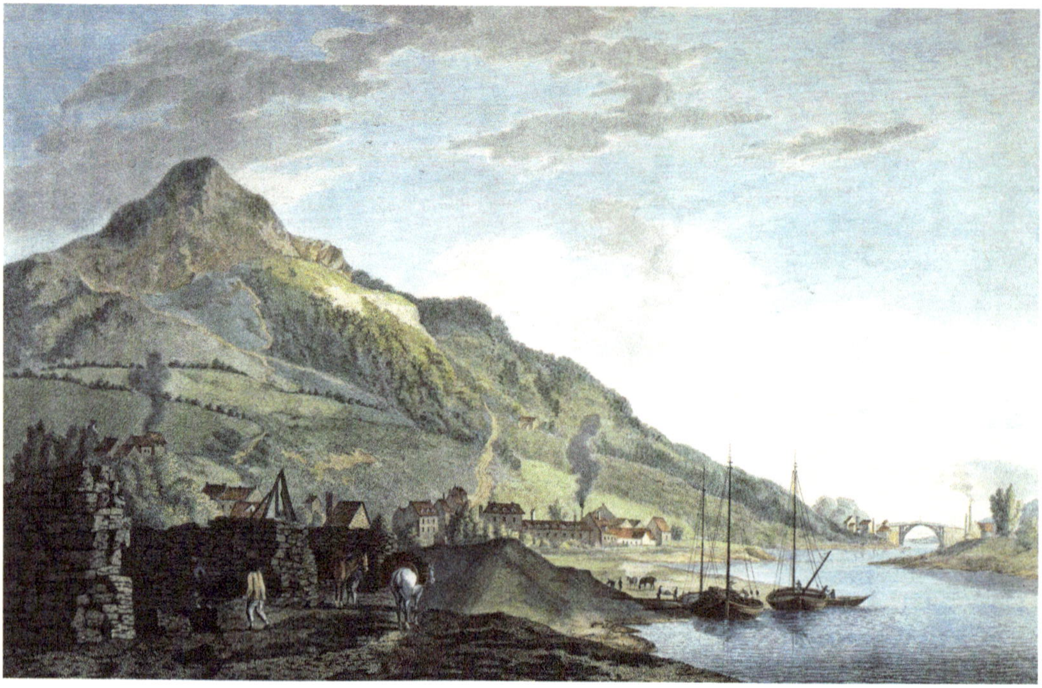

Meadow and Loadcroft Wharves

Above: The Coalbrookdale Company used Meadow Wharf, upstream from the confluence of the Coal Brook, and Loadcroft Wharf. Their railway reached the latter in 1757, but it was not until 1834 that the warehouse in the Gothic style, now the Museum of the Gorge, was built.
Below: The photograph from the early 1860s shows the plateway track and barges serving the wharf.

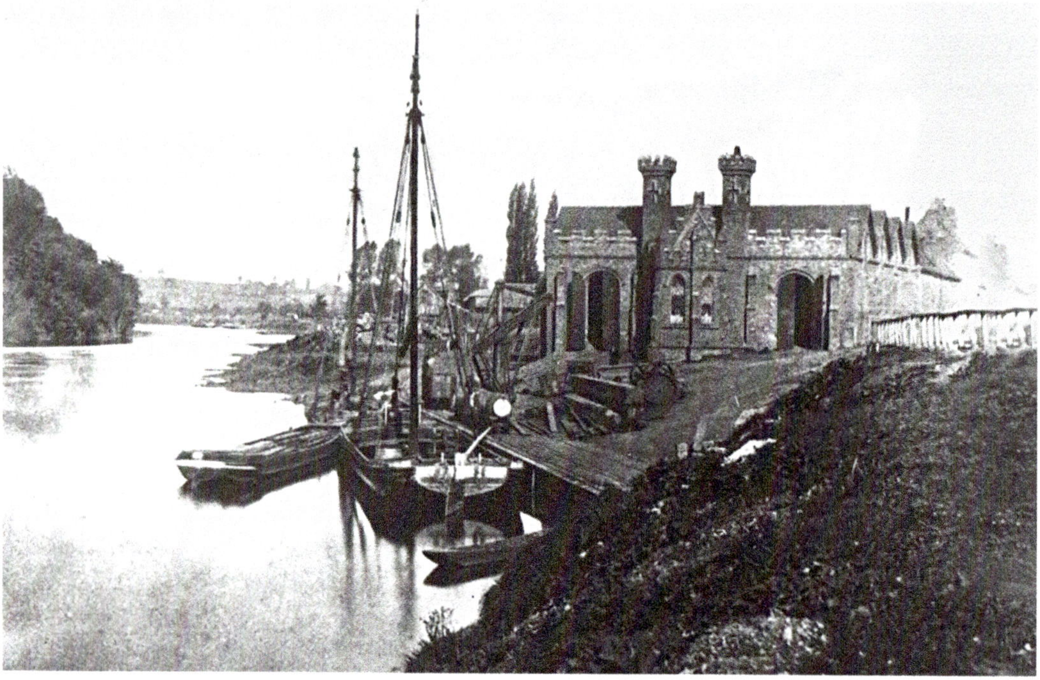

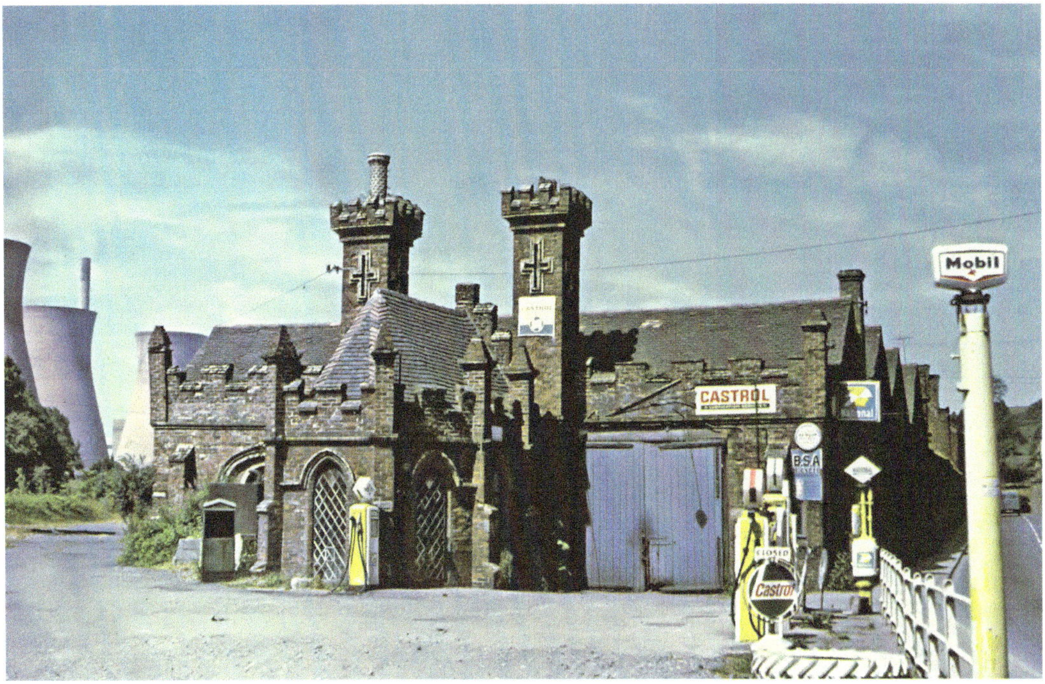

Museum of the Gorge

Following the closure of the wharf at the end of the nineteenth century, the warehouse took on several roles in succeeding years, including a mineral waters depot and a garage (above), before being converted by the IGMT into the Museum of the Gorge (below).

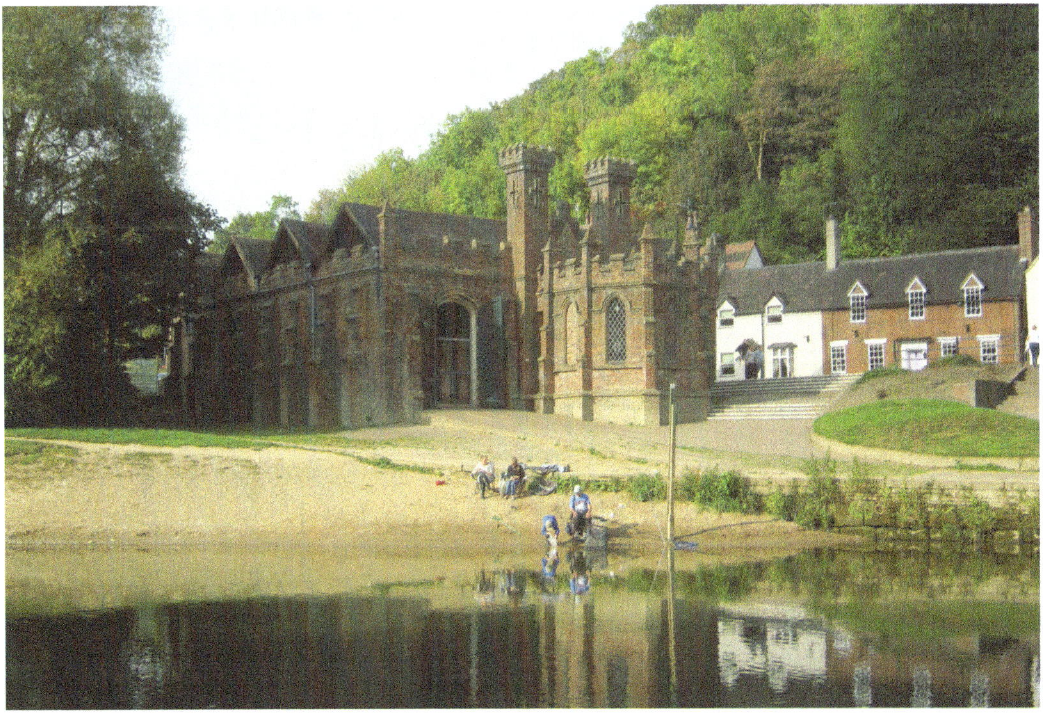

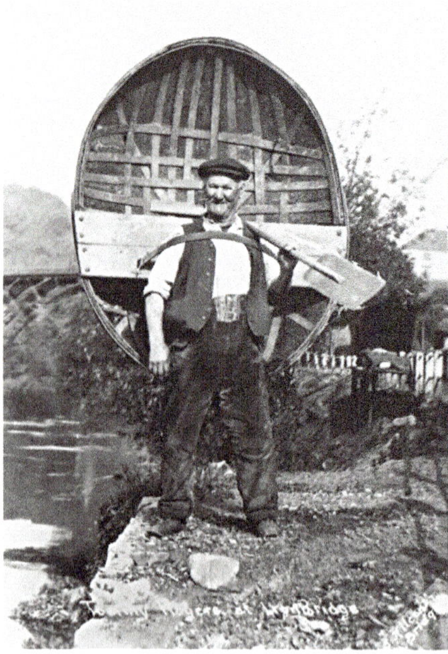 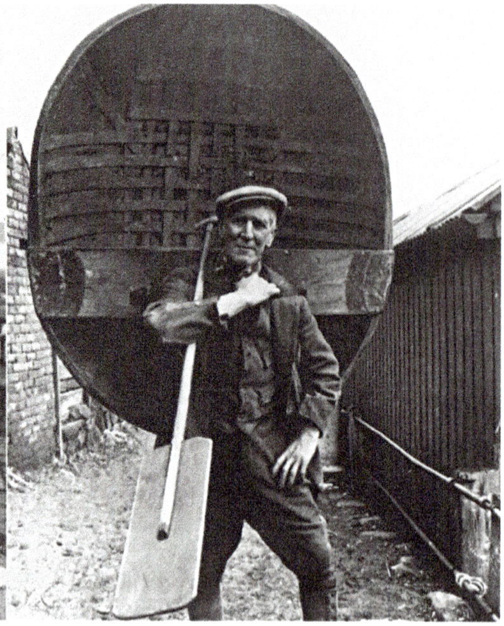

Coracles

Coracles were used for centuries on the upper reaches of rivers in western Britain, mainly for fishing. In the Ironbridge Gorge, several generations of the Rogers family were well known for their skill in making and using these craft. The construction of the coracle, with a wicker frame and cowhide covering, is shown in the early twentieth-century photographs of Tommy Rogers and his son Harry (above), both standing outside their riverside workshop, and Harry's son Eustace (below), who died in 2003, demonstrating how to manoeuvre the craft.

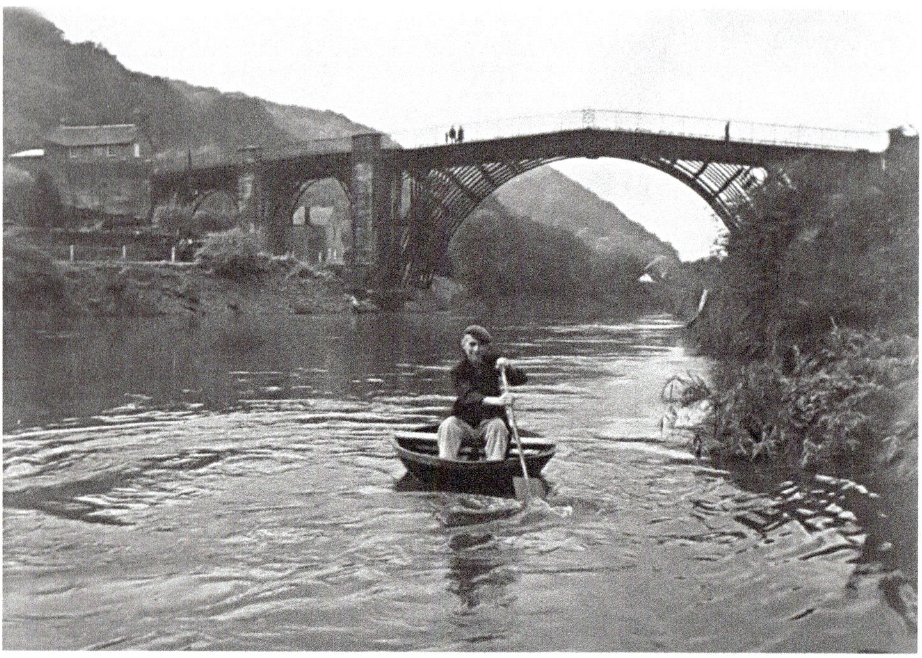

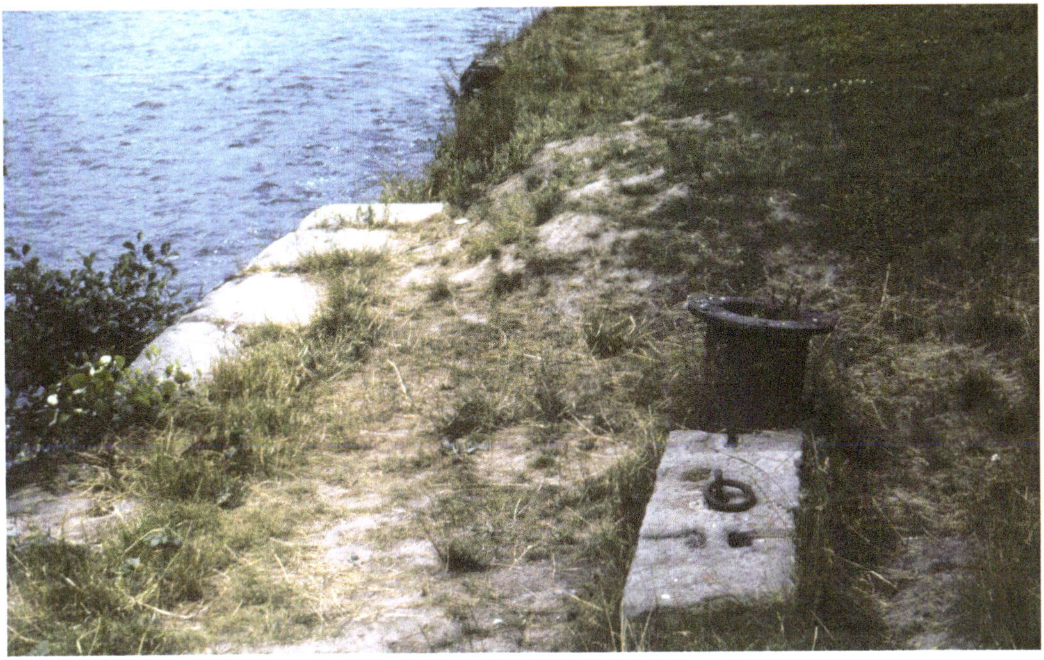

Coalport Wharf

Sixteen wharf sites have been identified in the Ironbridge Gorge. Those at Loadcroft and Coalport were two of the largest. The canal/river interchange at Coalport, established at the terminus of the Shropshire Canal in 1792, served the coal and iron trade along the northern and eastern edge of the Coalbrookdale Coalfield. These 1971 photographs show the cast-iron base of a pillar crane and a mooring ring (above) and the remains of the wharf wall, looking upstream (below).

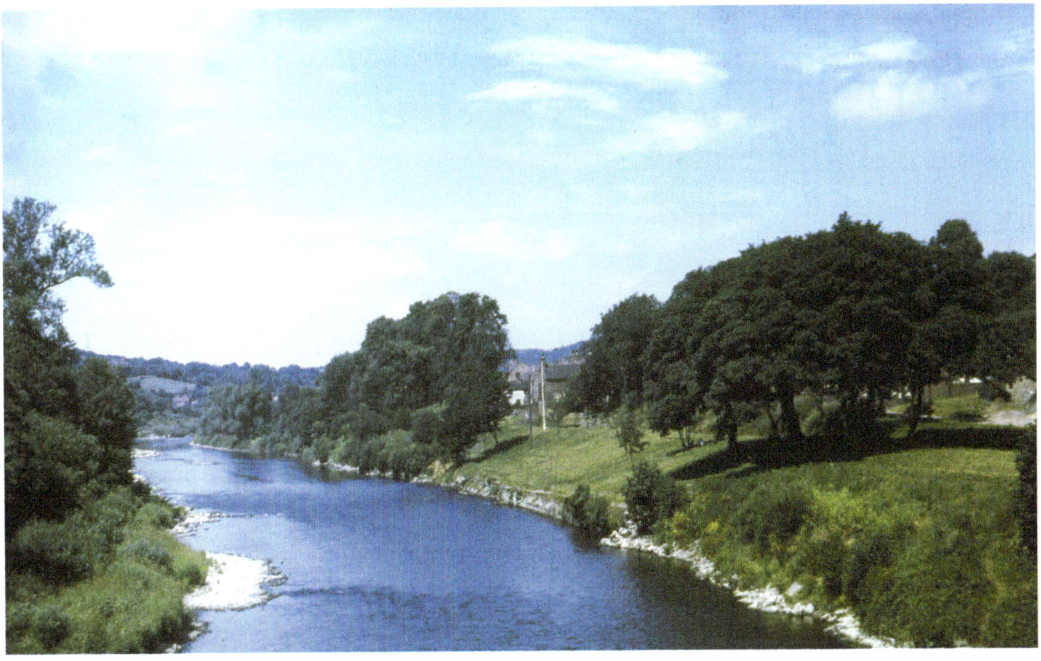

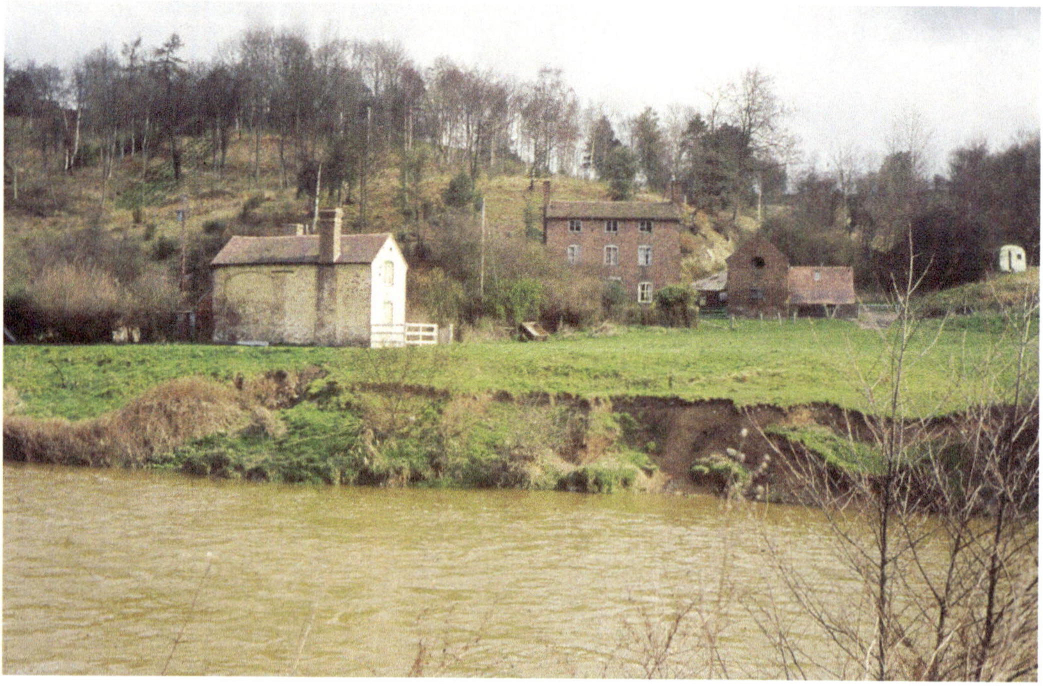

Other Wharves

A half-mile below Coalport Bridge, on the left bank of the river, was Sutton Wharf, the terminus of a short-lived railway carrying coal from the Oakengates area. The wharf building has survived (above). Further downstream, on the right bank, was a wharf serving Apley Forge, shown here around 1810.

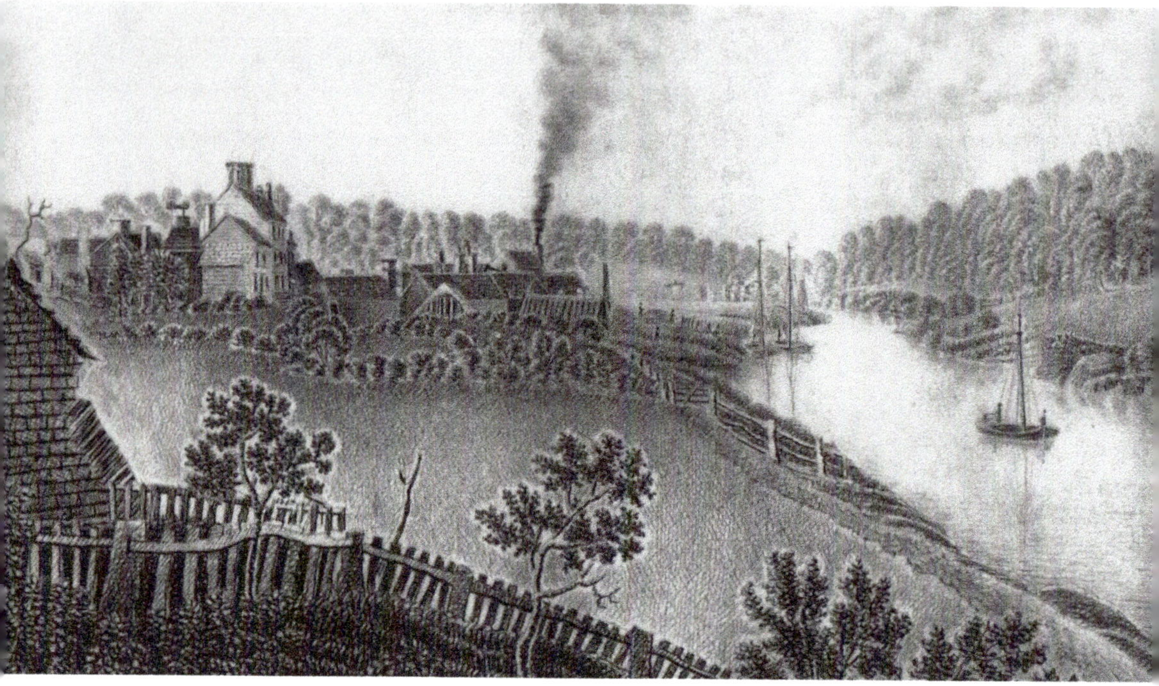

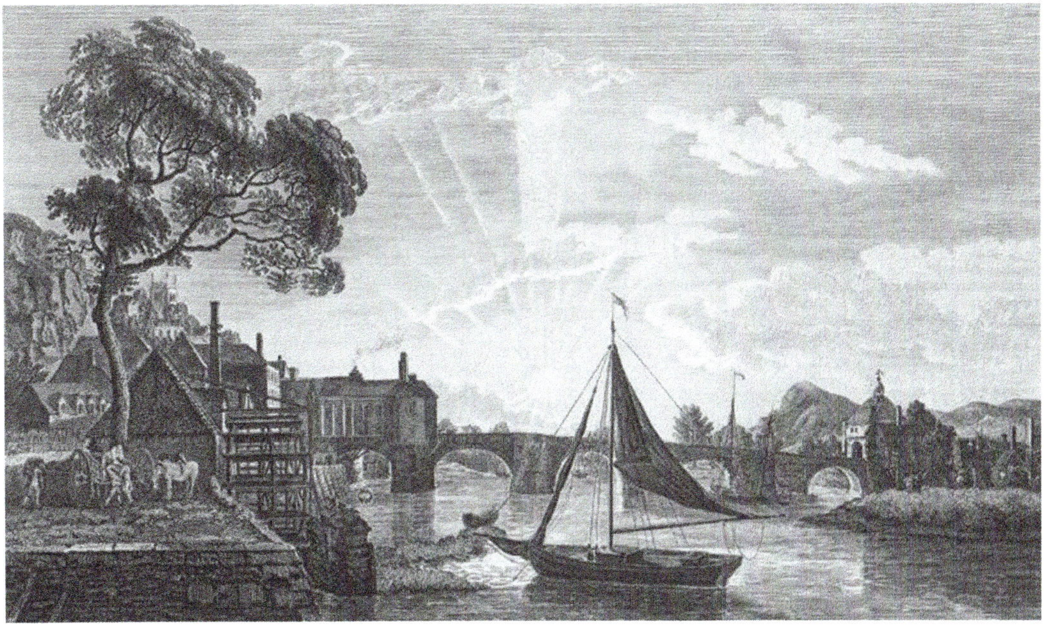

Bridgnorth

Bridgnorth had been an important river port since the Middle Ages, handling a variety of merchandise. There were wharves on the right bank of the river, upstream and downstream of the bridge, and barges were also unloaded on the left bank above the bridge. The main wharf was the Old Quay, shown between the waterwheel and the bridge in this late eighteenth-century engraving (above), and in a present-day view (below).

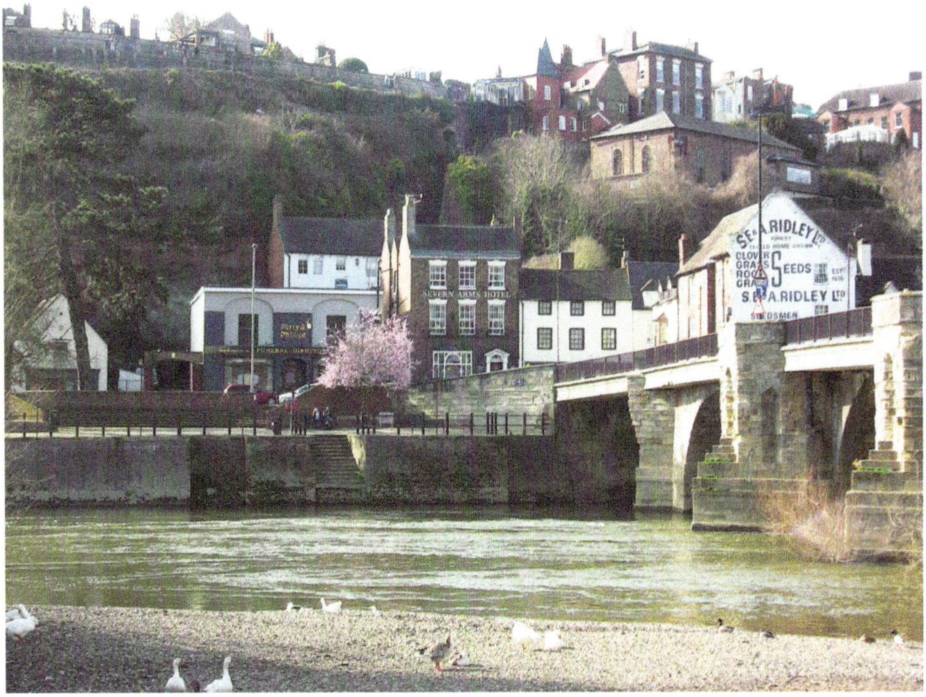

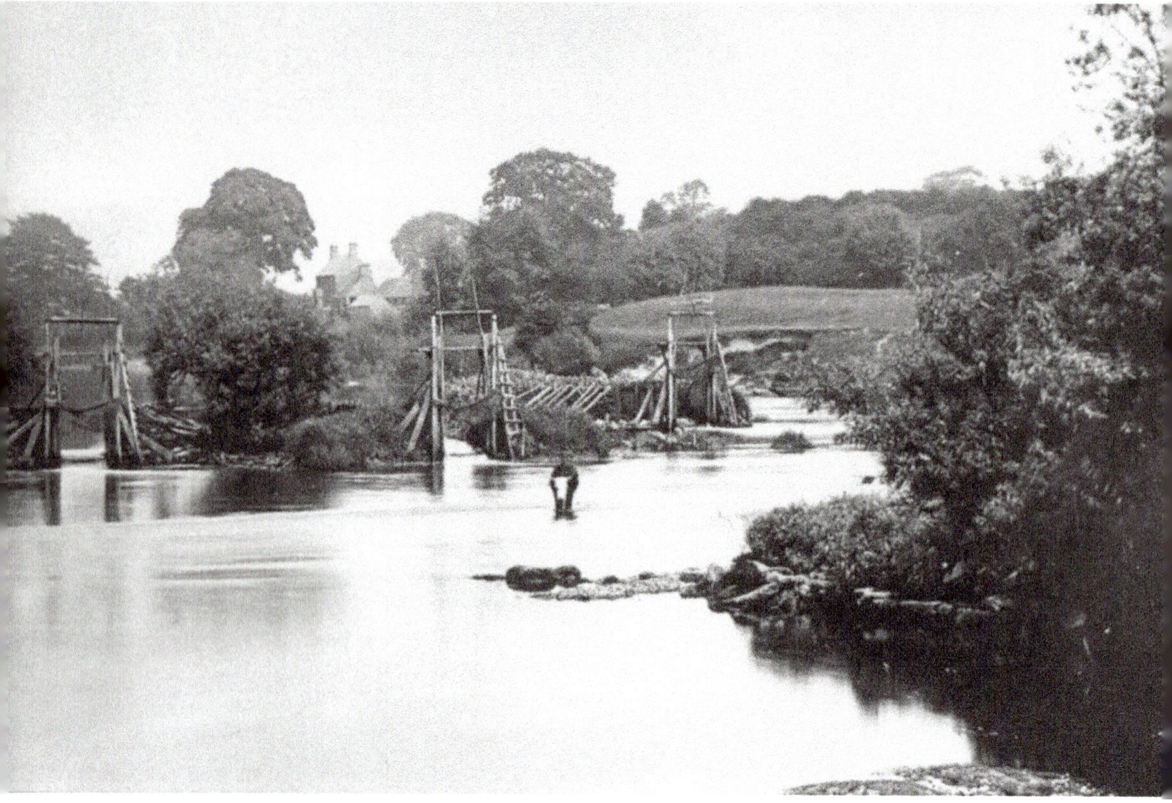

The fish weir at Preston Boats, a mile upstream from Atcham, was in use until 1912.

Hazards and Hindrances

There were a number of hazards and hindrances to navigation on the River Severn. At certain times of the year, particularly towards the end of winter and also following heavy rain in the Welsh mountains, flooding posed a major danger to navigation and to the communities along the banks of the river. Navigation could also be affected by ice, either from ice flows or by the surface of the river being frozen over. At times of extreme drought, shallows, which were caused by riffles in the river bed and a problem in normal times, became impassable. According to Thomas Telford, partly because of these natural conditions, 'During the whole of 1796, there were not two months in which barges could be navigated, even down the river, with a freight which was equal to defray the expenses of working them.'

In addition to these natural conditions, there were hazards and hindrances of the human kind. Fish weirs, which were fences of stakes that were built across the river in which basketwork fish traps were set, had necessitated the construction of barge gutters to enable vessels to bypass them. A particular danger was navigating a safe passage through one of the arches of bridges with one or more piers, while at the same time lowering the mast and sail.

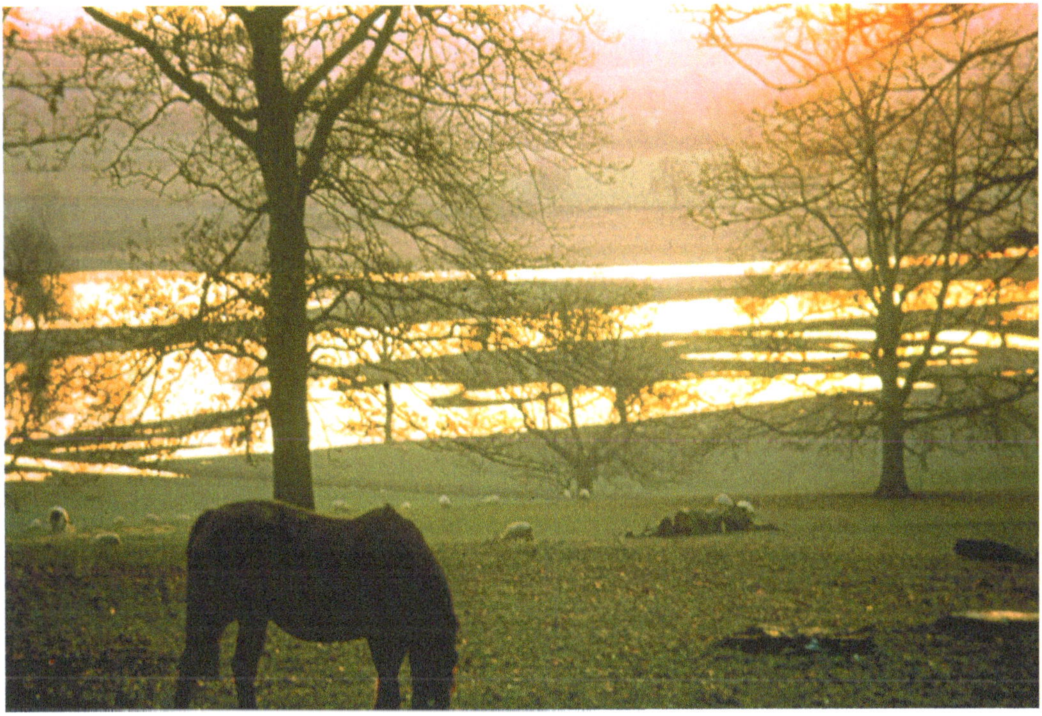

Floods

Flooding not only prevented vessels sailing, but also badly affected communities along the banks of the river and damaged bridges. Frequently, a lake was formed in the area between Atcham and Buildwas (above) and the large volume of water squeezing through the narrow Ironbridge Gorge caused damage to wharves and warehouses, flooding other buildings close to the river in the process – as seen here at the Boat Inn at Jackfield (below).

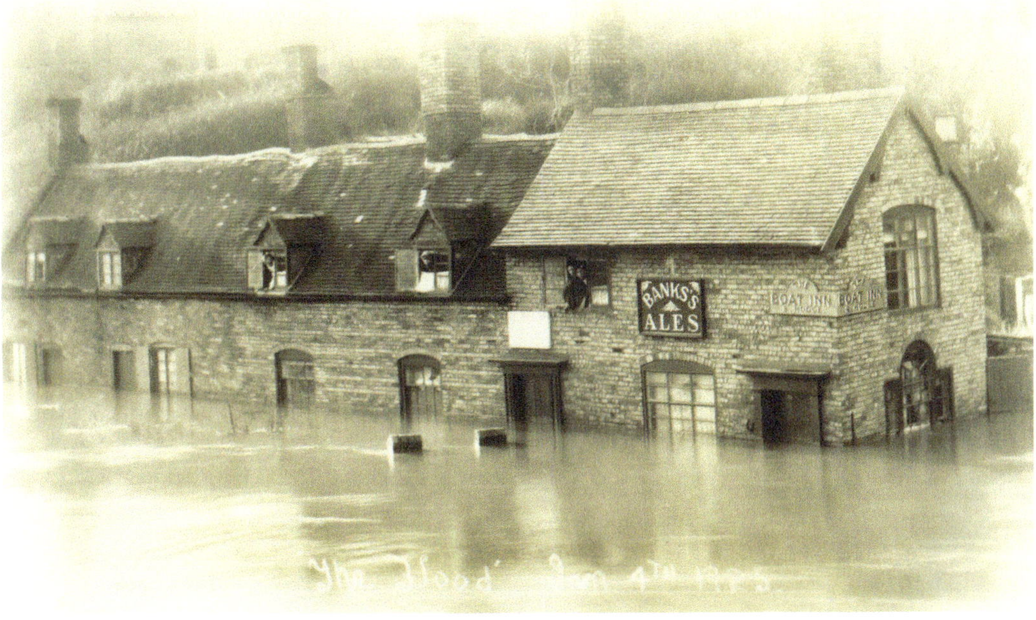

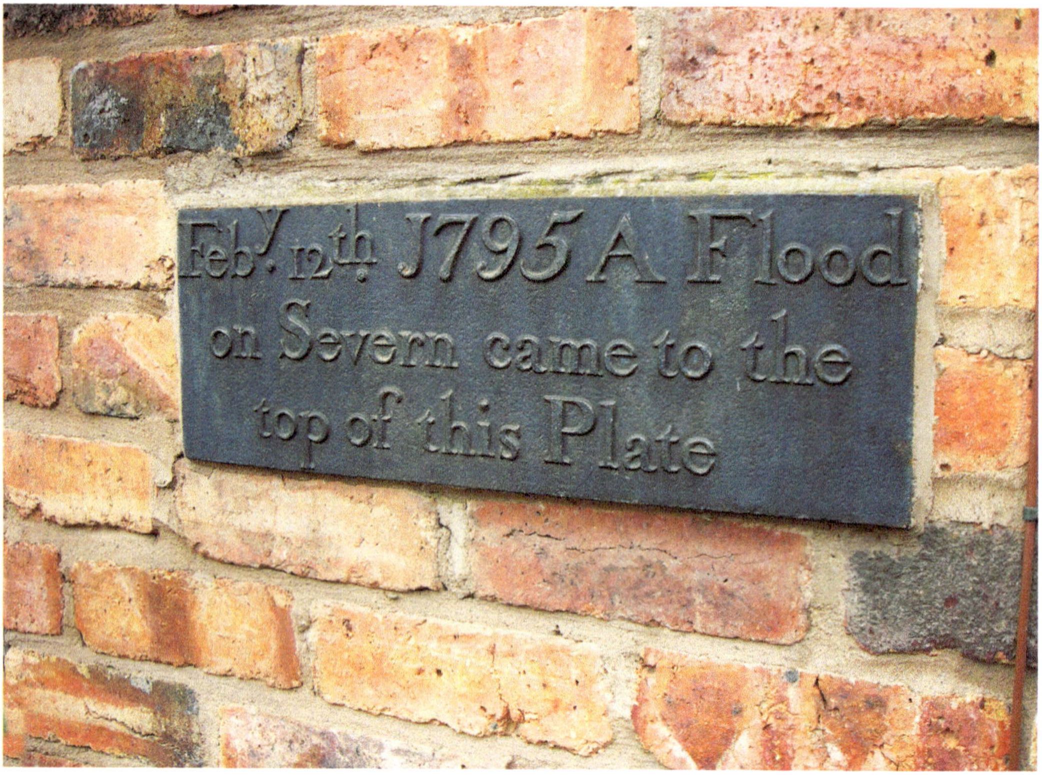

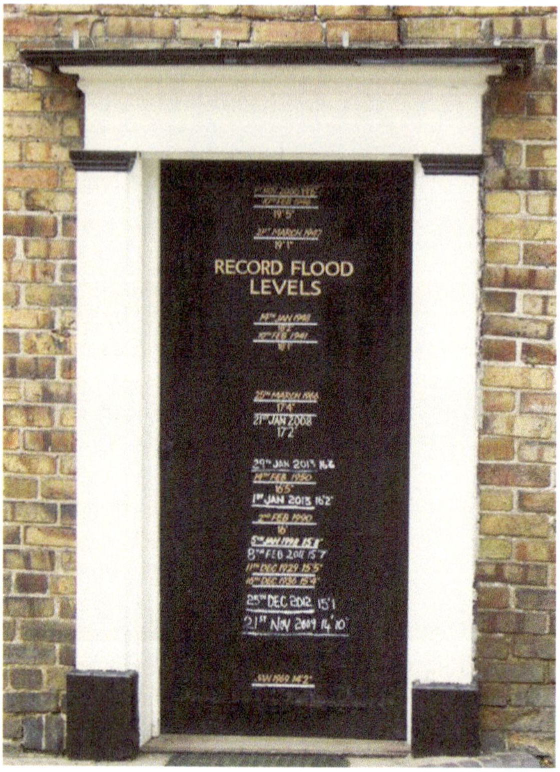

Recording floods

The levels of particularly severe floods in the Ironbridge Gorge have been recorded on two local buildings: that of the Great Flood of February 1795, where the water rose 20 feet above normal level, on a plaque on a shop wall at Dale End, Coalbrookdale (above); and other floods of the last two centuries on the door of the Boat Inn at Jackfield (left).

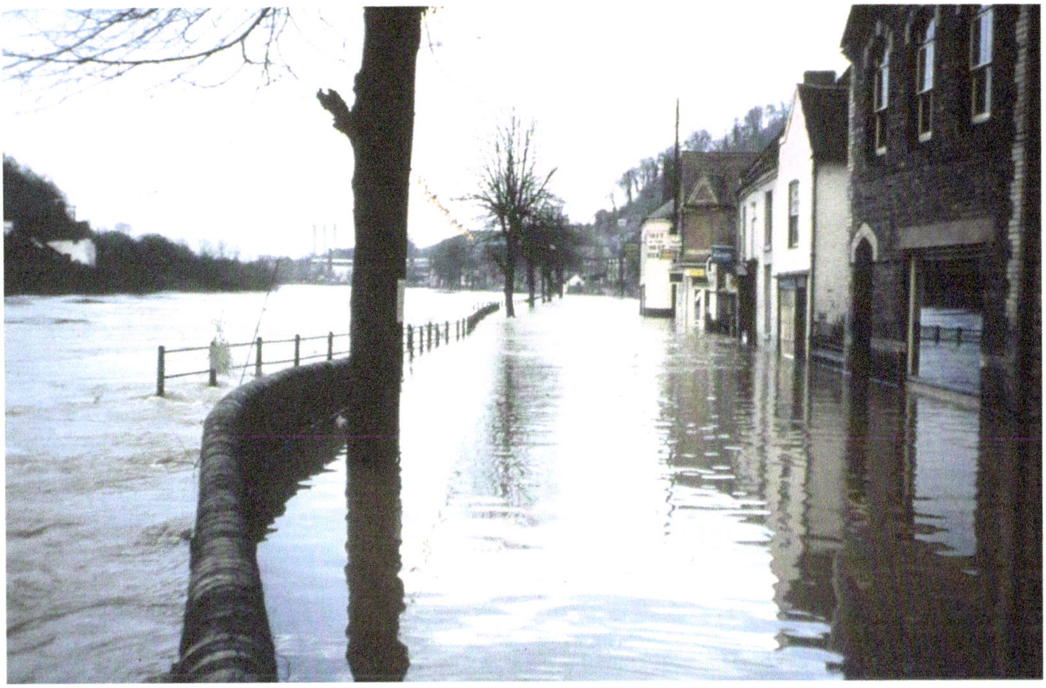

The Wharfage

Above: In the past, the Wharfage in Ironbridge was particularly prone to flooding.

Below: However, in recent years the erection of metal barriers prior to high water reaching the Ironbridge Gorge has alleviated the problem for local properties, though the riverside road has to remain closed to traffic while the barriers are in place.

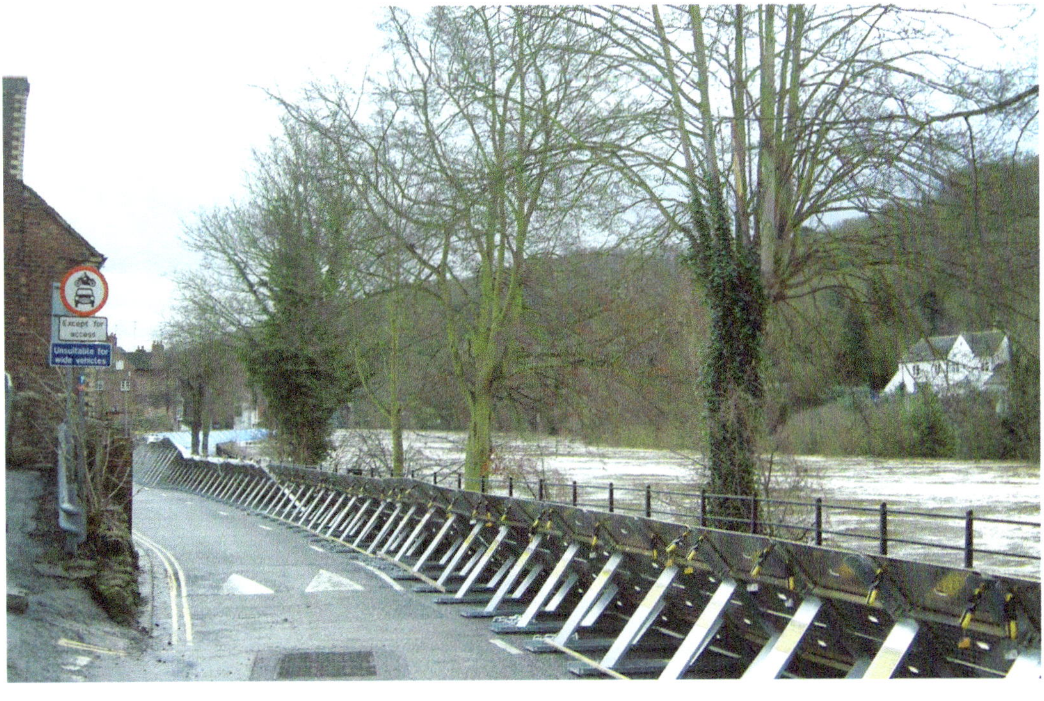

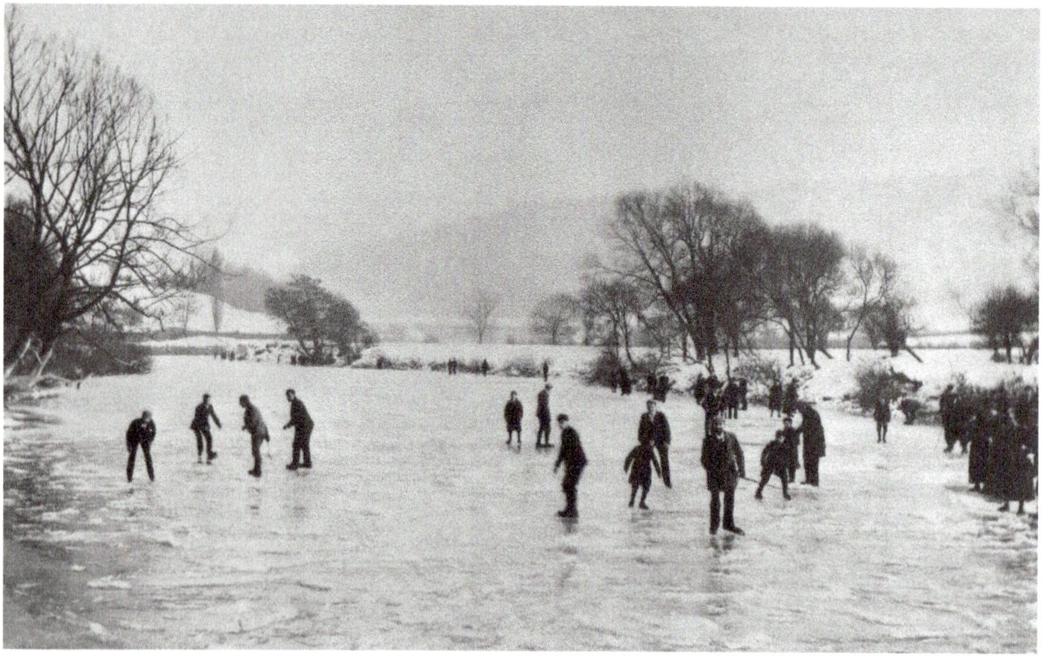

Ice

A less common natural hazard facing navigation on the river was ice. Ice floes would not necessarily prevent vessels from sailing, but they could cause damage. Obviously, if the river iced over navigation became impossible. Photographs at the beginning of the twentieth century, at Buildwas (above) and under the Albert Edward Bridge (below), record a frozen river, with local people taking the opportunity to walk, skate or ride on the ice.

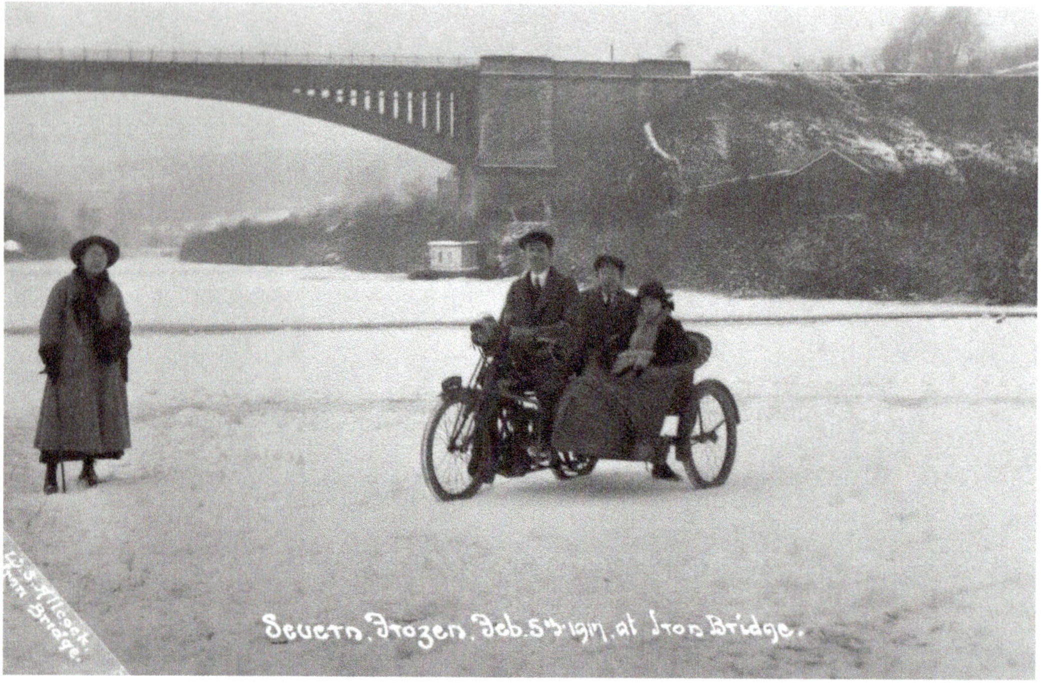

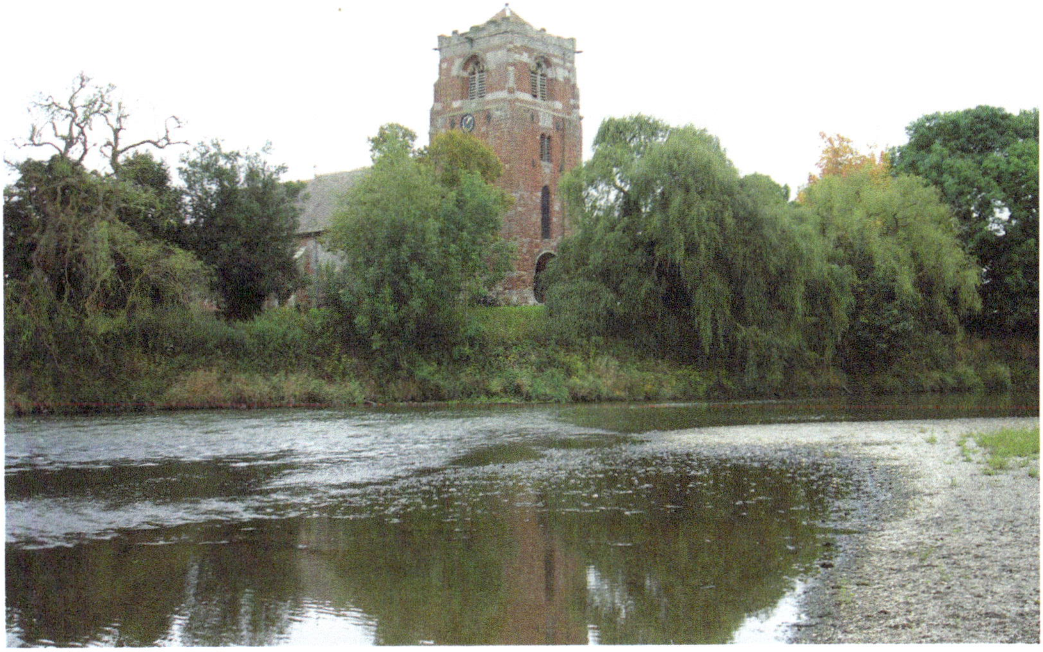

Low Water

During periods of very dry weather, low water levels became a problem for vessels, particularly where there were shallows in the river or fords, as at Atcham (above) and Dale End (below). At such times, heavy-laden vessels heading downstream waited for a 'fresh', a rise in river levels caused by rainfall in mid-Wales – going downstream on a 'fresh' was obviously hazardous.

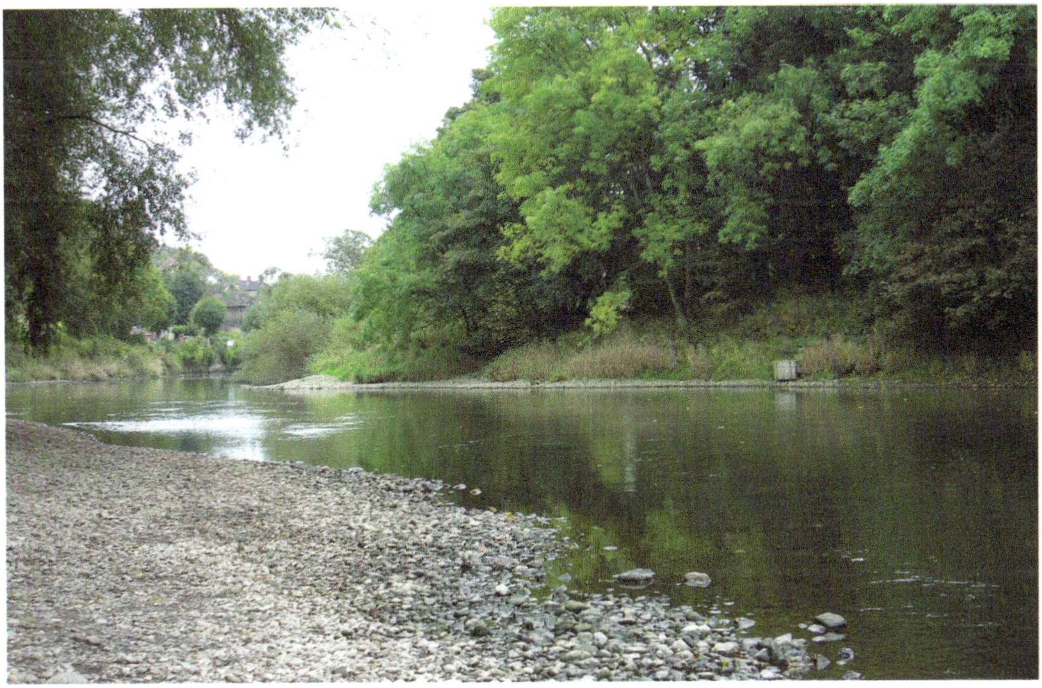

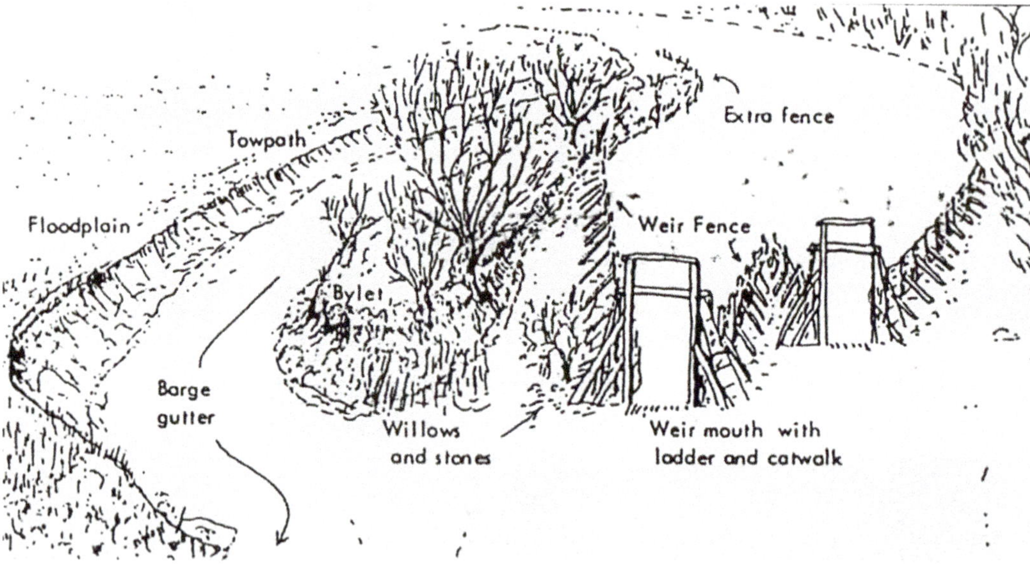

Fish Weirs

Above: Fish weirs were fences of stakes built across the river in which basketwork fish traps were set. They dated from the Middle Ages, and a survey of 1575 and archaeological evidence suggest there were some twenty or so fish weirs between Atcham and Bridgnorth. For vessels to bypass these, barge gutters were constructed, creating islands (bylets) in the river. All the fish weirs downstream from Atcham were out of use by the eighteenth century, and many of the barge gutters have now silted up.
Below: One of the remaining islands in the river is at Wroxeter, and this aerial view shows the barge gutter, which is the narrower of the two channels.

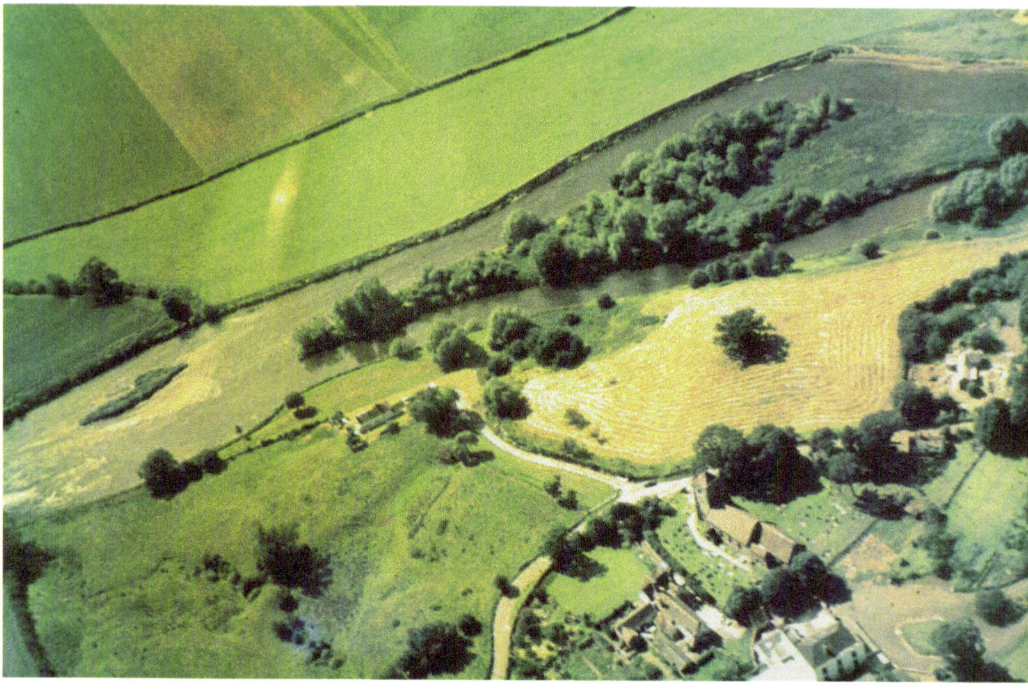

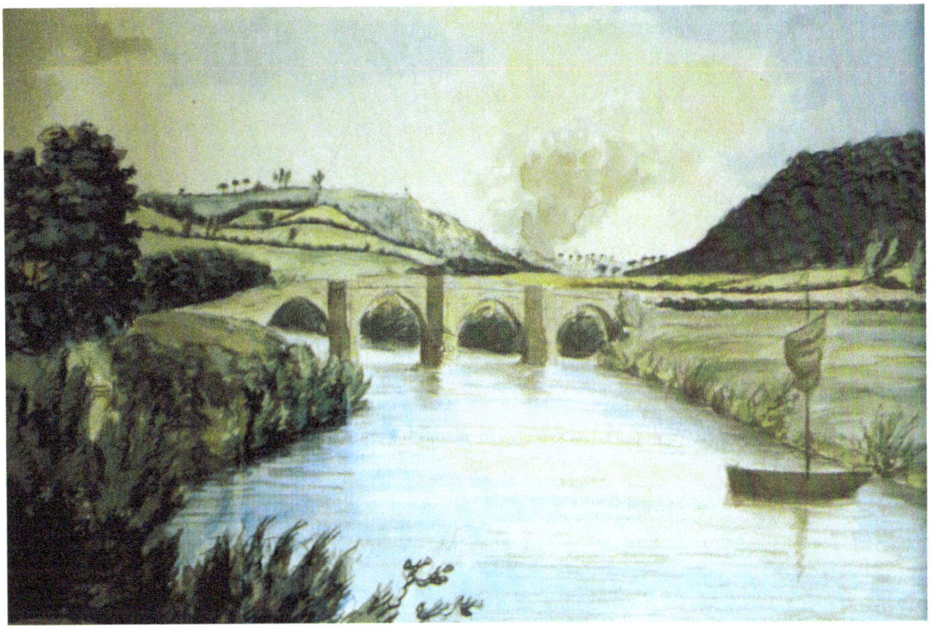

Dangerous Bridges

Above: The medieval bridges at Buildwas and Bridgnorth, each with low clearance and a number of piers, presented a hazard to steersmen of vessels on the river. In the late eighteenth century, wooden bridges at Preens Eddy (Coalport) and Cressage, with central piers, still posed a problem.

Below: John Gwynn's new stone bridge at Atcham (1776), replacing the mid-sixteenth-century eighteen-arch bridge, needed a distinct hump to give headroom for navigation through the central arch. Even then, a boat loaded with slates collided with one of its six piers in 1787. What was said to be the last commercial barge on the Upper Severn collided with Bridgnorth Bridge and sank in 1895.

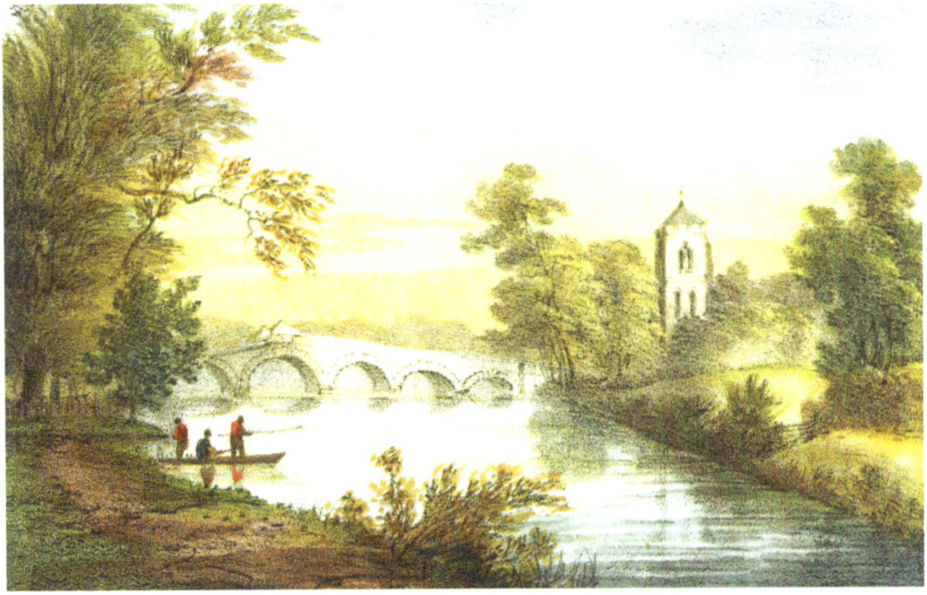

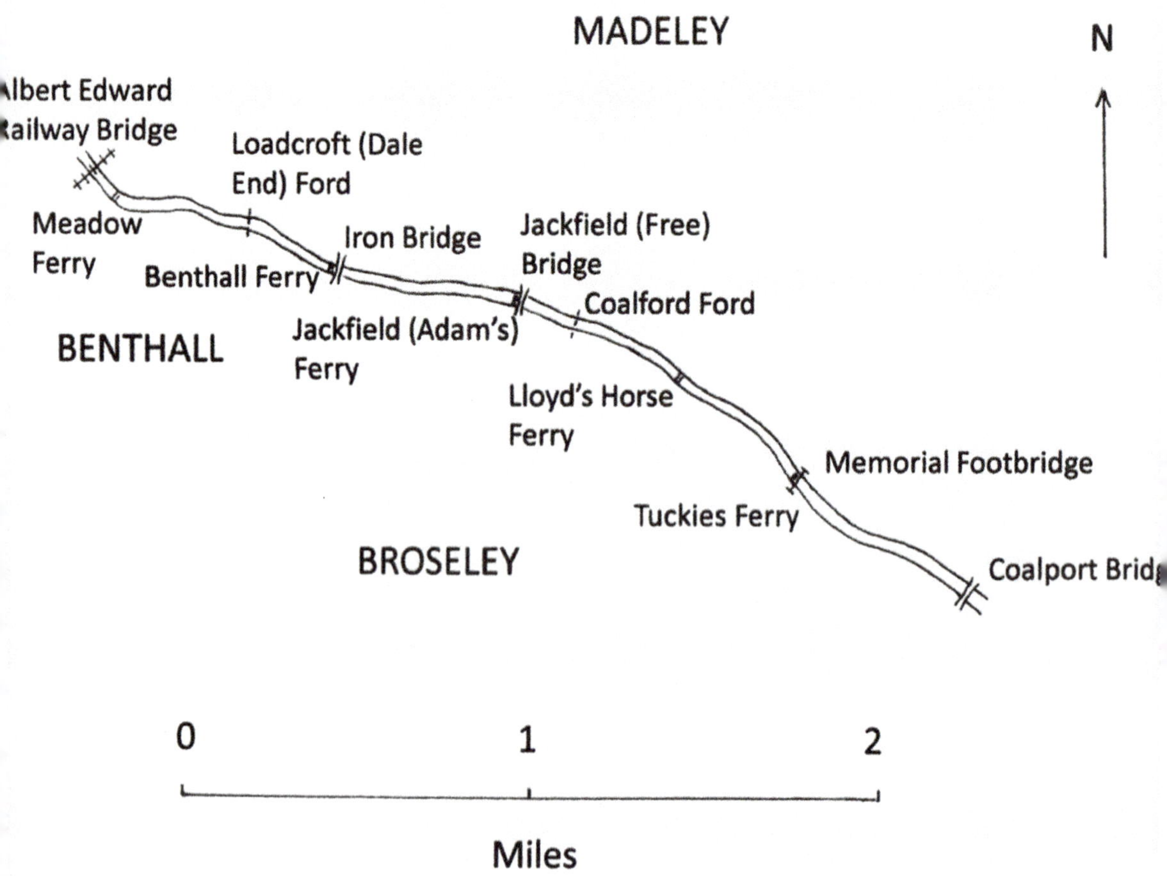

Fords, ferries and bridges in the Ironbridge Gorge.

River Crossings

In the past, rivers were vital arteries of communication and trade, but they have also been barriers. Need led to ways of crossing them, whether by fords, ferries or bridges. In East Shropshire, from early times the main crossing places of the Severn had been in the Atcham area, Buildwas and the Bridgnorth area. Later, specific needs resulted in crossings in the Ironbridge Gorge. Usually at such places the earliest way of crossing was by a ford, later by a ferry and finally by a bridge, but this was not always the sequence.

Between Atcham and Bridgnorth there are at least eight known sites of fords, and no doubt there were other unofficial crossings when conditions allowed. There were at different times a total of fourteen ferries, one of which, at the Lloyds in the Ironbridge Gorge, was a horse ferry, where the towpath switched from the left to the right bank of the river. Before 1700, there were only three bridges on this section of the river; in the late eighteenth century, two of these were replaced by new structures and three others were built. Today, with nineteenth- and twentieth-century replacements and new structures, there are fourteen bridges of various kinds on the river between Atcham and Bridgnorth.

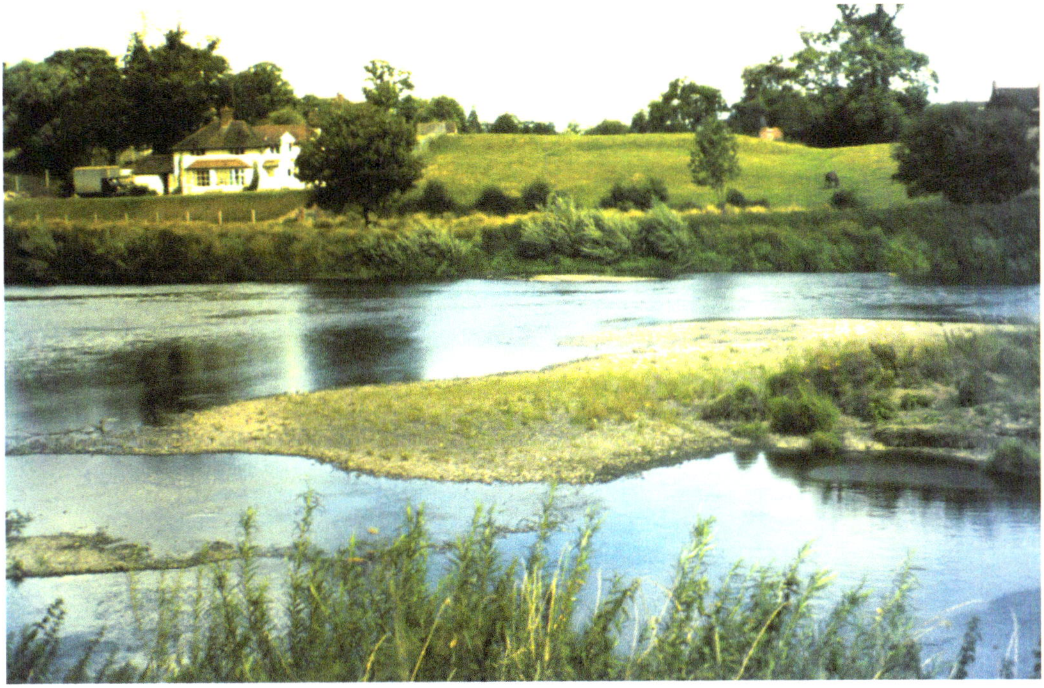

Fords

Above: Roman Watling Street crossed the Severn by a ford at the south-west corner of Wroxeter. The route was turnpiked in the eighteenth century but this section, together with the ford, was abandoned in 1829.

Below: Before bridges were built in the Ironbridge Gorge in the late eighteenth century, one crossing point was over the riffle (shallow water) at Loadcroft, Dale End, the site of which is shown in this late nineteenth-century photograph. Downstream, the name Coalford suggests another crossing, and below Coalport there was a ford at Gitchfield.

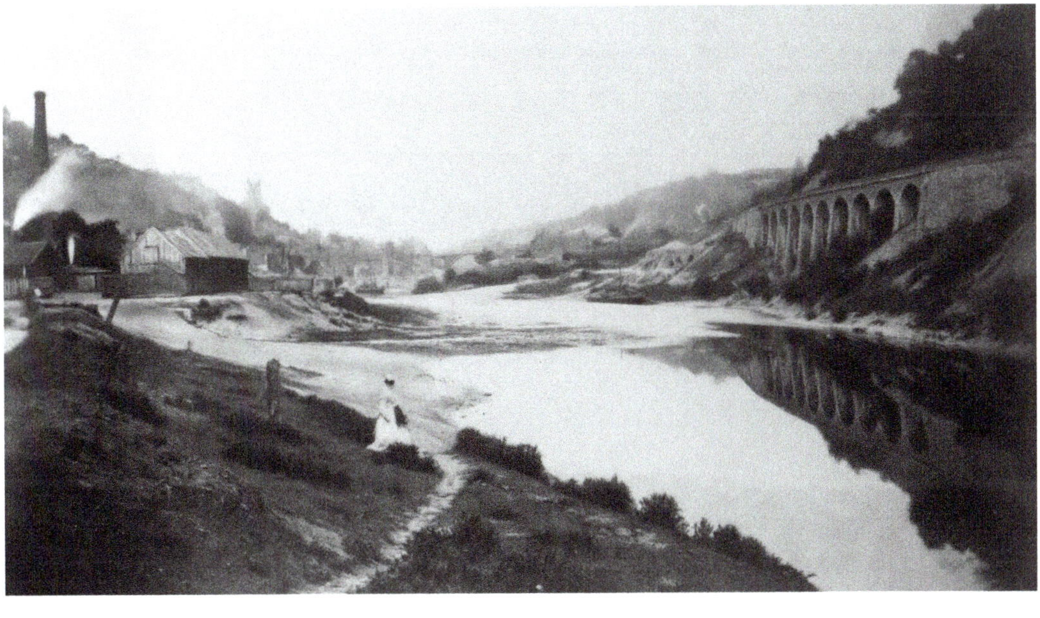

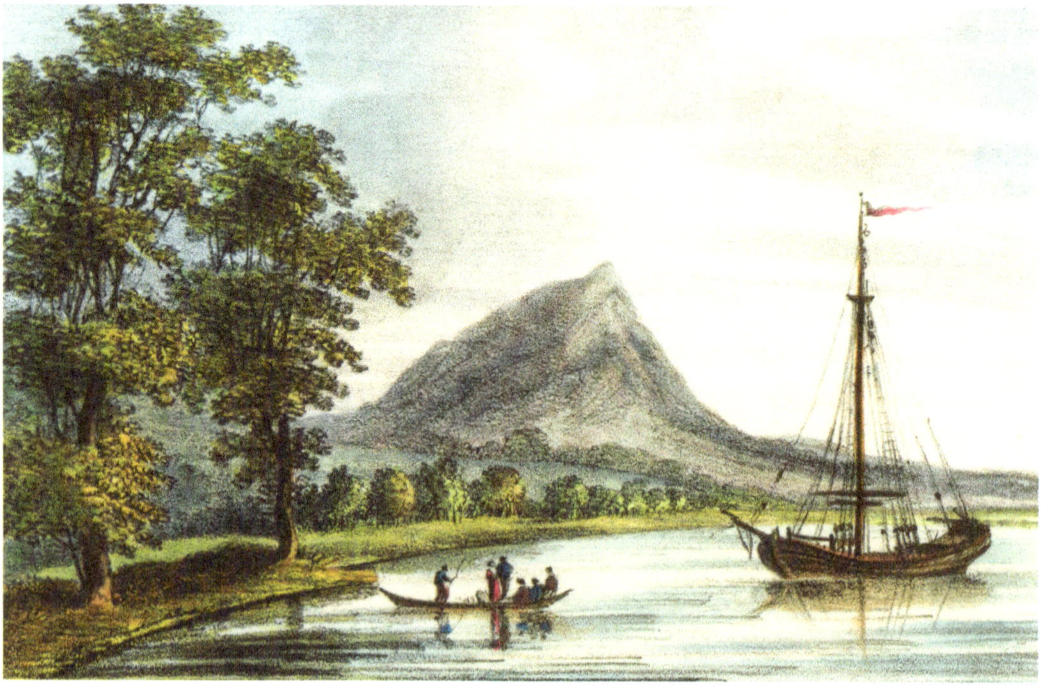

Ferries

Above: Two ferries upstream of the Ironbridge Gorge, at Cound Lane End and Buildwas, were recorded in Samuel Ireland's lithographs of the 1790s.

Below: At Buildwas, a temporary ferry was in use when the medieval bridge was damaged in 1791, and again following the destruction of the bridge by the Great Flood of February 1795.

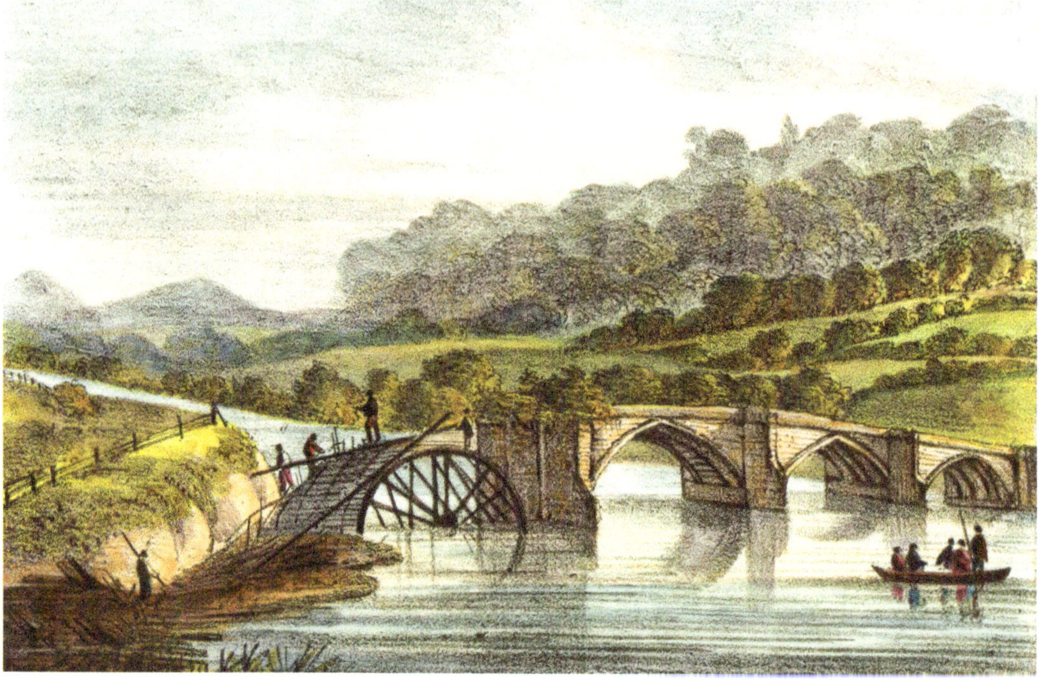

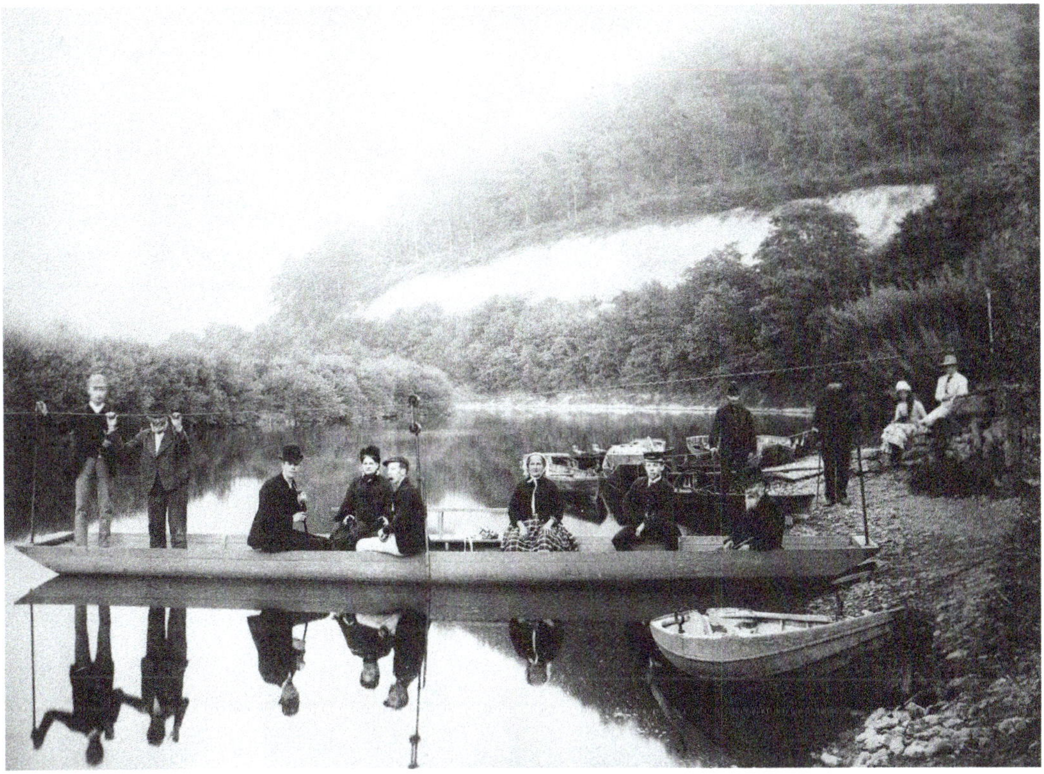

Meadow Ferry

Above: The punt-like ferry boat was pulled hand-over-hand along a wire, which was stretched across the river and ran through rollers on the side of the vessel.

Right: The ferry survived until the early 1950s, and the ferryman's cottage was demolished when land was being cleared for the construction of the cooling towers for the new Ironbridge B power station in the mid-1960s.

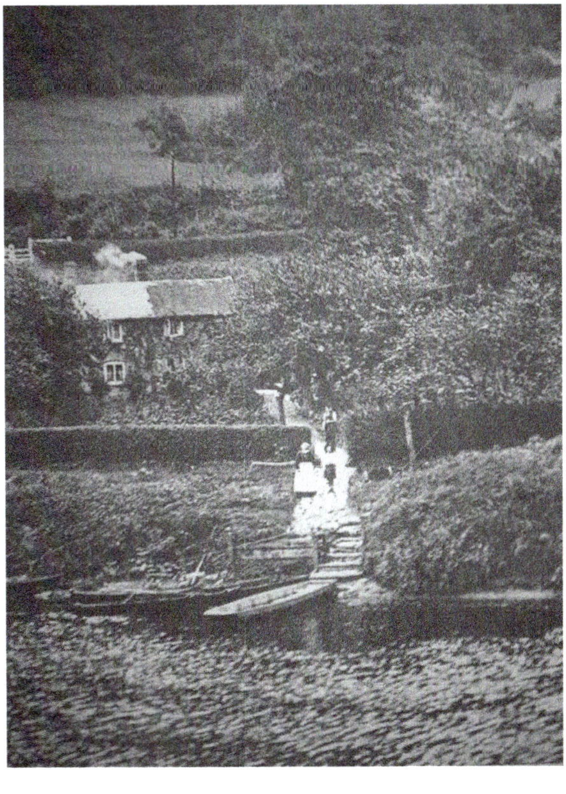

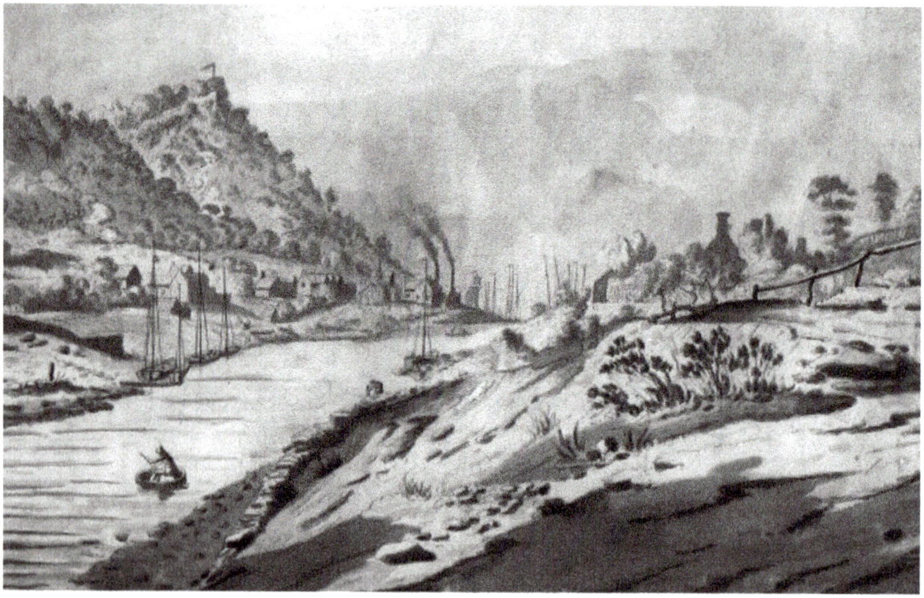

Benthall Ferry

The ferry, at a point where the Benthall Brook enters the Severn, was operating in the mid-eighteenth century, but the petition for a bridge that was presented to Parliament in February 1776 stated that those involved in local industries 'frequently are put to great inconveniences, delays and obstructions by reason of the insufficiency of the present ferry over the River Severn, particularly in winter.' William Williams' sketch of 1776 (above) shows the site of the ferry, and his 1780 painting (below) shows the ferry before its closure, with passengers in similar boats admiring the new iron bridge.

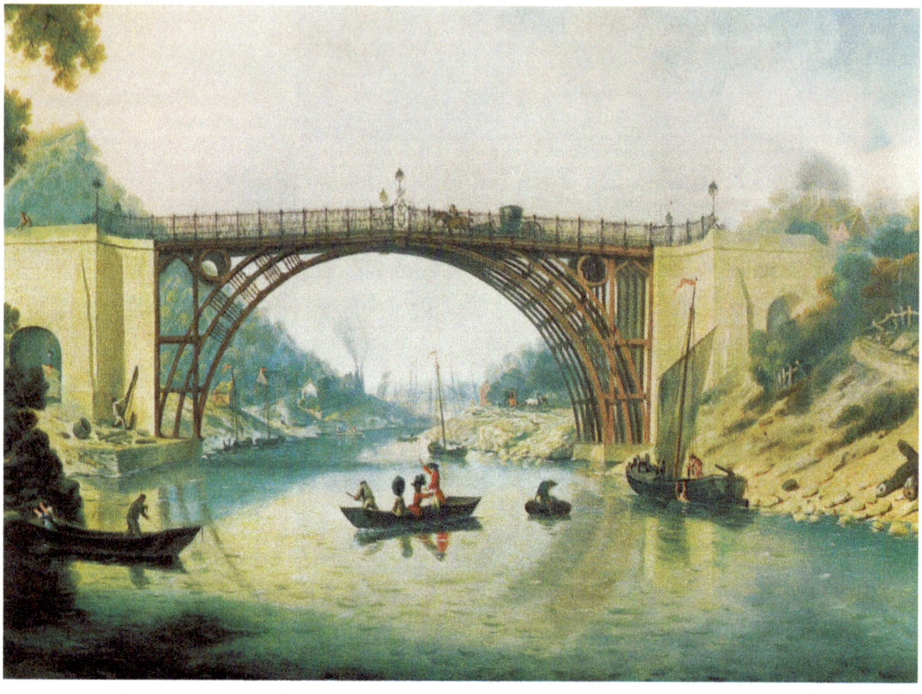

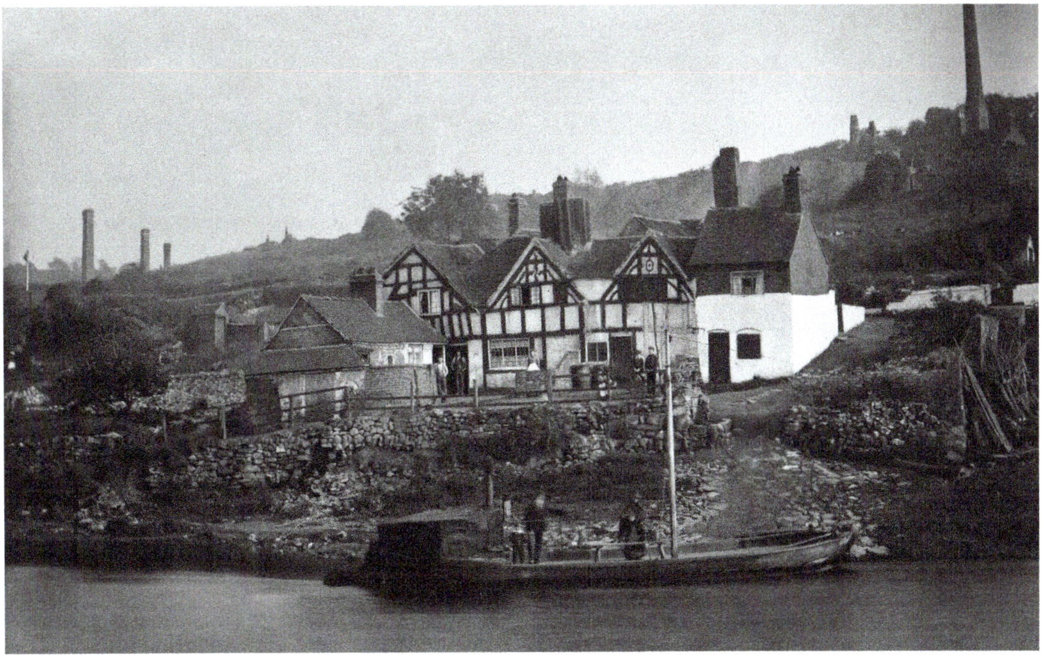

Jackfield Ferry

Above: This ancient ferry was sometimes known as Adam's ferry after Adam Crumpton, ferryman and miner, who in 1654 built the substantial timber-framed building that later became the Dog & Duck public house.

Below: The new ferry boat, built in 1894, was propelled across the river by its large rudder being angled into the current; it had a life of only fifteen years, being made redundant by the opening of the Free Bridge in 1909.

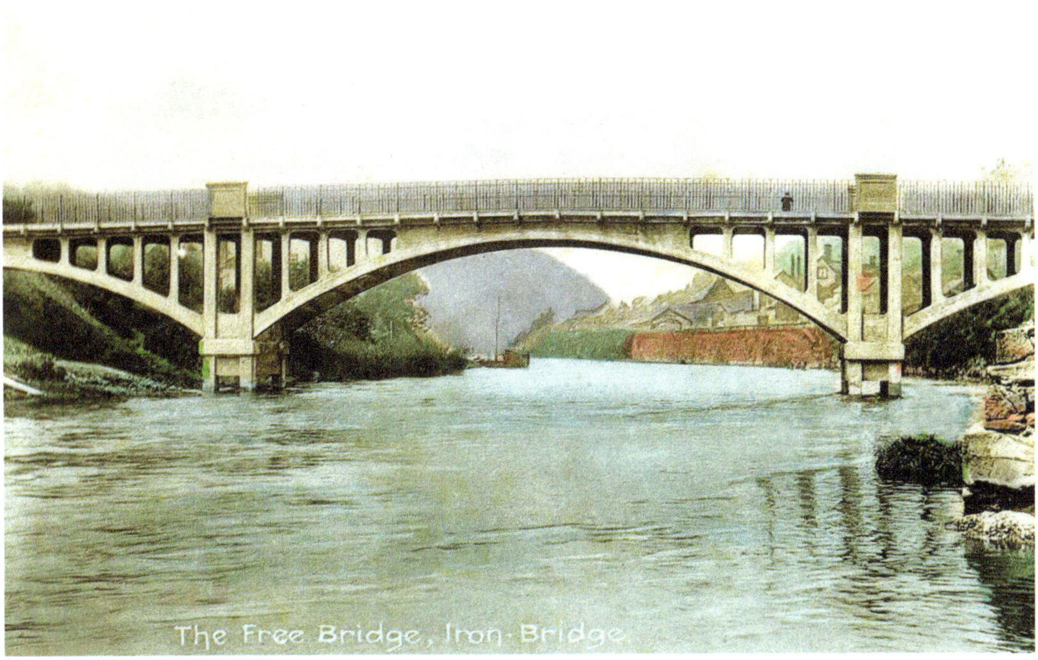

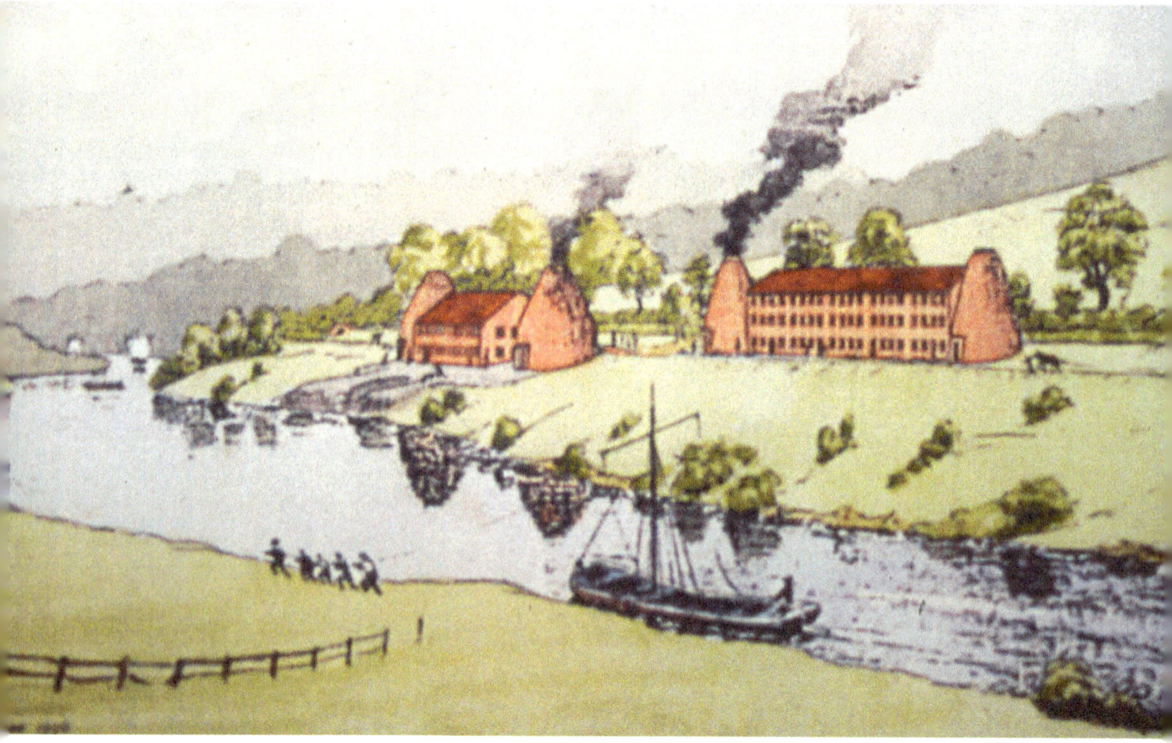

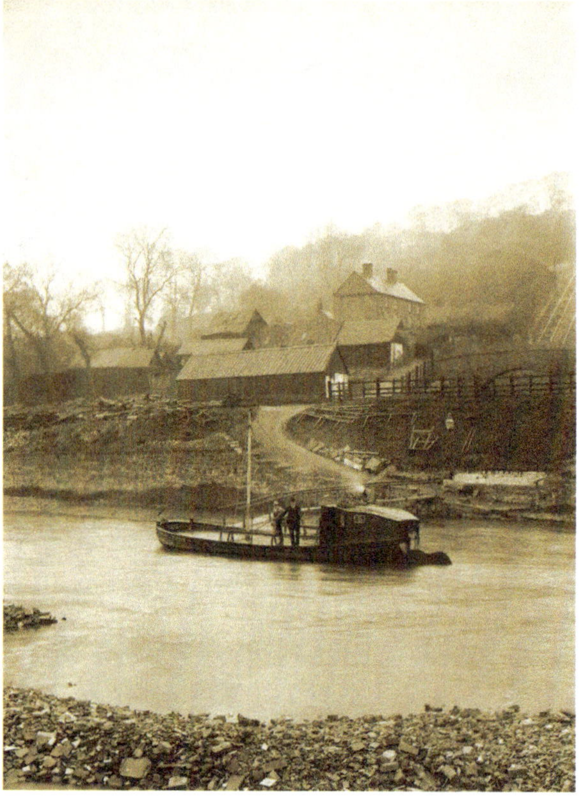

Coalport Ferry

This was sometimes known as the Tuckies or Werps ferry and originated with the development of Coalport in the early 1790s. The first ferry boat (depicted in the middle distance of this reconstruction, above) capsized in October 1799 with the loss of twenty-eight workers returning home from the Coalport China Works. The type of vessel used a hundred years later (below) is considered to be a converted Severn trow. Concern over the condition of the ferry led to its closure and eventual replacement by the memorial footbridge in 1922.

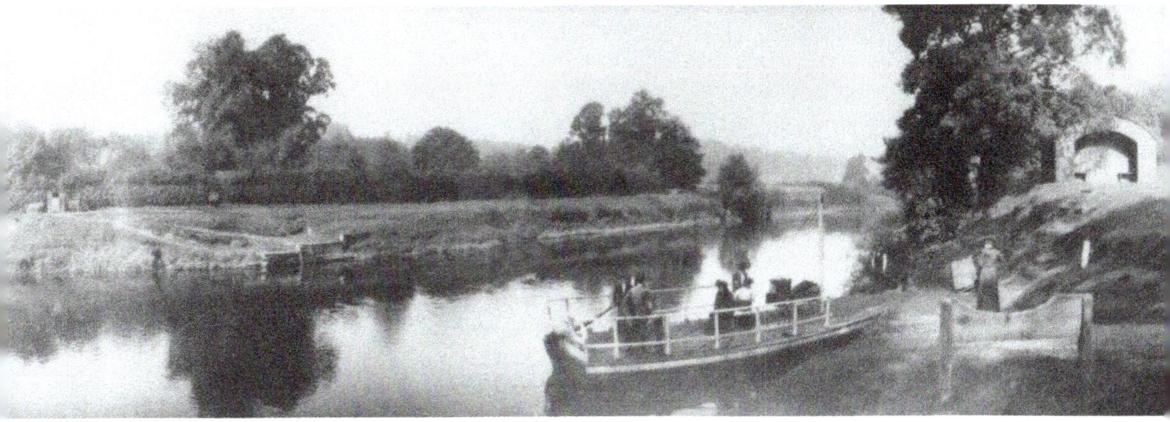

Apley Ferry

There were in fact two ferries at Apley, connecting the parish of Stockton on the left bank with the parishes of Linley and Astley Abbots on the right bank, and serving Apley Park, the residence of the Whitmore family and later the Fosters. The upper ferry (above), dating back to the late fifteenth century, would have provided the hall with access to Linley station on the newly opened Severn Valley Railway (SVR) in 1862. The lower ferry is shown in a mid-nineteenth century engraving (below).

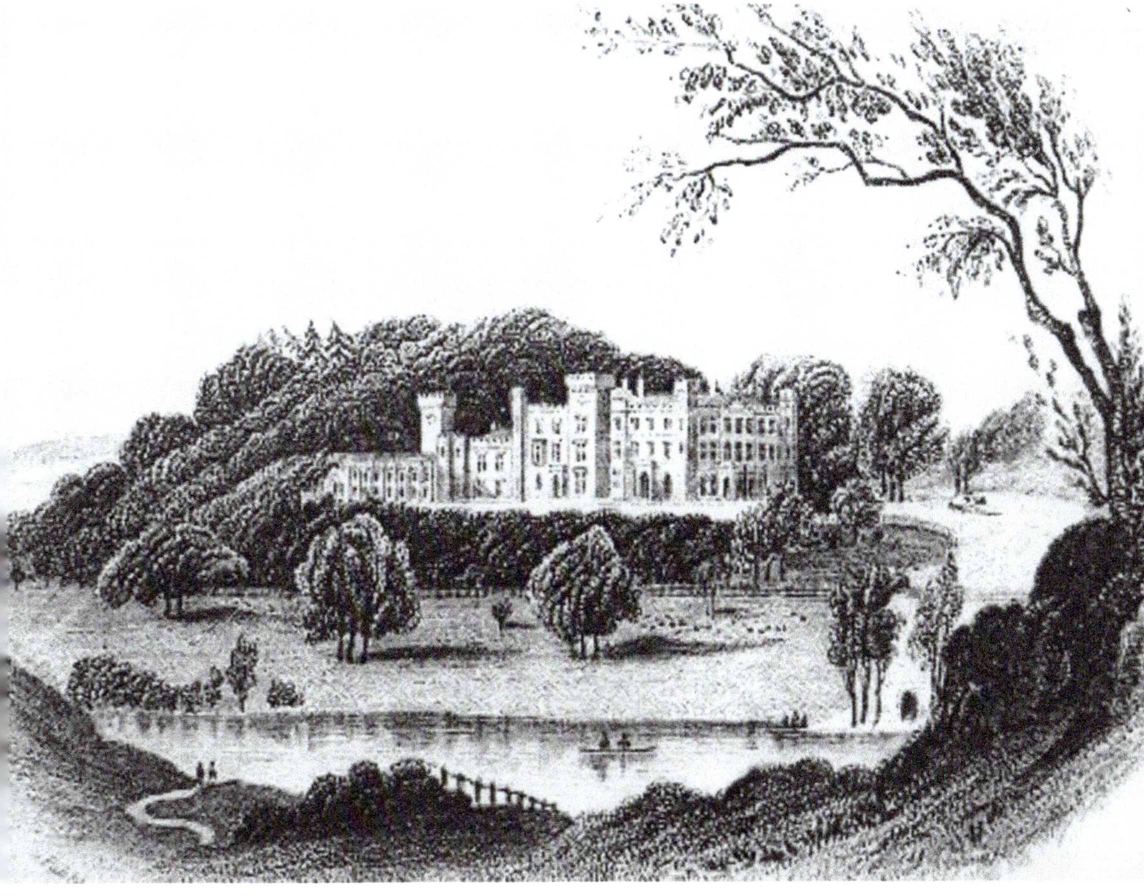

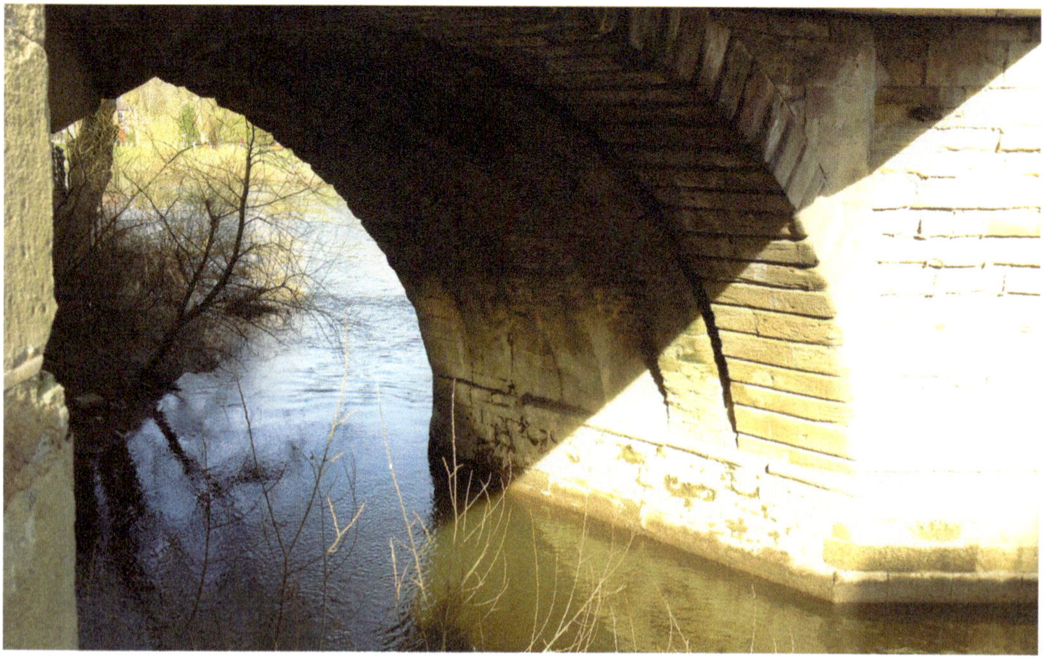

Stone Bridges

Above: There were medieval stone bridges across the Severn at Atcham, Buildwas and Bridgnorth. At Bridgnorth, the bridge has undergone many changes, but the original ribbed western arch survives in the present structure.

Below: The medieval bridge at Buildwas survived until 1795. John Gwynn's stone bridge at Atcham replaced an earlier structure in 1776, and was itself superseded in 1929.

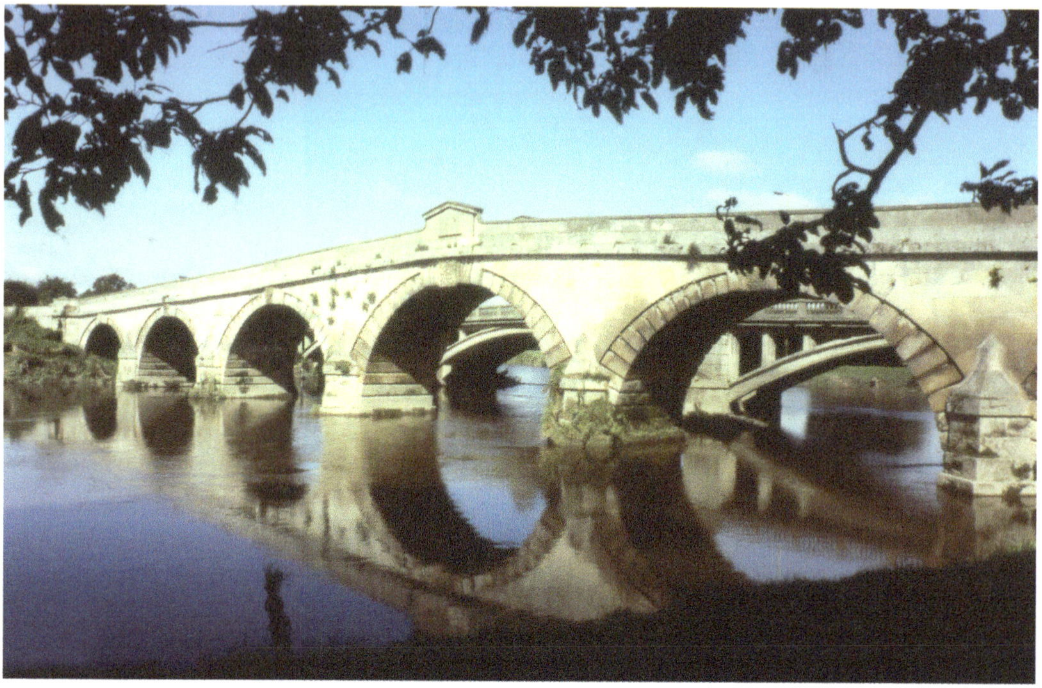

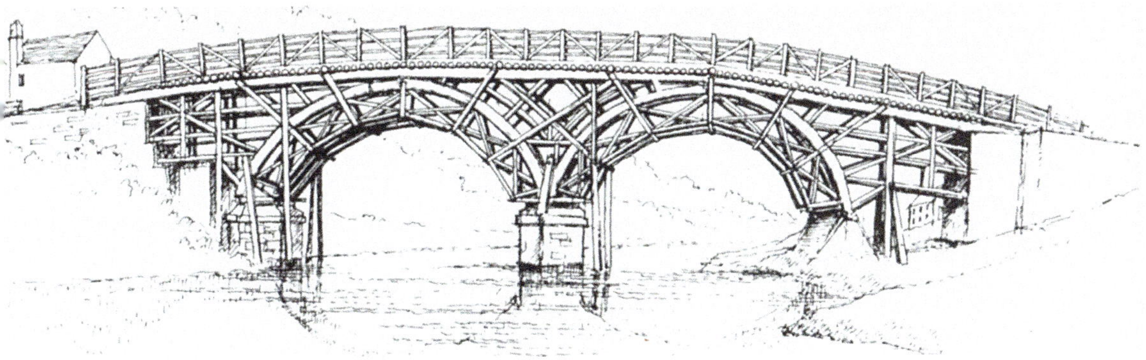

Wooden Bridges

Two wooden bridges were built over the Severn in the late eighteenth century. The bridge at Preens Eddy (Coalport) had two timber-frame arches with a midstream masonry pier (above); it opened in April 1780, but was destroyed by the Great Flood of 1795. The timber bridge at Cressage, of five spans on four timber trestle piers and stone abutments, was designed by Thomas Telford and opened in April 1801 (below).

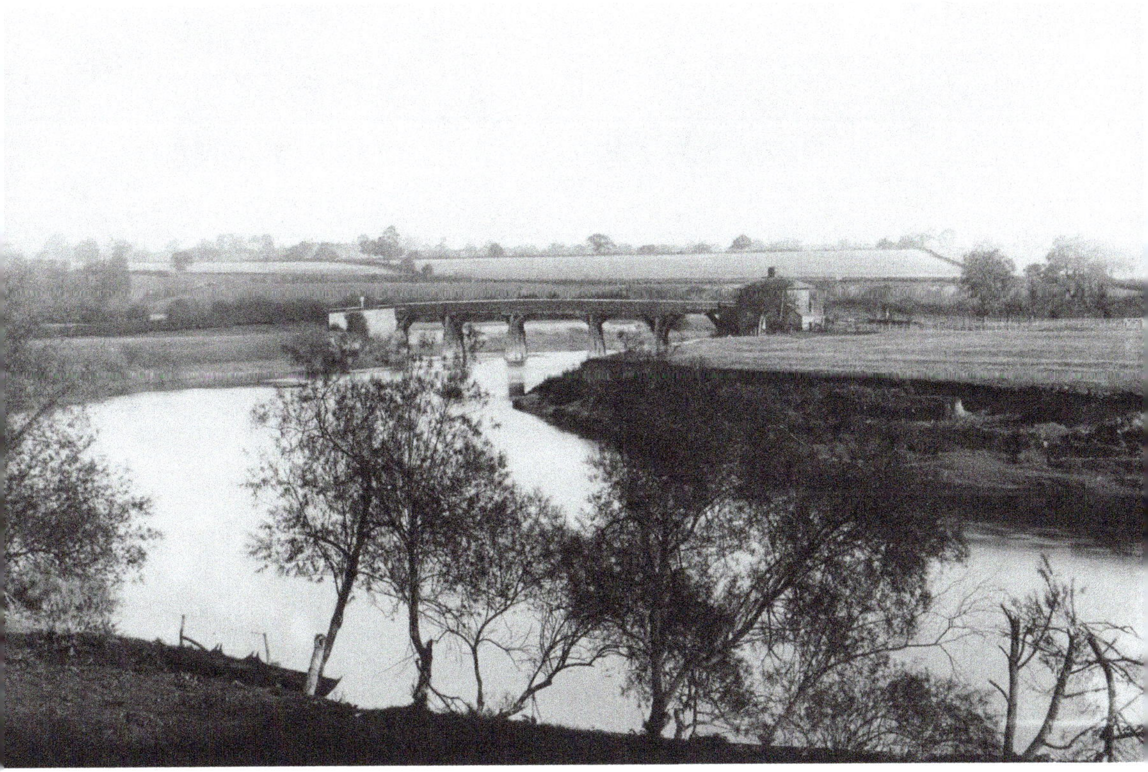

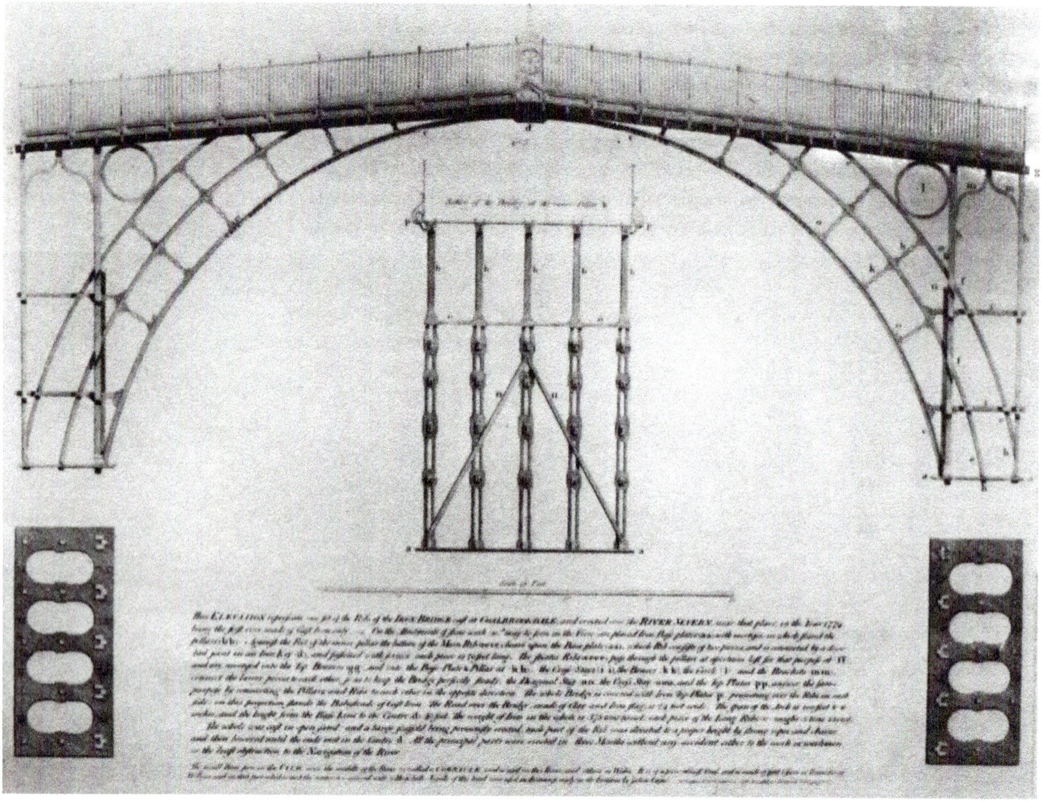

Iron Bridges

Above: The first iron bridge, designed by Thomas Farnolls Pritchard, sponsored by John Wilkinson and built by Abraham Darby III, was opened on 1 January 1781. Although much visited and admired, it was not copied for another decade.

Below: Locally, the example of the single-span, cast-iron structure withstanding the devastation of the Great Flood in 1795 influenced Thomas Telford in his design for the new Buildwas Bridge, opened the following year.

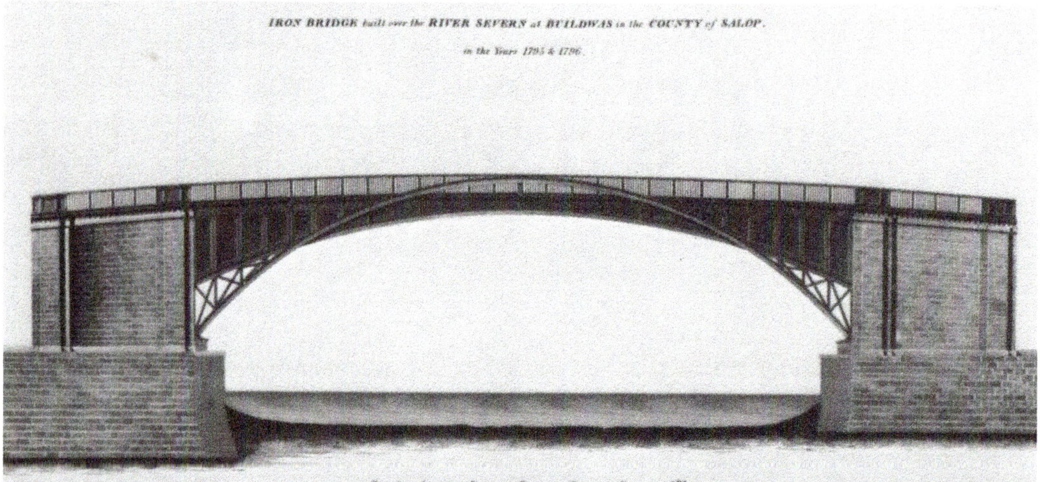

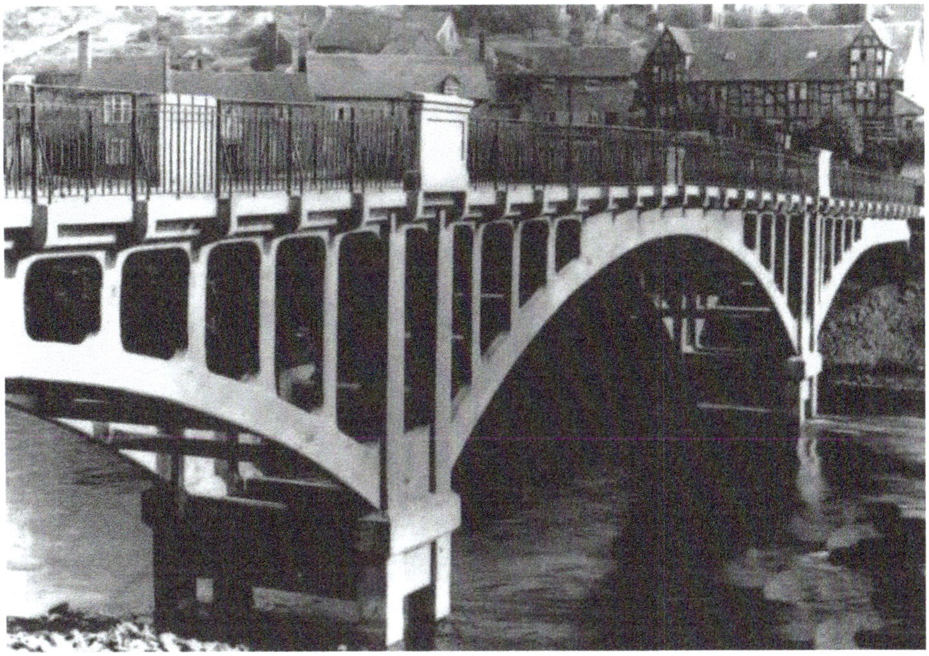

Reinforced Concrete Bridges

Three reinforced concrete bridges, designed by L. G. Mouchel, were built on this section of the river in the early twentieth century. At Jackfield, a bridge incorporating an open spandrel central arch was financed by local subscription and replaced the ferry in 1909 (above); being toll-free, it was always known as the Free Bridge. Telford's timber bridge at Cressage was replaced by three segmented arches of hollow construction in 1913 (below). The bridge at Atcham, built alongside Gwynn's bridge, opened in 1929.

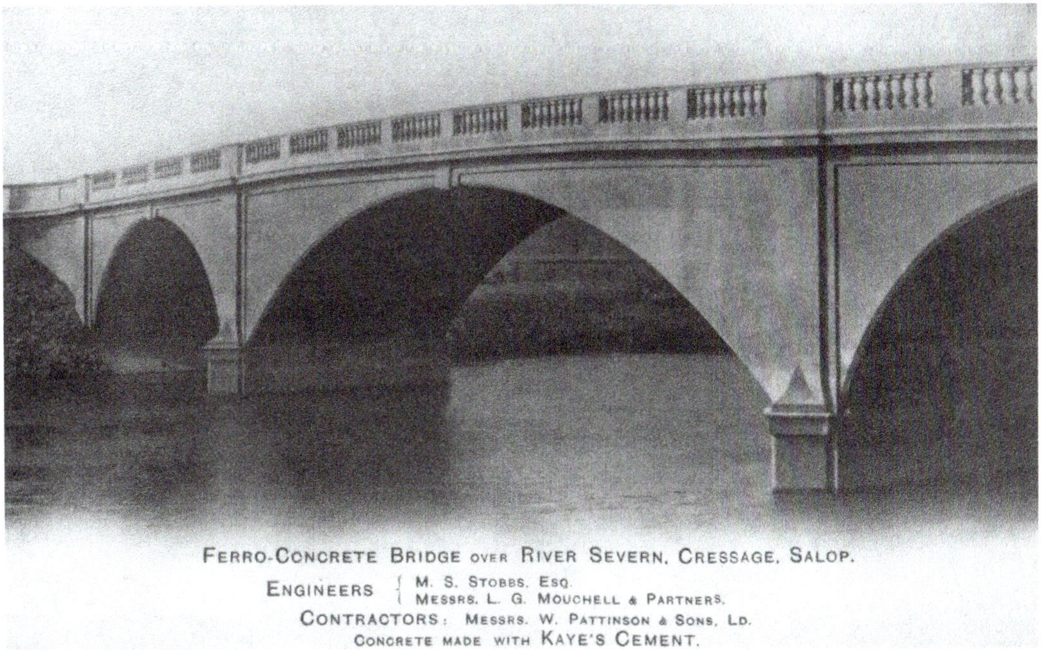

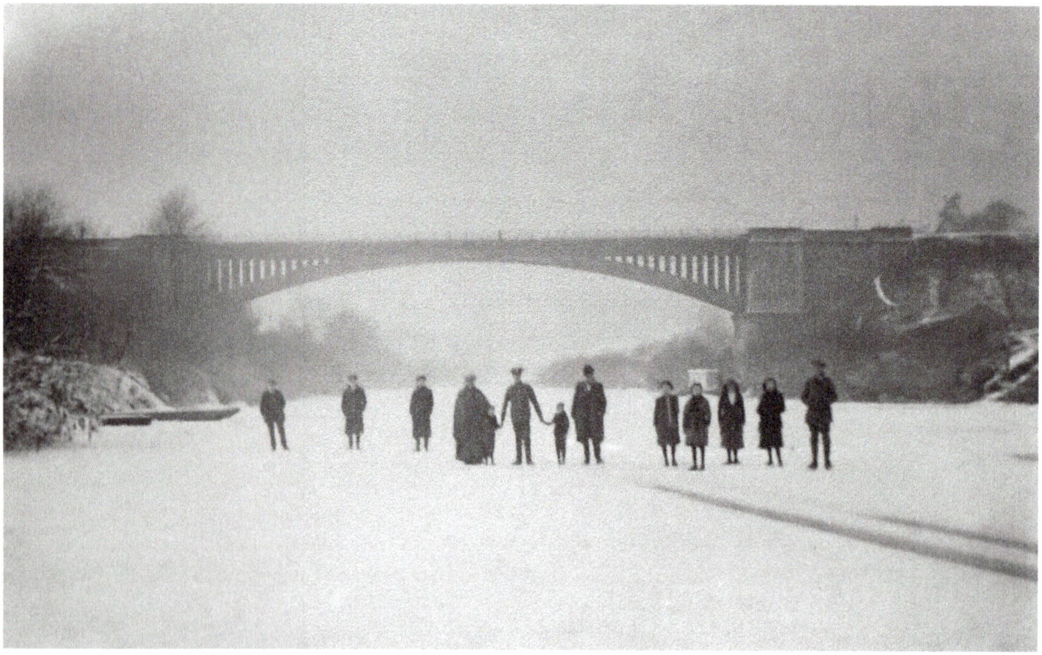

Railway Bridge

Opened in 1864, the Albert Edward Bridge, which carried the Wenlock Railway over the river at Coalbrookdale, was designed by John Fowler and cast by the Coalbrookdale Company. When built, it was said to be 'the largest cast-iron arch carrying a double line of railway that has yet been erected anywhere in the world'. Now single track, the bridge is still used by trains carrying fuel (formerly coal, now biomass) to Ironbridge power station.

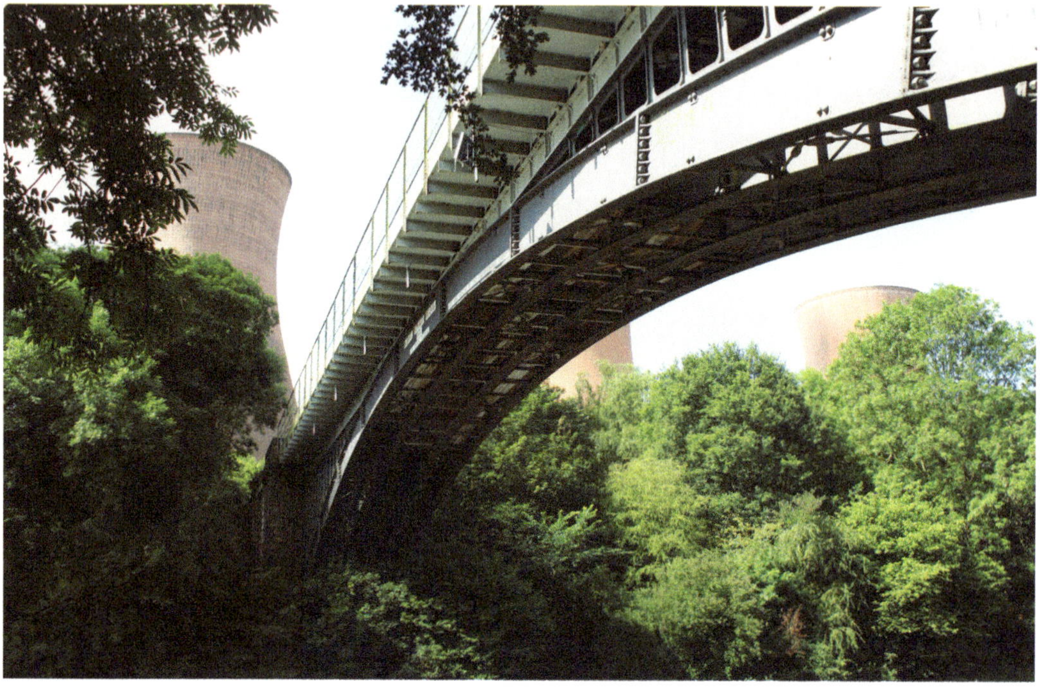

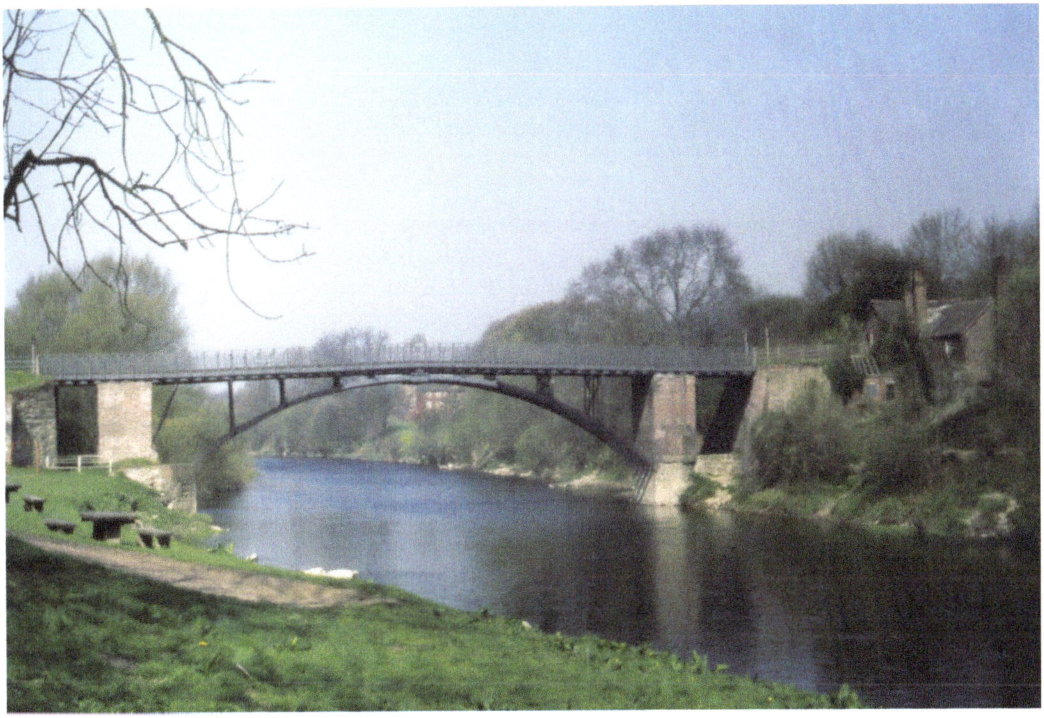

Replacement Metal Bridges

At Coalport, the original two-span timber Preens Eddy Bridge was rebuilt as a single-span structure, with two iron ribs and a timber deck, following the Great Flood of 1795. This was later developed into an all-iron bridge with five ribs in 1818 by John Onions of Broseley (above). Telford's Buildwas Bridge of 1796, damaged over the years by ground movement, was replaced in 1905 with a Pratt truss steel girder bridge, constructed by the Horsehay Company (right).

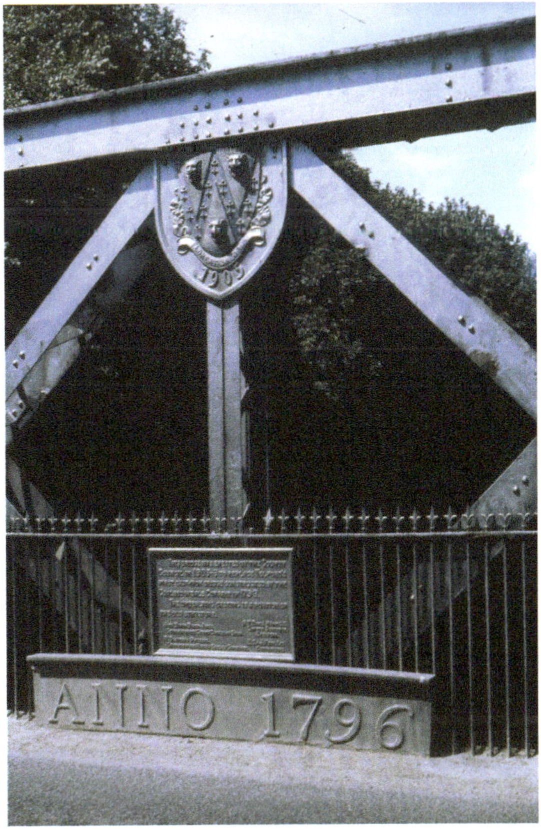

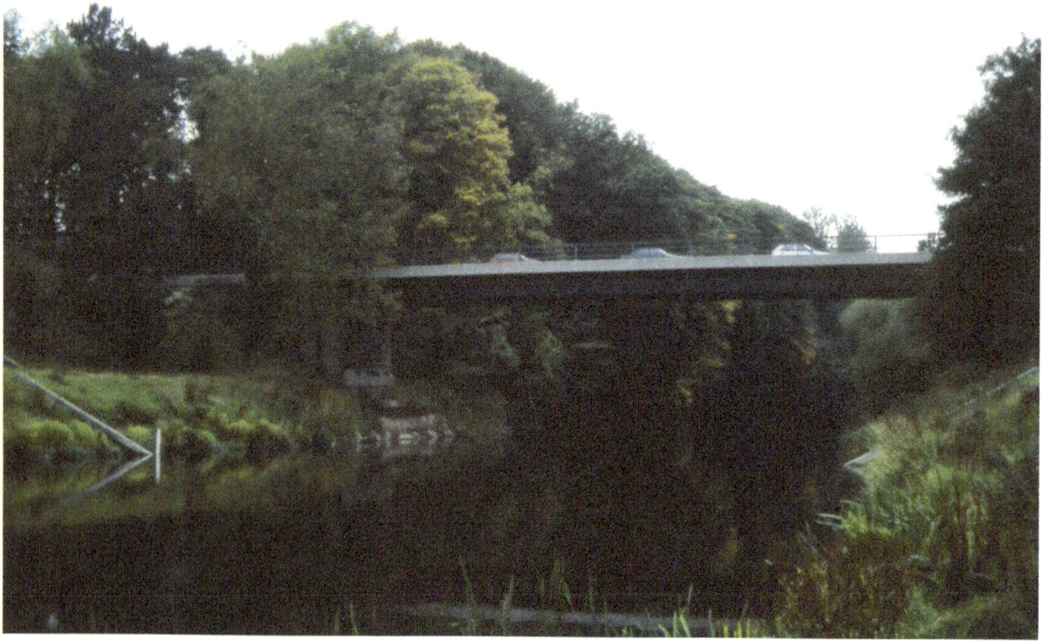

Late Twentieth-Century Bridges

Two of the early twentieth-century bridges failed to see the century out, again as a result of damage caused by earth movement. The 1906 Buildwas Bridge was replaced by the present structure in 1992 (above); this is a steel girder bridge carried on concrete abutments and piers. The 1909 Free Bridge was replaced in 1994 by this cable stay design with an overall span of 57 metres and a steel tower of 30 metres (left).

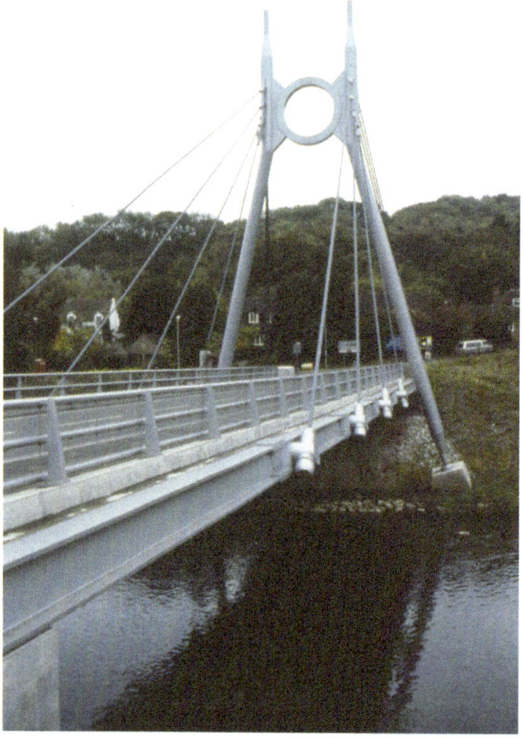

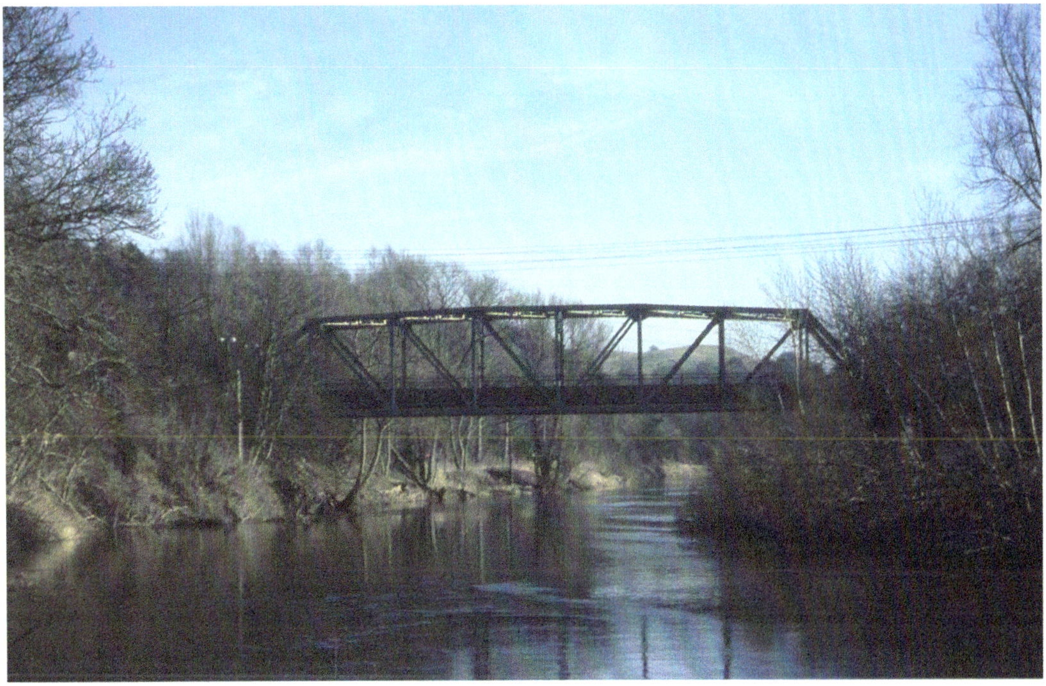

Power Station Bridges

Above: Access to the power station, which was constructed at the entrance to the Ironbridge Gorge in the early 1930s, was provided by this Pratt truss steel girder bridge.
Below: The bridge has been closed to traffic since the building of a three-span concrete structure, some 400 yards downstream, to serve the new power station that opened in the late 1960s.

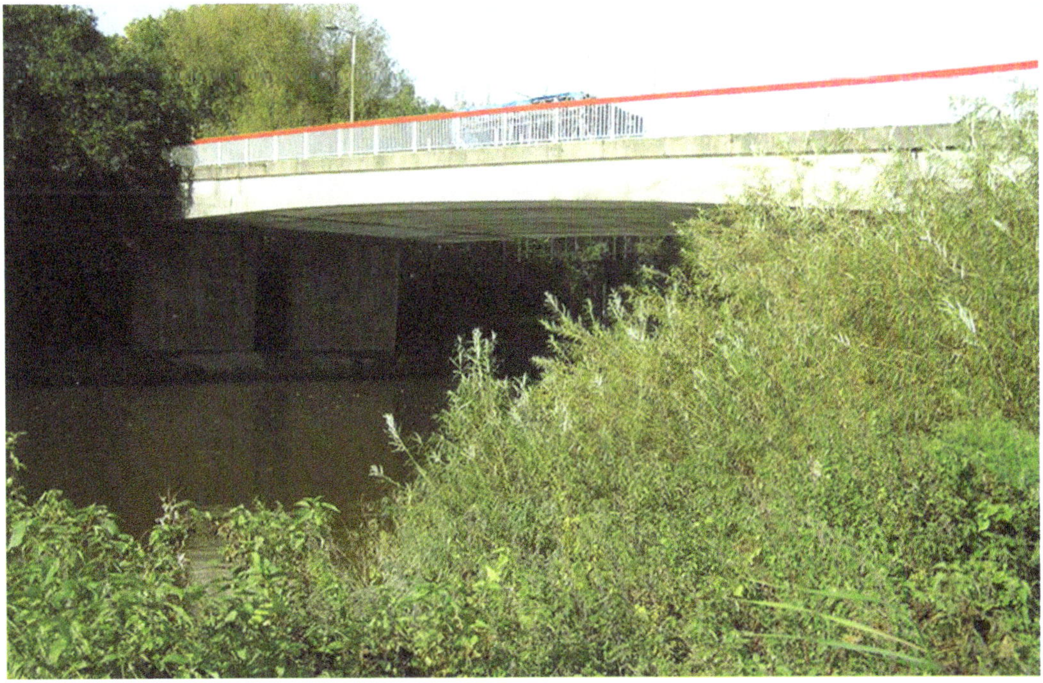

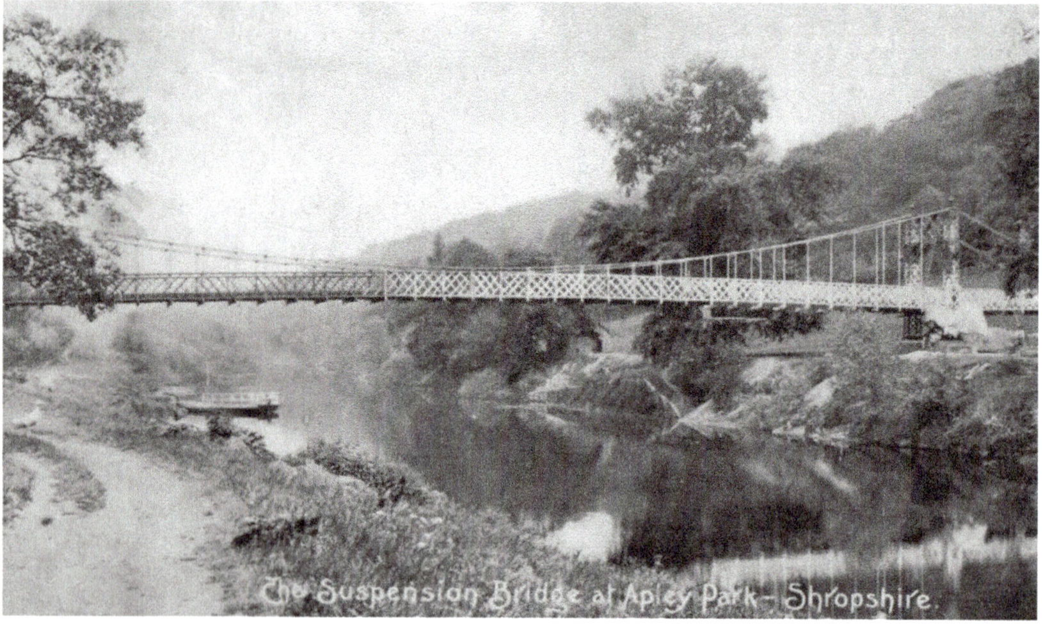

Other Bridges

Above: The suspension bridge at Apley was built in 1905 for the private use of Apley Park. When residents of the estate were given permission to use the bridge to get to the SVR station at Linley, the ferry here closed.

Below: The footbridge at Coalport, built to replace the ferry, was opened in 1922 as a memorial to those locally who died in the First World War; the names of the fallen of the Second World War were subsequently added. The bridge was restored by Shropshire County Council in 2000.

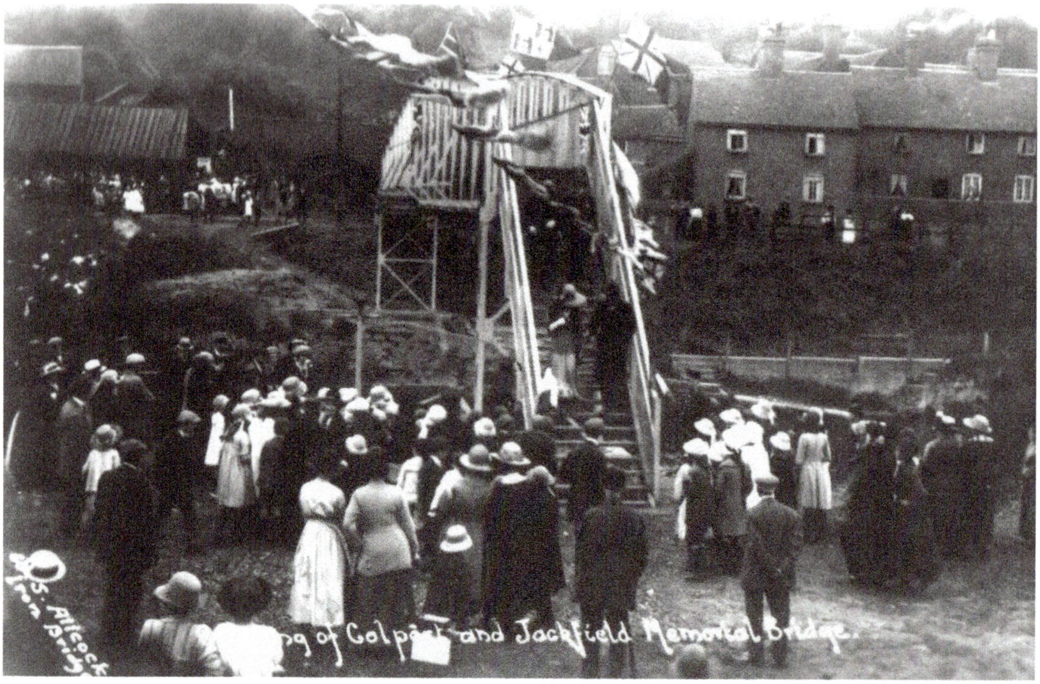

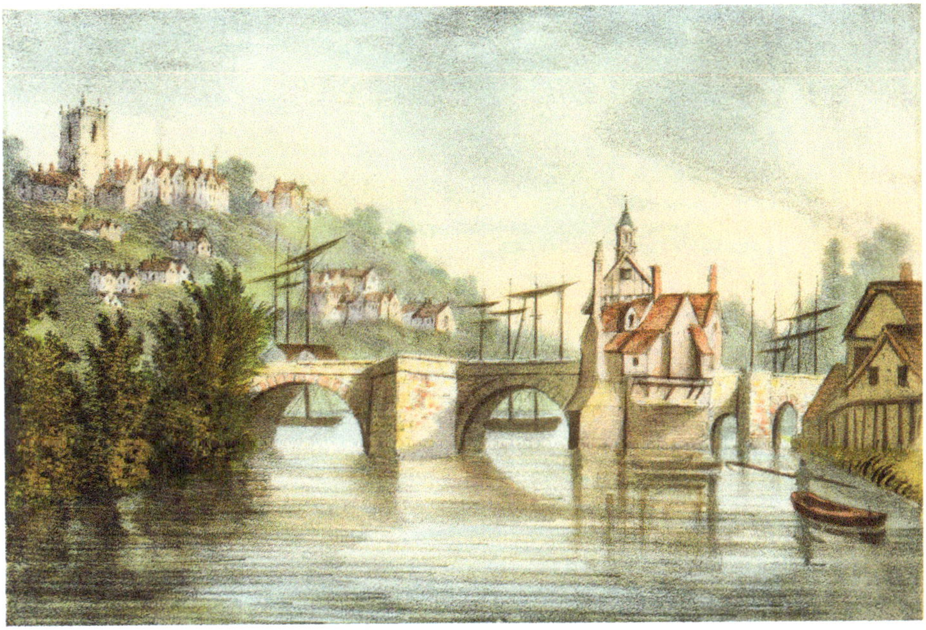

Bridgnorth Bridge

Above: The original medieval stone bridge of eight arches was reduced to seven by 1700, and four of these arches are shown in this early 1790s painting. Following damage caused by the Great Flood of 1795, some of the rebuilding proposed by Thomas Telford was carried out by Thomas Simpson in 1813 and a section was widened by John Smallman ten years later. *Below*: Reduced to six arches and considered 'the handsomest structure on the Severn', the bridge continued in this form until 1960, when the volume of vehicular and pedestrian traffic required an overall widening and strengthening.

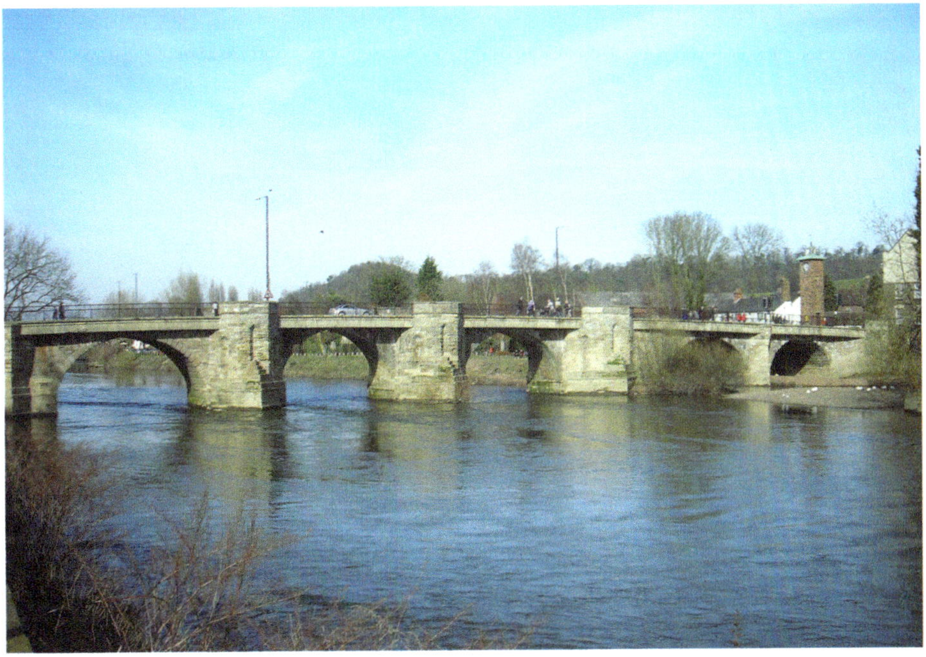

Part II

2

The Canal Network

The canals of East Shropshire were built in three distinct stages over a period of sixty years in the late eighteenth and early nineteenth centuries. The Donnington Wood Canal was completed in 1767; the Wombridge, Ketley, Shropshire and Shrewsbury Canals were built in the decade between 1787 and 1796; and the Newport Branch of the Birmingham & Liverpool Junction Canal (B&LJC) opened in 1835. The first three, shorter, canals were privately owned, but the other three longer ones required Acts of Parliament to authorise their construction and also shareholders to raise the necessary capital.

Apart from the Newport Branch, which was built to carry the 70-foot narrowboats used on the national network, the canals of East Shropshire were tub-boat canals built to serve the coal, iron and clay industries that were developing on the Coalbrookdale Coalfield. Designed to cope with the undulating nature of the area and the shortage of surface water, tub boats were 20 feet in length and 6 feet 4 inches wide; they were square ended and flat bottomed for use on inclined planes rather than locks; they could carry 3, 5 or 8 tons of cargo and were pulled in trains by horses. Originally made of wood, later tub boats built by the Lilleshall Company were made of iron.

The tub-boat canals were linked to the River Severn at Coalport, and only after the opening of the Newport Branch of the B&LJC in 1835 was the network connected to the national canal system at Norbury Junction, just inside Staffordshire. Competition from railways led to a decline in the use of canals, and in fact the London & North Western Railway took over ownership of the three local public canals. Over the next century, sections both private and public were closed, and the final length of canal from Shrewsbury to the main line of the Shropshire Union Canal at Norbury Junction was officially abandoned in 1944. A trust set up in 2000 aims to reopen this section.

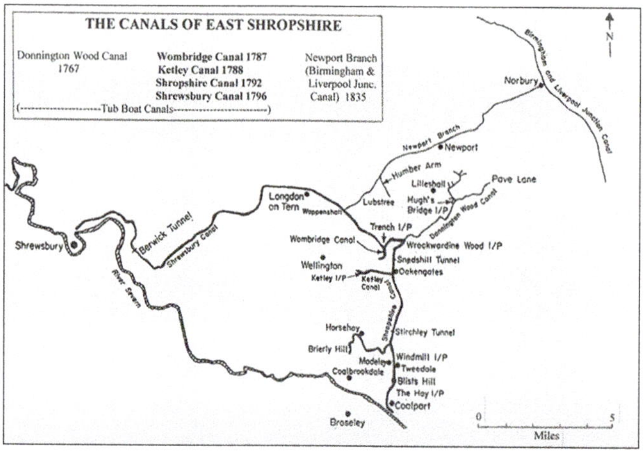

The canals of East Shropshire.

3

The First Canal

The Donnington Wood Canal was the first canal to be built in Shropshire. Earl Gower, owner of the extensive Lilleshall estate in East Shropshire, was brother-in-law to the Duke of Bridgewater. Knowing of the Duke's new canal, opened in 1761, which carried coal from Worsley to Manchester, Earl Gower wanted something similar to help him develop the mineral resources of his own estate. In 1764, he took into partnership the brothers John and Thomas Gilbert, and three years later the new company opened a 5½-mile canal from a coal mine at Donnington Wood to a roadside wharf at Pave Lane, on the Newport–Wolverhampton turnpike road. Later, a branch canal carried coal to limestone quarries and kilns in the Lilleshall/Pitchcroft area, from which lime for agricultural purposes and limestone for furnaces in the Donnington Wood area were transported.

The new Lilleshall partnership, which was formed in 1802 and later became the Lilleshall Company, leased the canal and in 1825 built a short arm to their new Lodge furnaces. However, the development by the Lilleshall Company of its own standard gauge railway from the early 1850s onwards led to the decline of the canal. With the closure of the Lilleshall limeworks in the 1870s, the section of the canal east of Muxton Bridge became disused, and part of the former canal bed was converted into a driveway to Lilleshall Hall. After 1882, only the western mile of the canal leased by the Lilleshall Company was still in use, and this was abandoned in the first decade of the twentieth century.

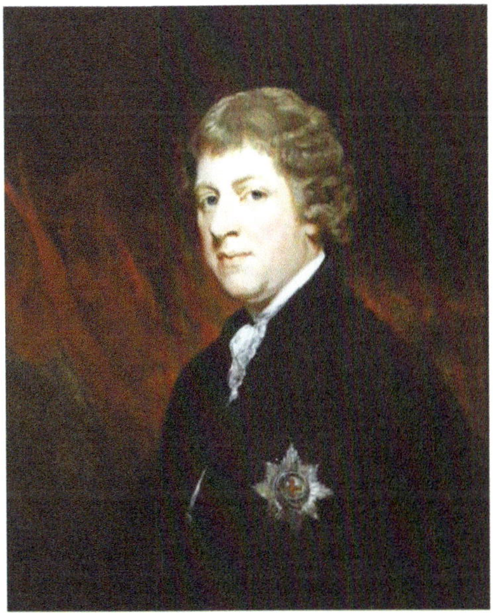

Earl Gower, later Marquess of Stafford (1721–1803).

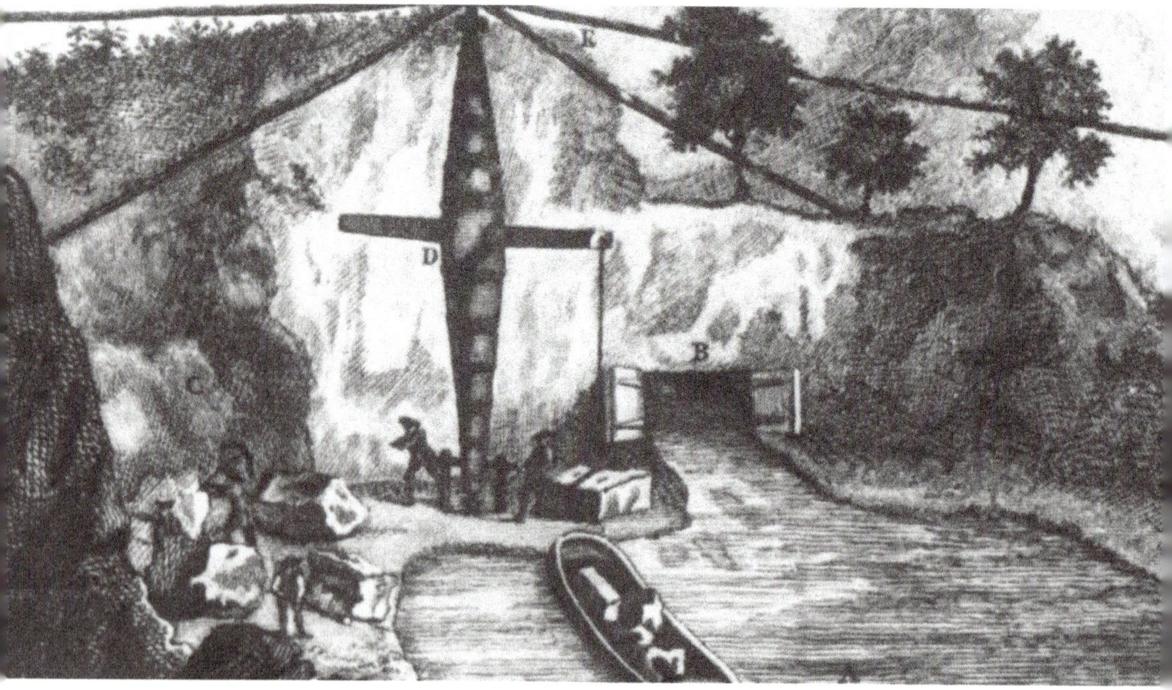

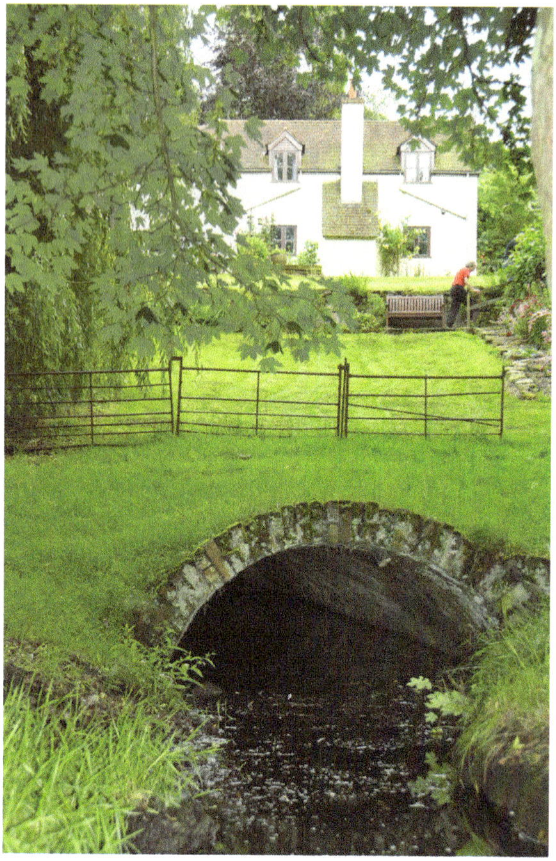

Tunnels

Above: As at Worsley on the Duke of Bridgewater's canal, some of the seams of coal in the mine at Donnington Wood were navigable and boats could travel into the workings. Below at Hugh's Bridge, where the level of the Lilleshall branch was 42 feet below that of the main line, a system of a tunnel and two vertical shafts was used at first to pass materials between the two canals, later to be replaced by an inclined plane.

Left: The tunnel entrance can still be seen.

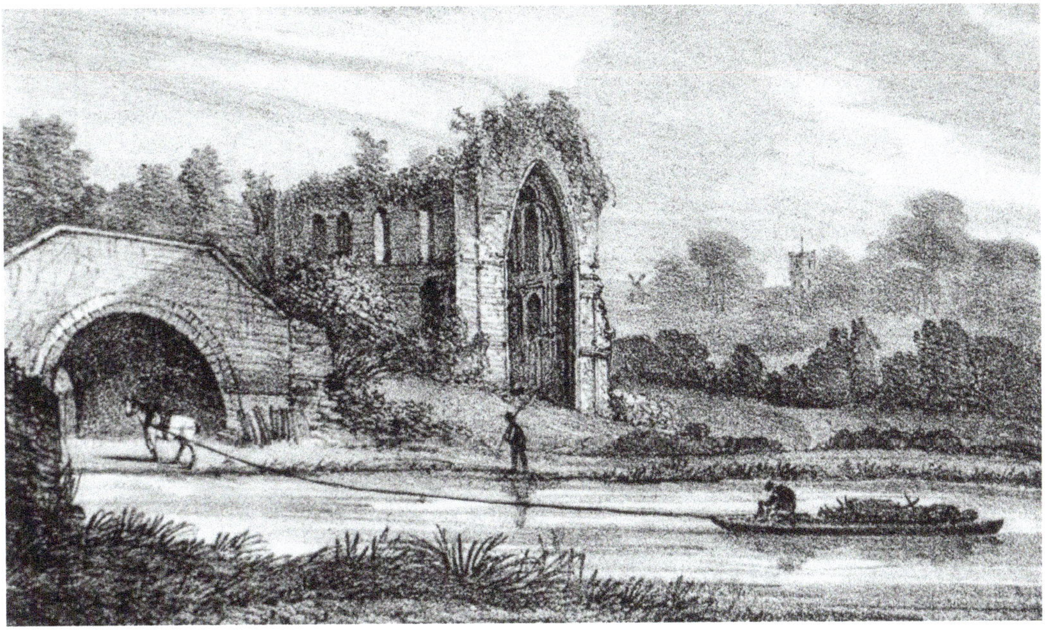

Tub Boats

The main traffic on the canal – coal from Donnington Wood to Pave Lane and the Lilleshall limeworks, lime from the limeworks stone to the furnaces at its western end and lime for agricultural use – was at first carried in 3-ton tub boats.
Above: The 1790s engraving perhaps rather inaccurately portrays such a boat being towed past Lilleshall Abbey.
Below: The photograph of a mine pumping engine at Donnington Wood in the late nineteenth century includes an iron tub boat on the canal.

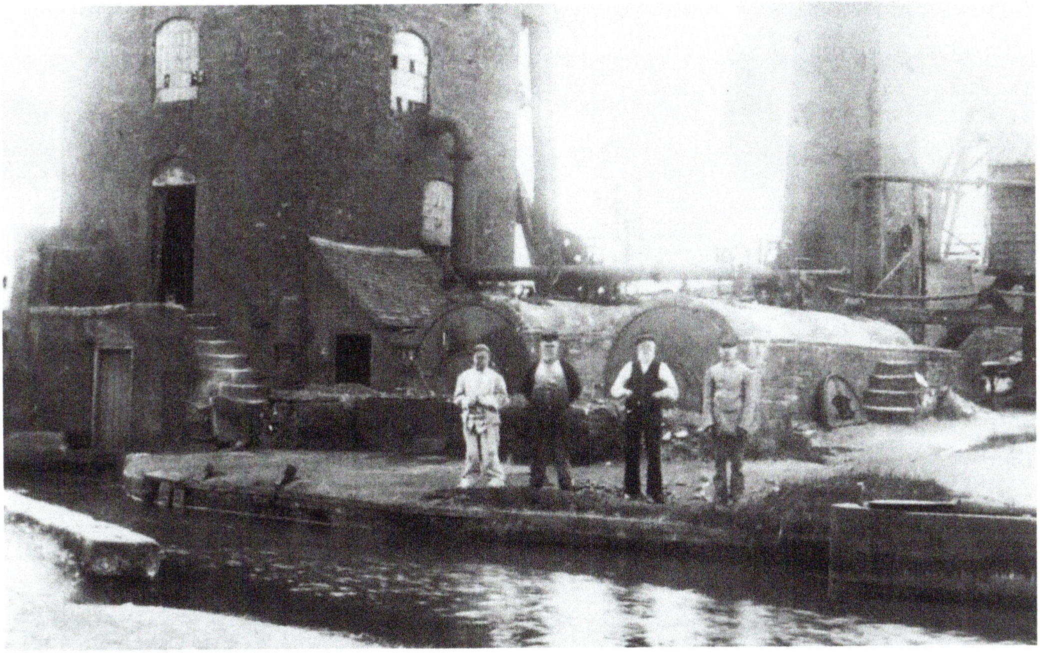

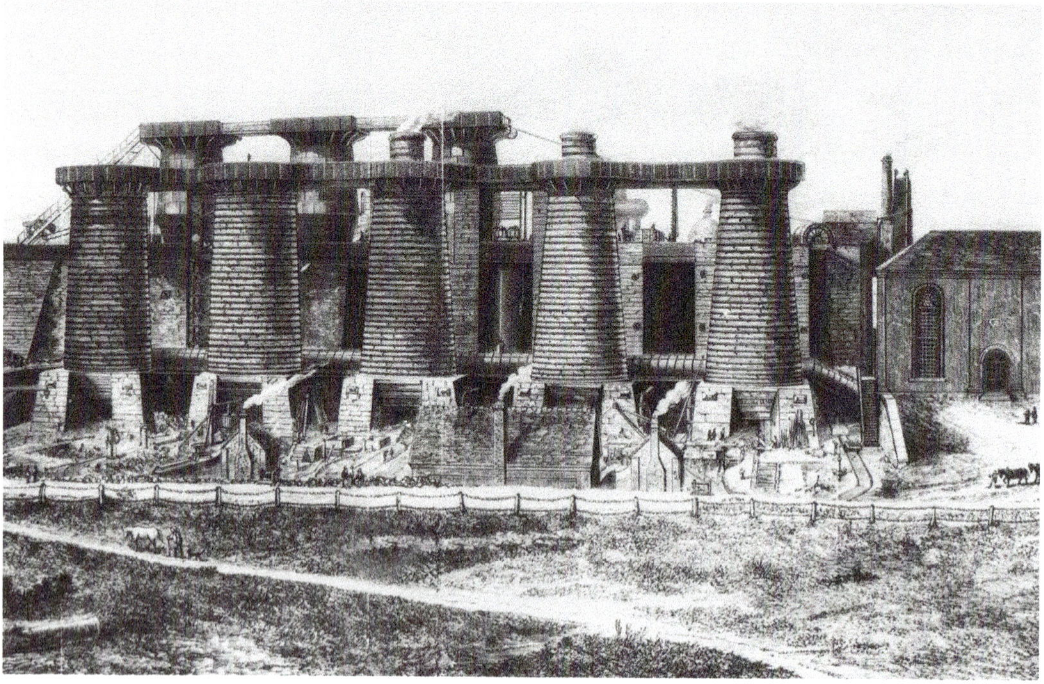

Lodge Furnaces

Above: The Lodge furnaces were famous for the quality of their cold-blast iron. The original two furnaces were extended to five by 1859. They were served by an arm of the canal.
Below: The remains of the furnaces, which were blown out in 1888, and the canal arm can still be seen in Granville Country Park.

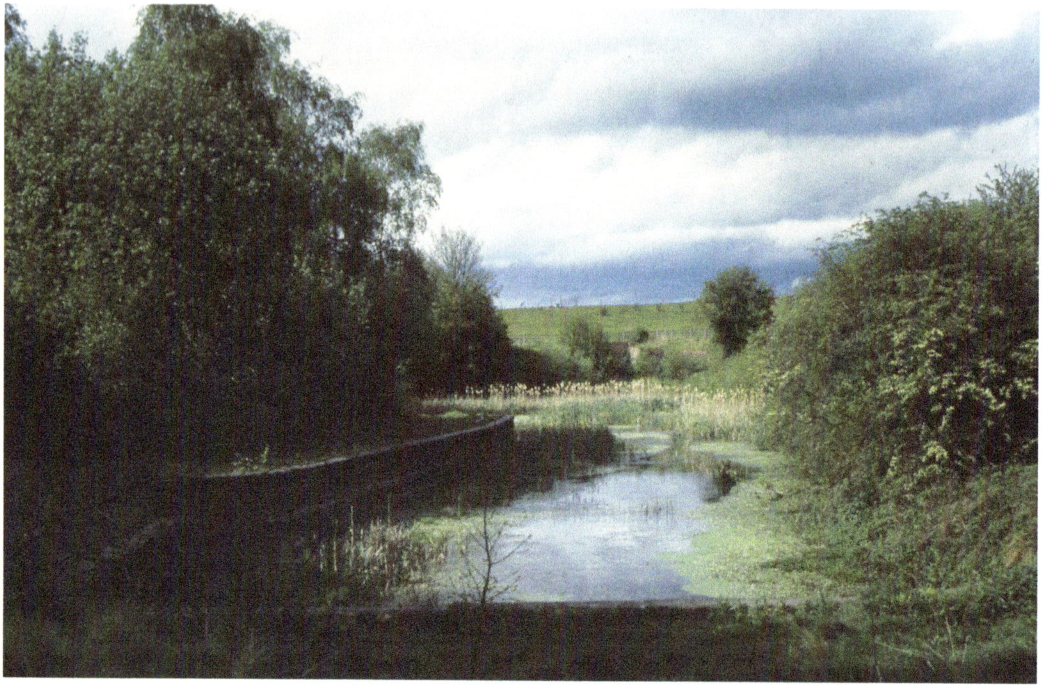

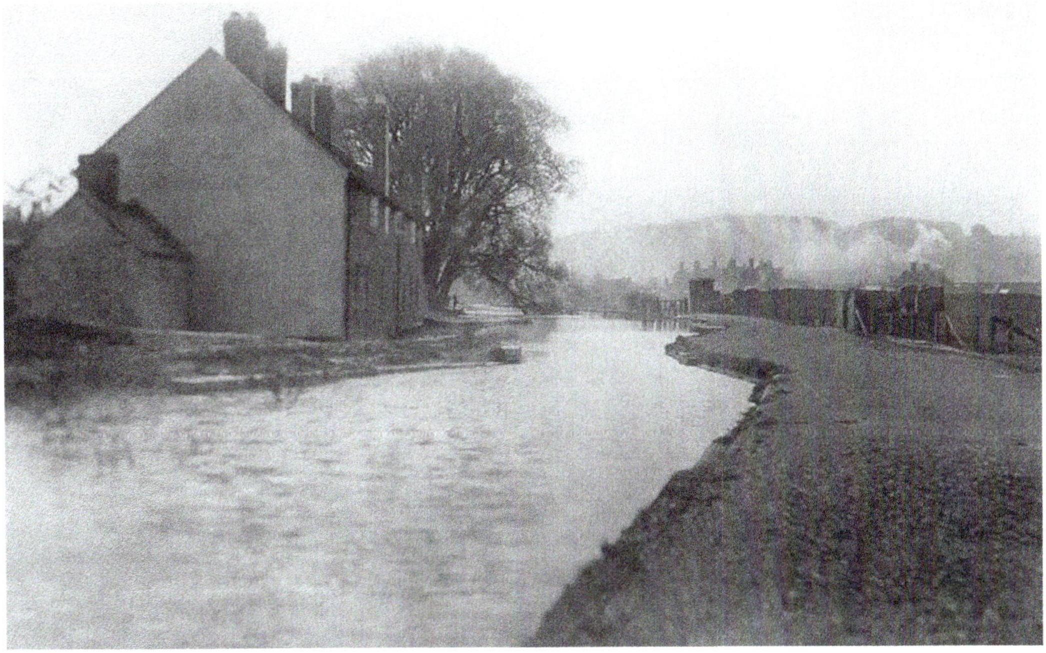

Other Industries

Other industrial sites of the Lilleshall Company were served by the Donnington Wood Canal. The early twentieth century photograph (above) shows the canal near the site of the Old Yard, where boats had been made and later a wide range of manufacturing duties had been undertaken. The shell of Muxton Bridge Colliery's engine house (below) can still be seen alongside the bed of the canal.

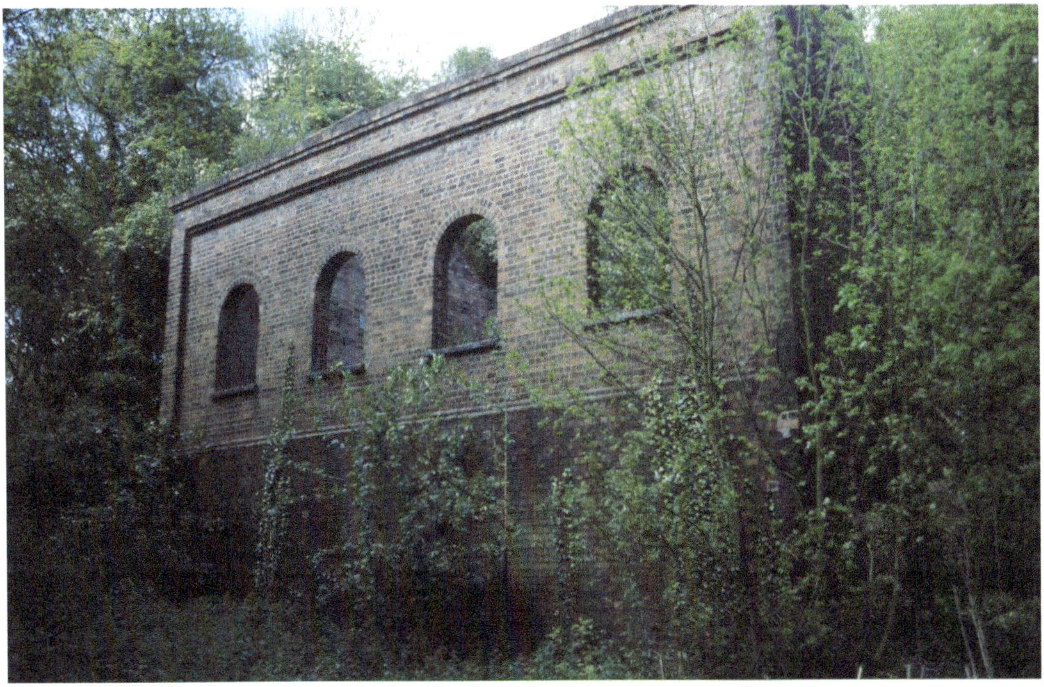

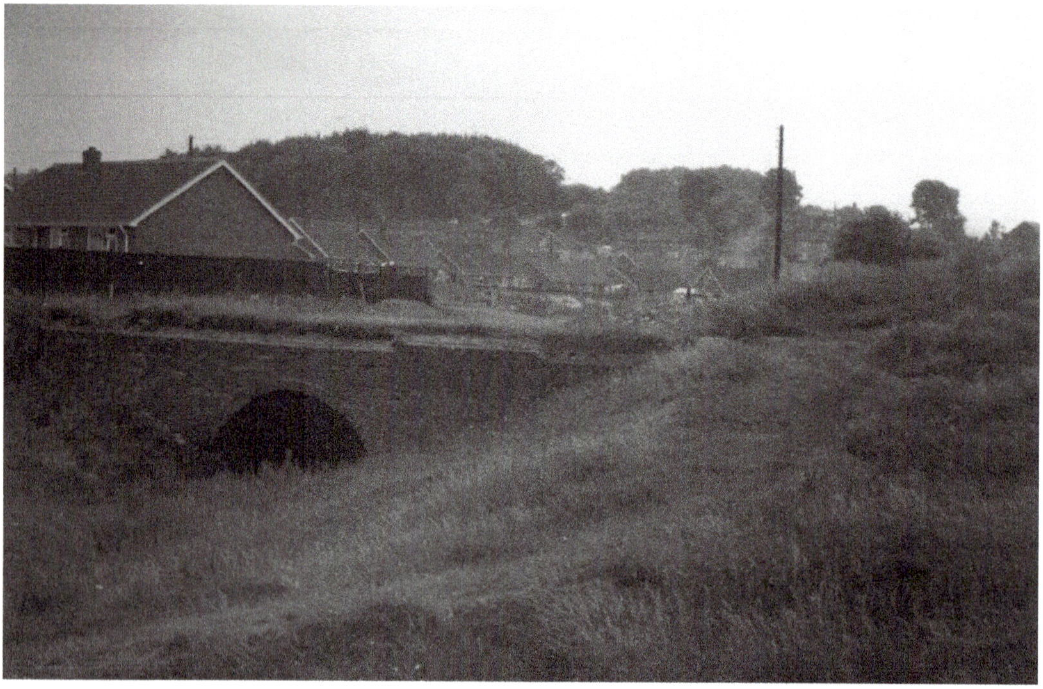

Bridges

Several bridges and bridge remains can still be seen along the course of the canal today. Pictured are the first bridge at Donnington Wood (above) and the final bridge, which carries the road from Pitchcroft to Pave Lane (below).

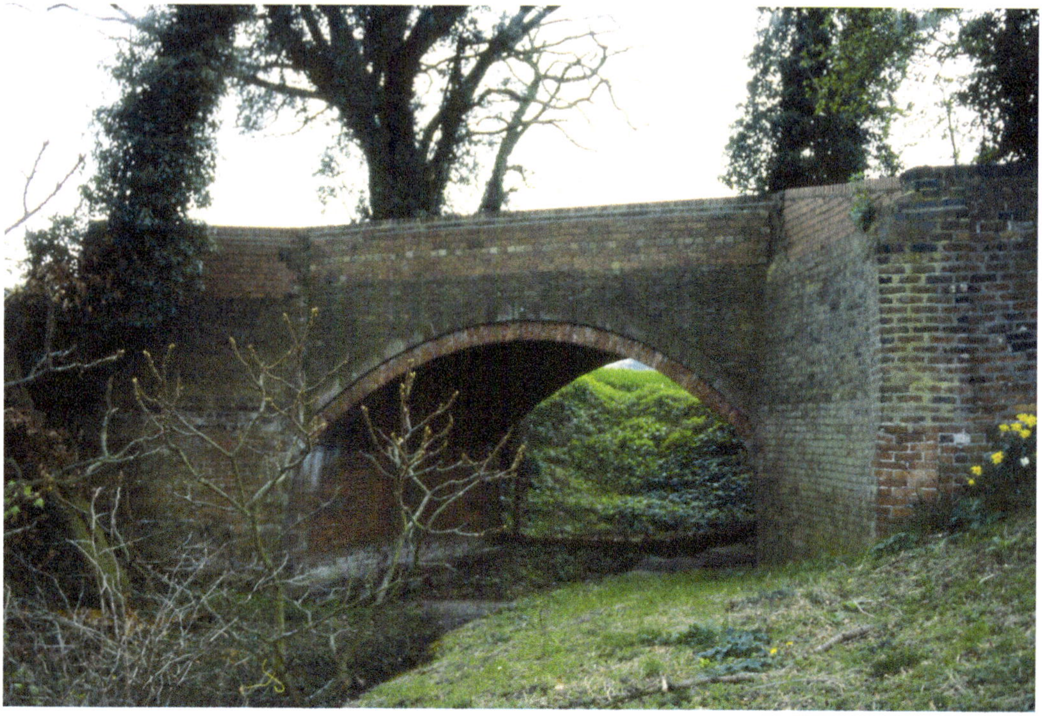

4

William Reynolds' Private Canals

William Reynolds and his half-brother Joseph took over the management of Ketley ironworks from their father Richard in 1782, and two years later built new furnaces at Donnington Wood. Needing supplies of raw materials, William discovered valuable deposits of coal and ironstone near the surface on nearby Wombridge Common, and in 1787 constructed a 1¾-mile canal on the level from west of Wombridge church to Donnington Wood furnaces, at a cost of £1,640. The canal also served a glassworks that was built by the Reynolds brothers in 1792. When the Shrewsbury Canal, from Donnington Wood to the county town, was surveyed in 1792 the new company purchased a little over a mile of the eastern end of Reynolds' Wombridge Canal for £820. The remaining part of the Wombridge Canal later served two ironworks in the area but was abandoned by the 1840s.

In 1788, to maintain supplies of raw materials for Ketley ironworks, William Reynolds leased land to build a canal to carry coal from the Oakengates area at Snedshill. To overcome a difference in level of 73 feet at the western end of the 1½-mile canal, Reynolds built the first canal inclined plane in this country. Using a counterbalancing system, descending 8-ton tub boats loaded with coal or ironstone and carried on wheeled cradles, and pulling up boats that were empty or carrying lighter iron goods. When, by 1792, the Ketley Canal was joined to the new Shropshire Canal, Reynolds was able to link up with the other ironworks in which he had interests at Donnington Wood, Horsehay and Coalbrookdale. At the end of the Napoleonic Wars, Ketley ironworks closed and, although re-established in 1818, the inclined plane and lower level of the Ketley Canal did not reopen. However, the section of canal serving Ketley coal wharf, adjacent to the Holyhead Road, remained open until the 1850s.

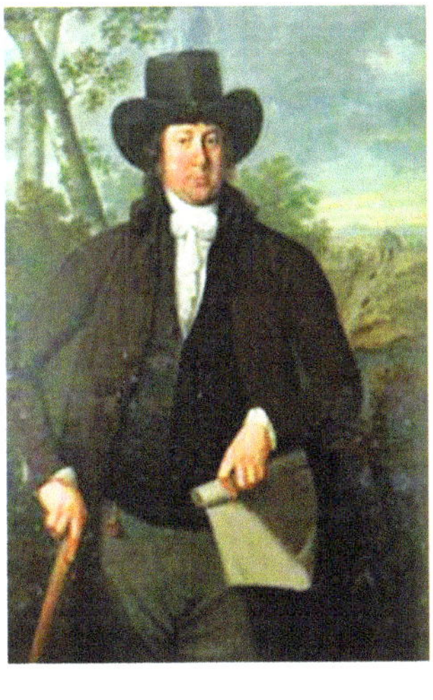

William Reynolds (1758–1803).

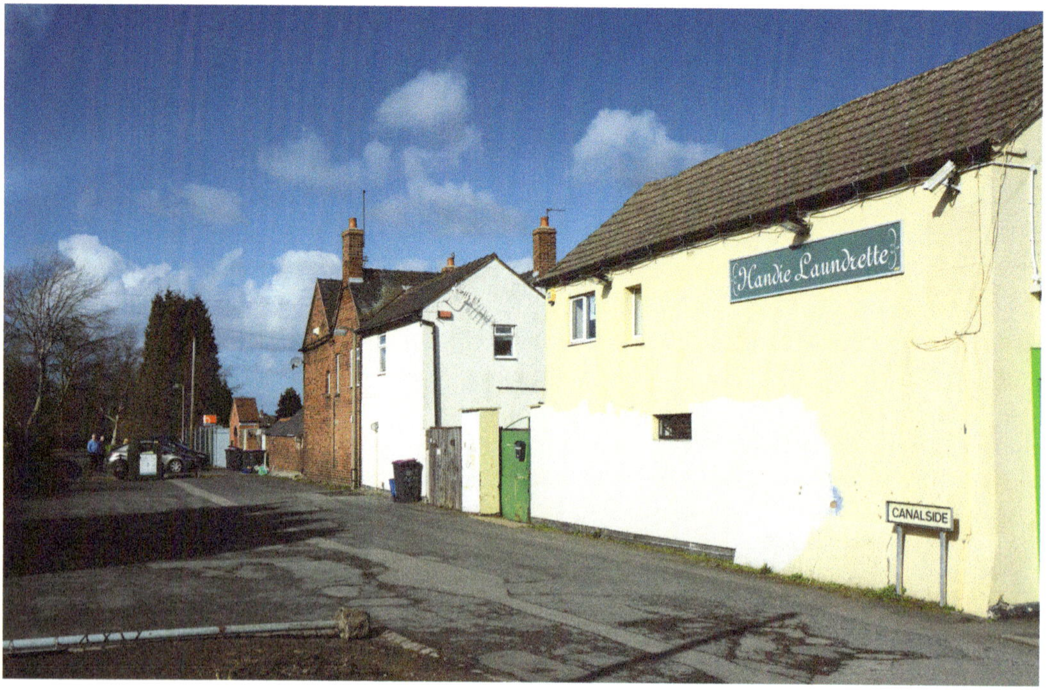

Wombridge Canal

Above: The course of the Wombridge Canal beyond Furnace Lane, Wrockwardine Wood, is used as an entrance to lock-up garages, and is now named Canalside.
Below: It continues as a pathway and passes the site of Reynolds' glassworks, with the parish church in the background.

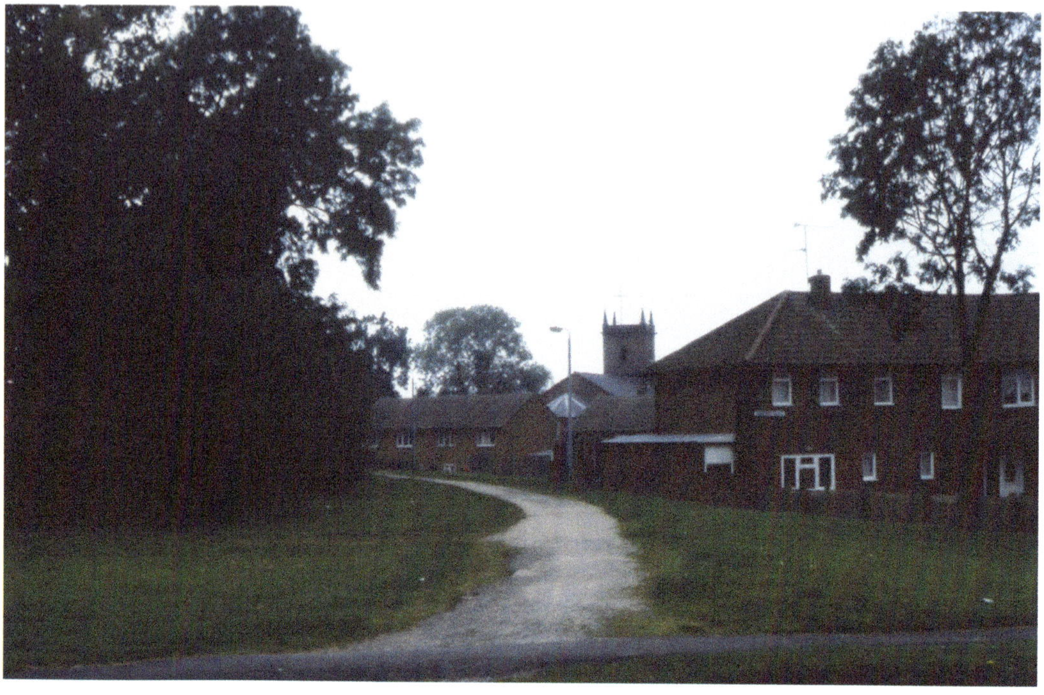

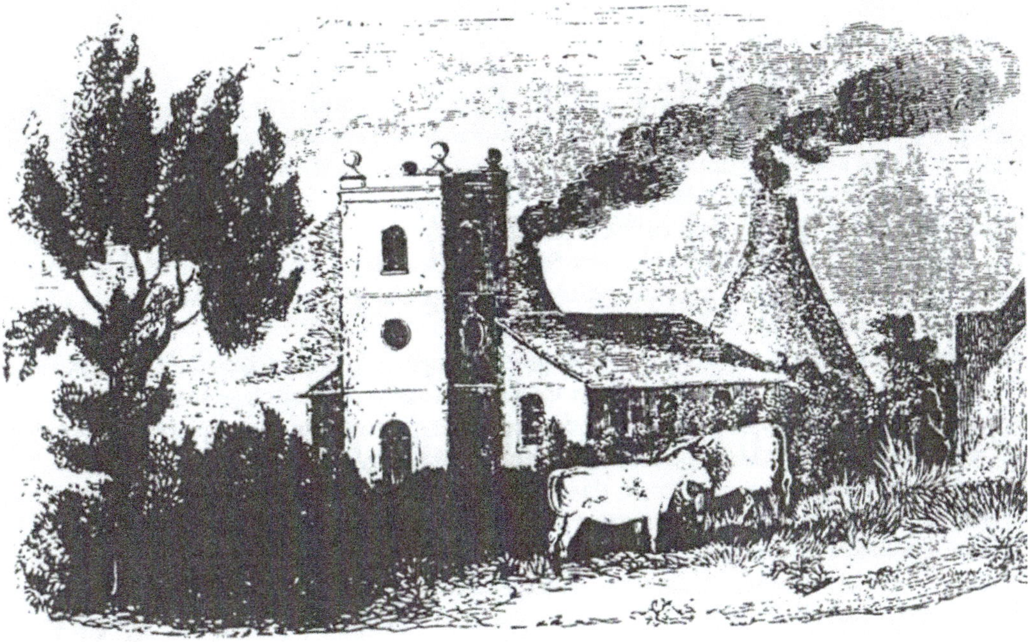

Glassworks And Teague's Bridge

Above: The two cones of the glassworks are shown on an engraving made after the Church of Holy Trinity was built in 1833.

Below: The sectional iron bridge, which carried the original Teague's Bridge Lane (now Wombridge Road) over the canal, is shown prior to removal to storage at IGMT, with The Bridge public house in the background.

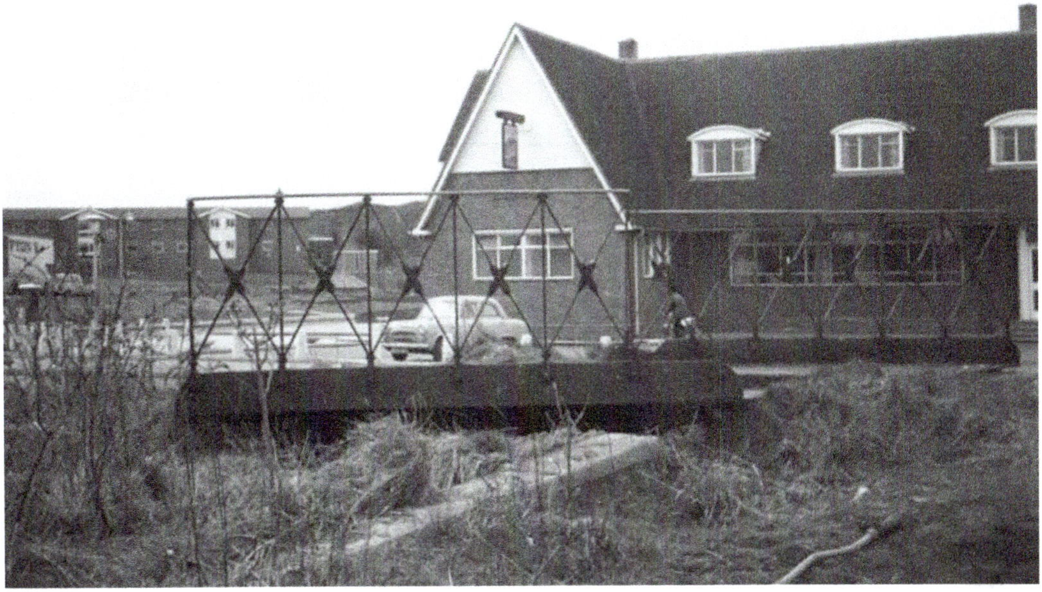

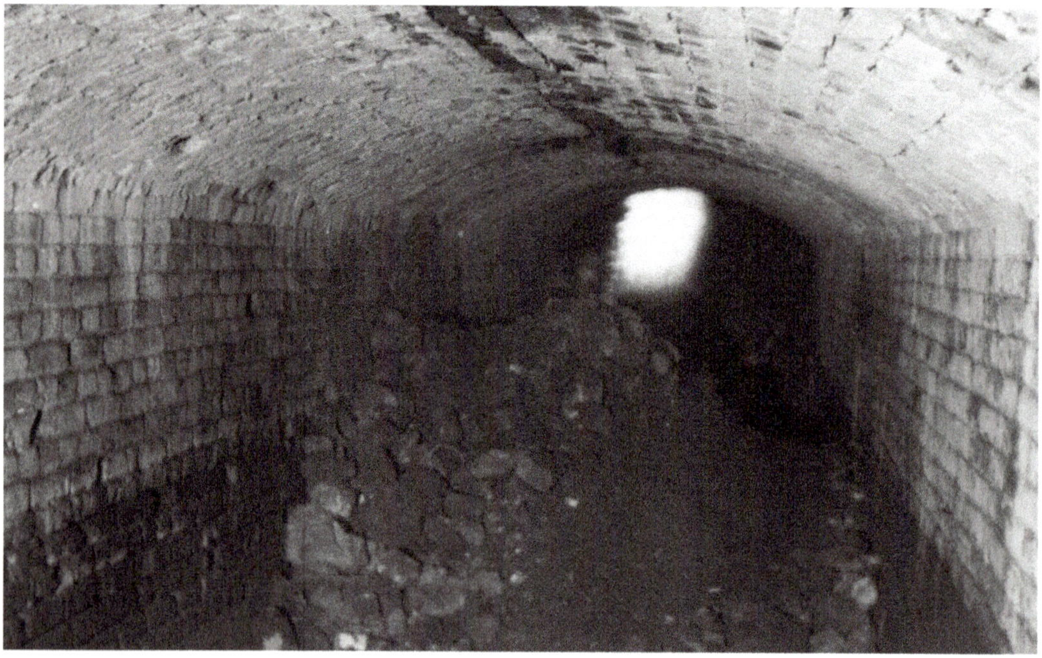

Wombridge Tunnel

South of Wombridge church the canal passed through a short tunnel, which was rediscovered during building work in 1965 (above), before terminating in the area of Wombridge Common shown in the lower photograph. From here, a tramway was later built to serve the New Hadley furnaces of John Wilkinson, opened in 1804. A new arterial road, Wombridge Way, now crosses this area from left to right.

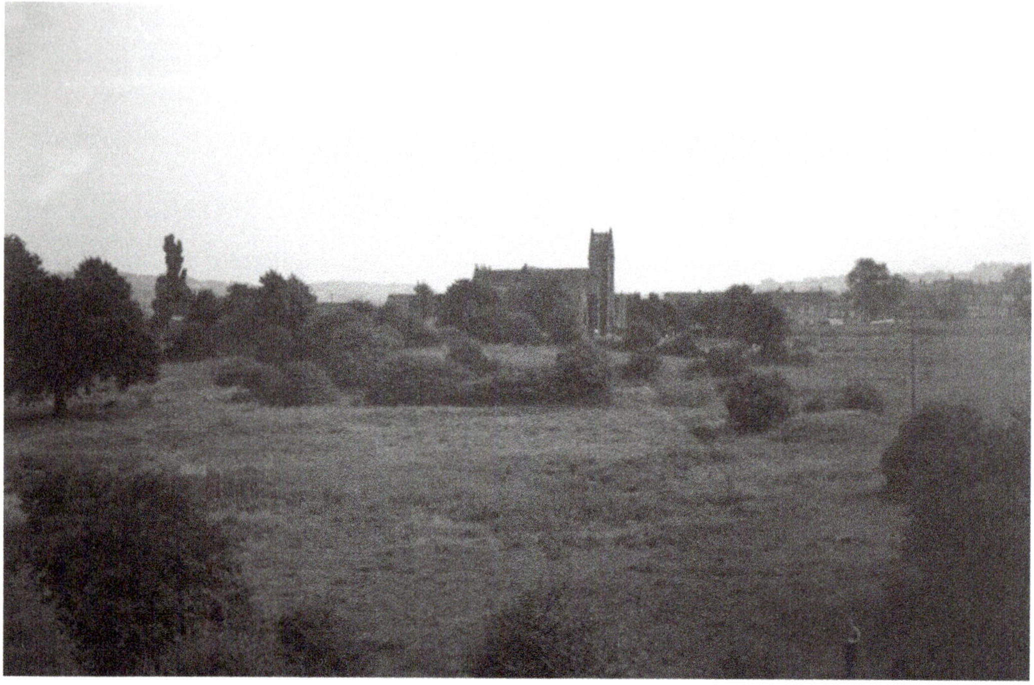

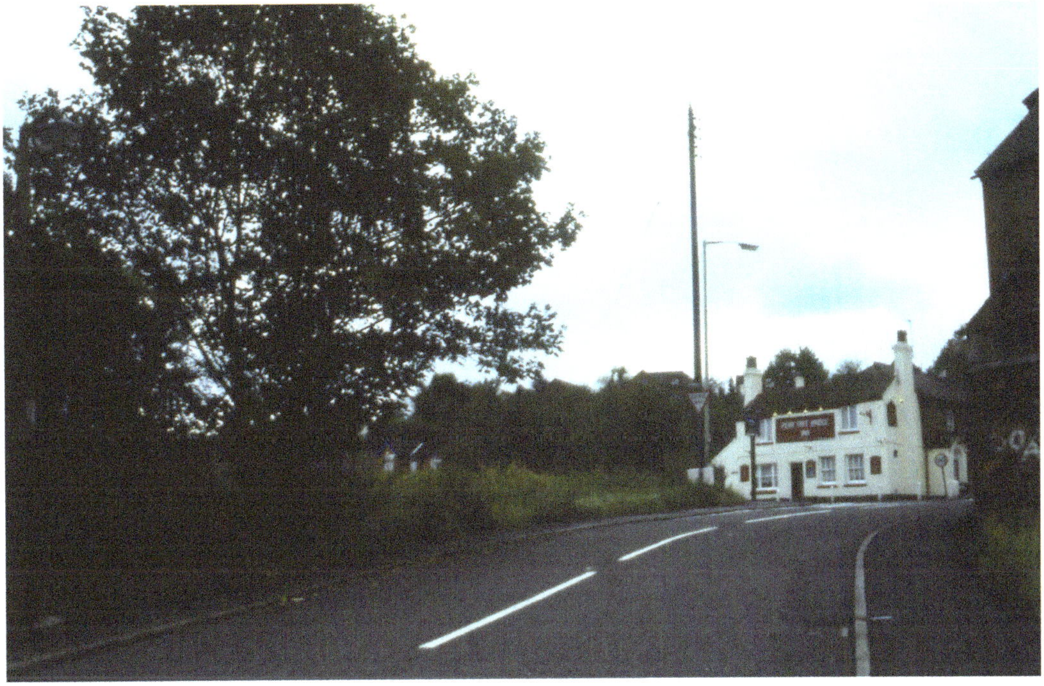

Ketley Canal

Of the bridges that were built on the upper section of the Ketley Canal, the only remains are a slight hump in Charlton Street as it approaches the former public house named after Pear Tree Bridge (above), and the scrolled stone block in Hartsbridge Road (below).

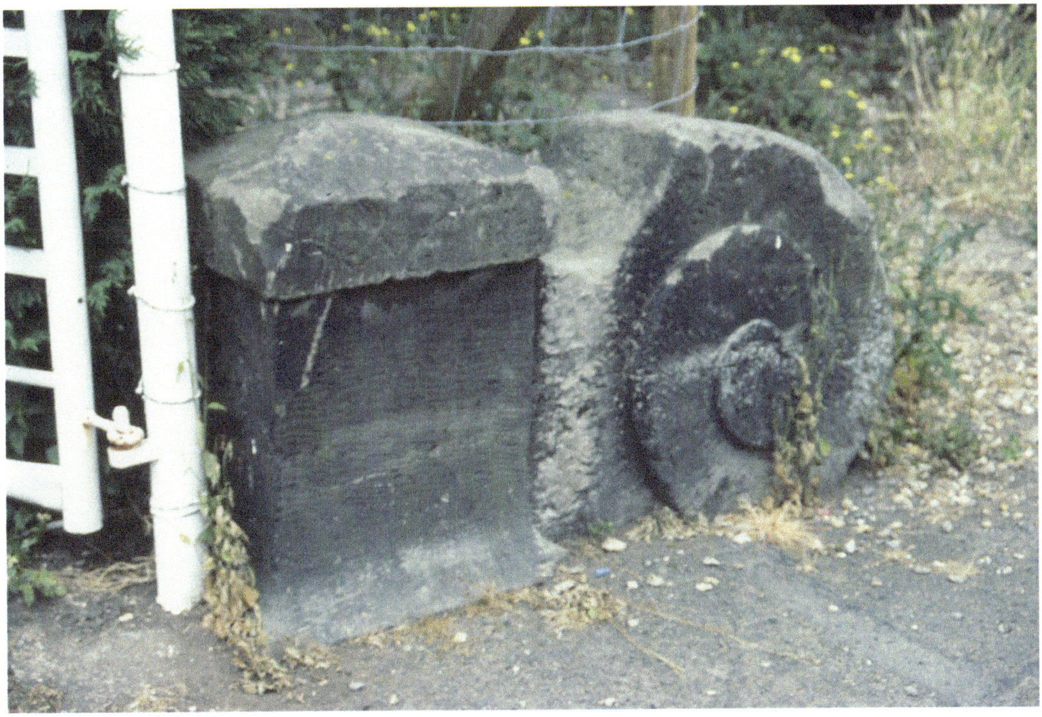

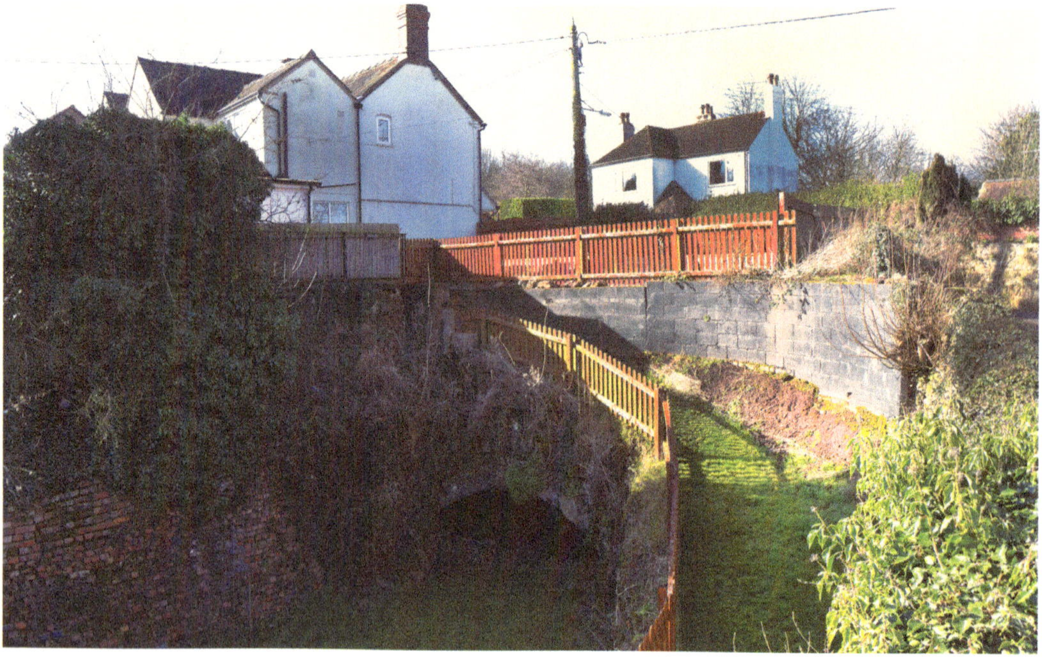

Tunnel And Remaining Canal Bed

Above: The eastern portal of the tunnel that carried the canal beneath Potters Bank can still be seen. Below the western portal has been filled in, but there is a remaining section of canal containing water.

Below: The former site of Ketley coal wharf has been built over.

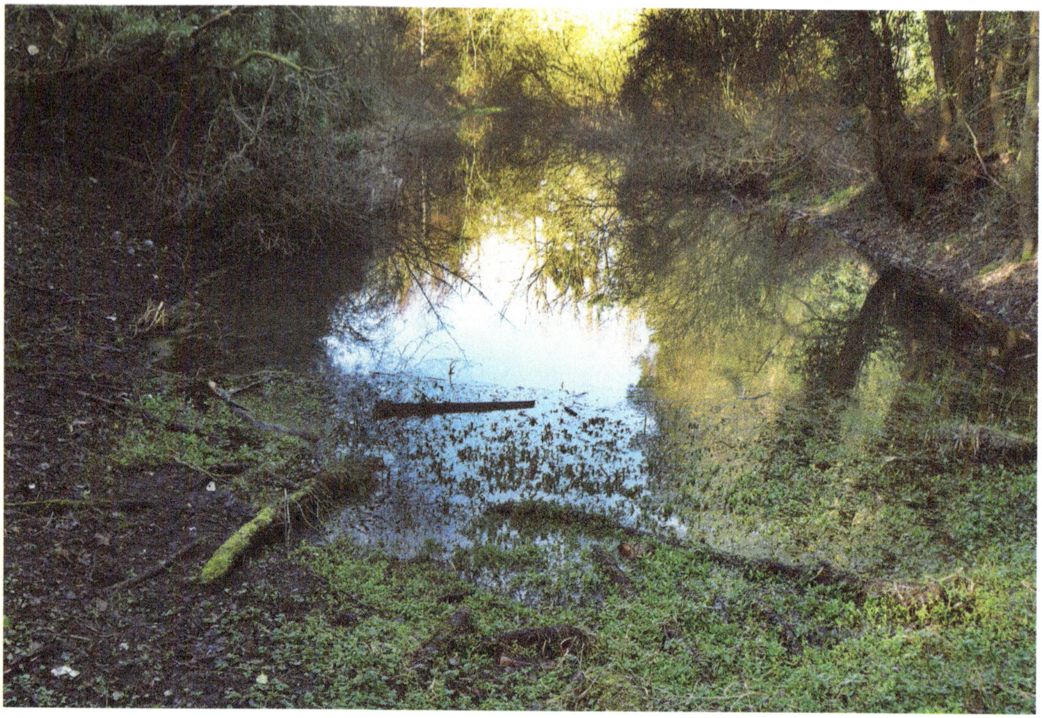

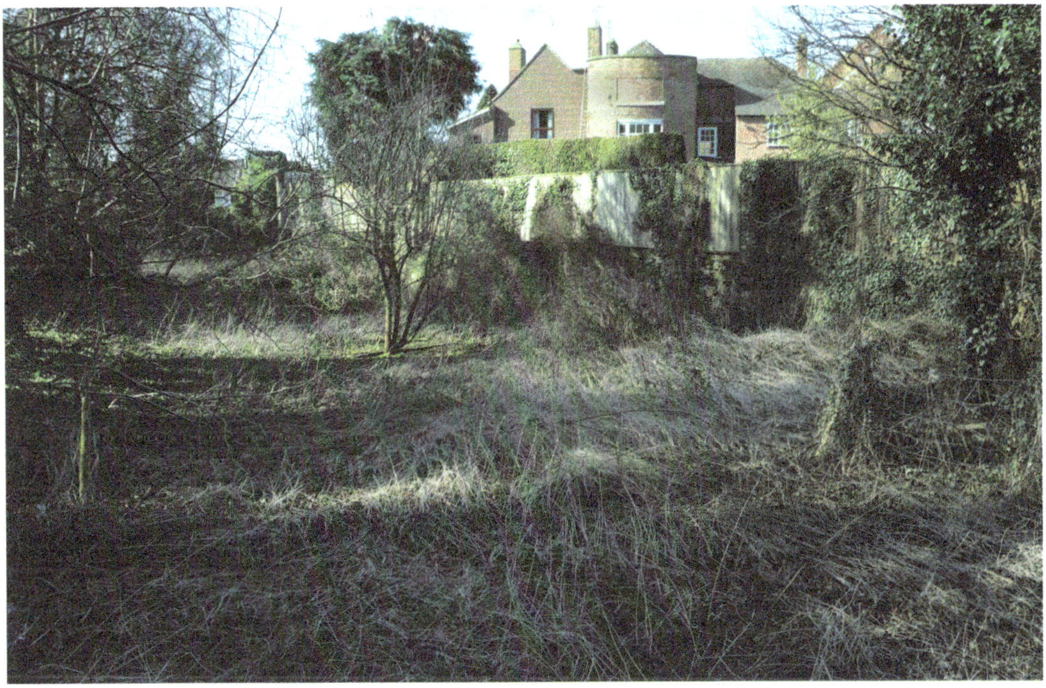

Ketley Inclined Plane

Above: At the back of Ketley Hall, the overgrown depression that was once the basin at the top of the inclined plane can still be seen.

Below: An image of the inclined plane, showing lock chamber, winding drum and descending boat on cradle, was depicted on a trade token issued by the Coalbrookdale Company in 1789.

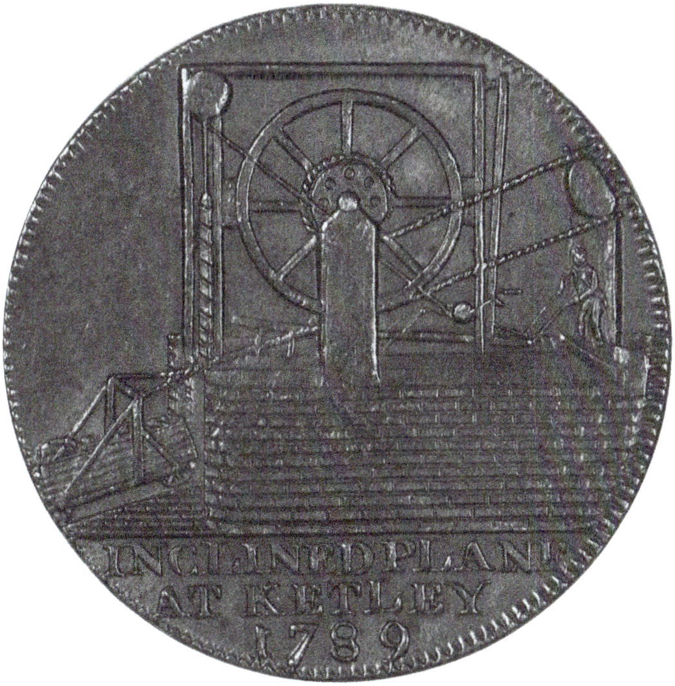

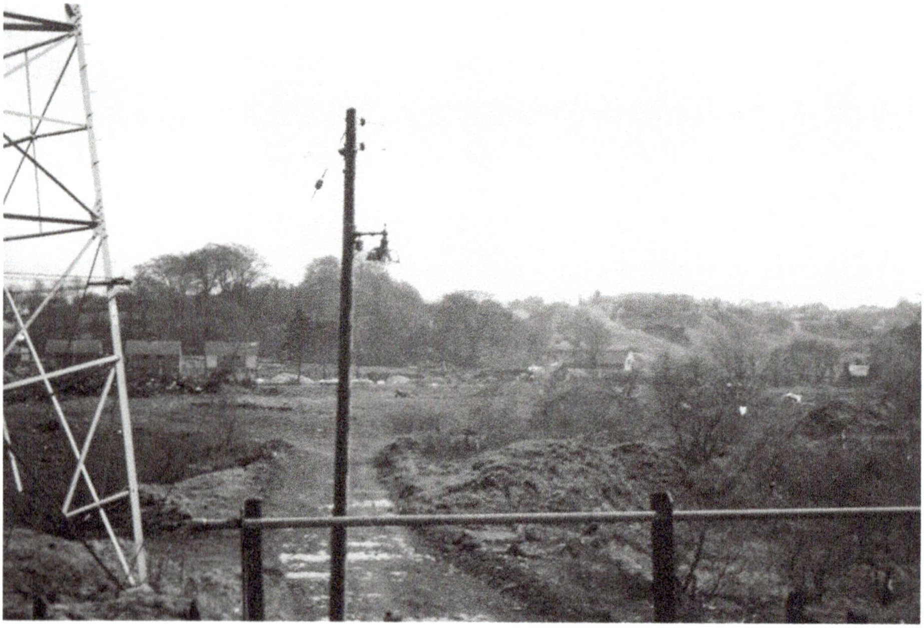

The Incline Today

Above: The course of the inclined plane is no longer obvious, but the change in level between the original top and bottom sections of the canal can be seen in the view of the housing estate that was being built in the early 1960s.
Below: An estate road near the top of the inclined plane has been appropriately named 'The Incline'.

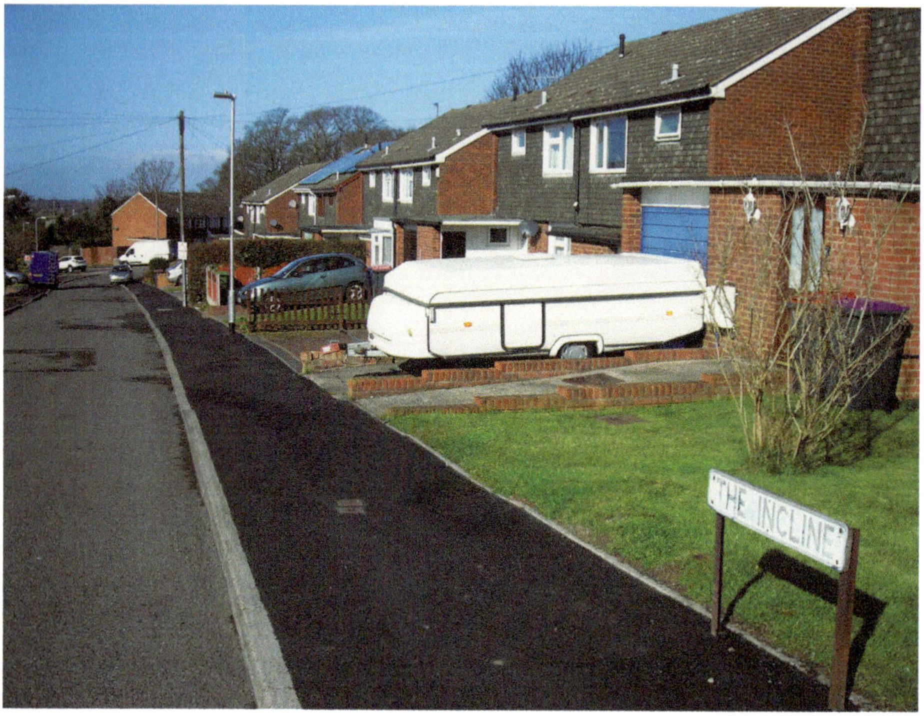

5
The Shropshire Canal

The promoters of the Shropshire Canal – mainly local ironmasters and coal mine owners – required an Act of Parliament to enable them to purchase land for its construction and to raise the capital of £50,000 from shareholders. Opened in 1792, the canal ran southwards from the Oakengates area, $7\frac{3}{4}$ miles to the River Severn at Coalport and with a $2\frac{3}{4}$-mile branch to Coalbrookdale. The undulating nature of the land through which it was built, and the shortage of surface water, required the construction of three large inclined planes, three tunnels, two reservoirs, a small aqueduct and a tunnel-and-shafts system. Its construction, mainly the work of William Reynolds, impressed Thomas Telford, who later wrote:

> This canal, carried over high and rugged ground, along banks of slipping loam, over old coal mines and over where coal mines and iron stone are now actually worked under it, is satisfactory proof that there is scarcely any ground so difficult, but where, with proper exertions and care, a convenient water conveyance may always be obtained.

Most of the traffic on the canal – coal, ironstone and pig iron – was carried in 5-ton tub boats from mines and works along the eastern edge of the Coalbrookdale Coalfield to other works and to Coalport. Here, cargoes were transhipped to barges on the river and carried to markets downstream. By the 1830s the canal was realising an annual dividend averaging 8 per cent. However, its deteriorating condition, caused mainly by subsidence, led to mounting complaints from users; the ailing canal was purchased in 1858 by the London & North Western Railway (LNWR), who closed it and replaced it with the Coalport Branch railway. The middle 3 miles of railway were built alongside or on the bed of the canal, but most of the section of the canal from the bottom of the Windmill inclined plane to Coalport remained in use until the closure of Blists Hill furnaces in 1912.

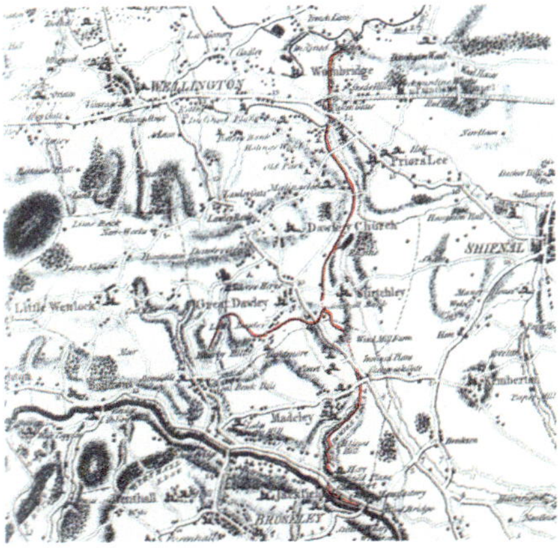

The Shropshire Canal (marked in red) on Baugh's map of Shropshire, 1808.

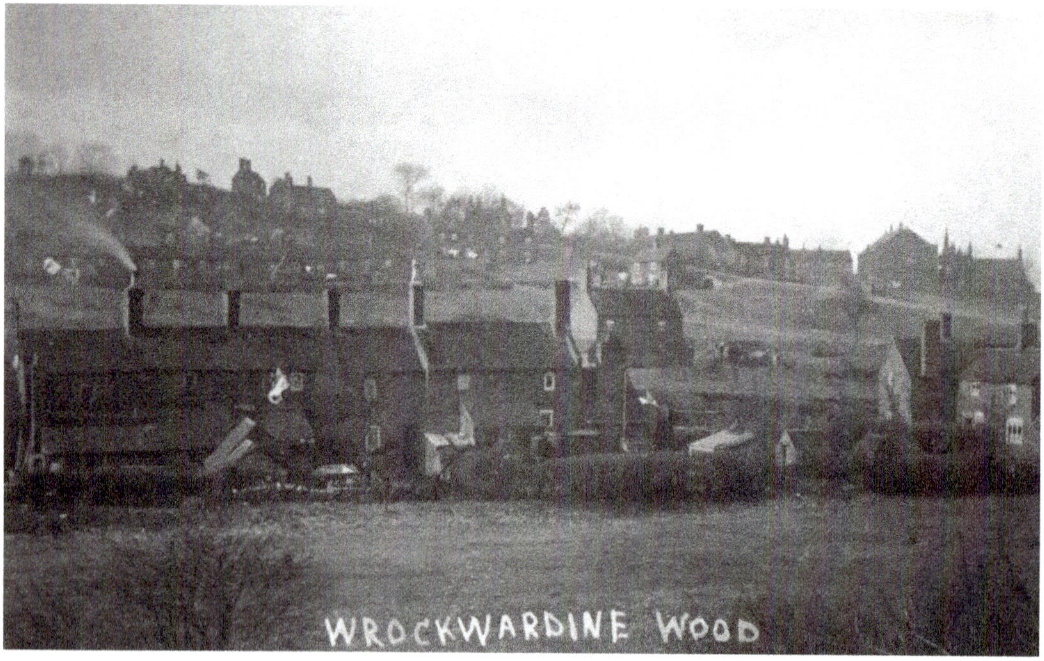

Wrockwardine Wood Inclined Plane

Within 100 yards of its junction with the Donnington Wood and Wombridge Canals, the Shropshire Canal climbed 120 feet by a 320-yard inclined plane. Tub boats carrying coal, ironstone and limestone up the slope needed the services of the steam engine at the top. A late nineteenth-century photograph (above) shows the gradient of the redundant incline. Correspondingly, the 1960s view, looking up the incline (below), shows it before the bottom third was obliterated by a new roadway.

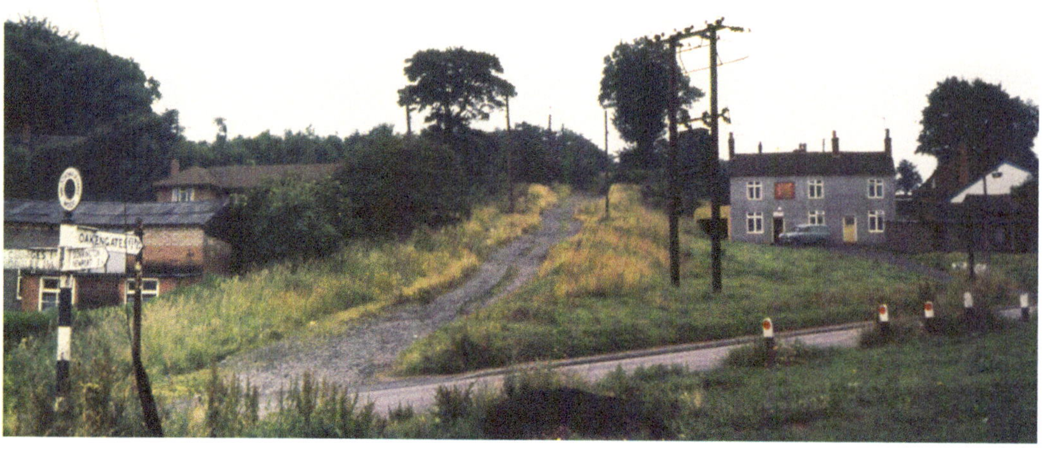

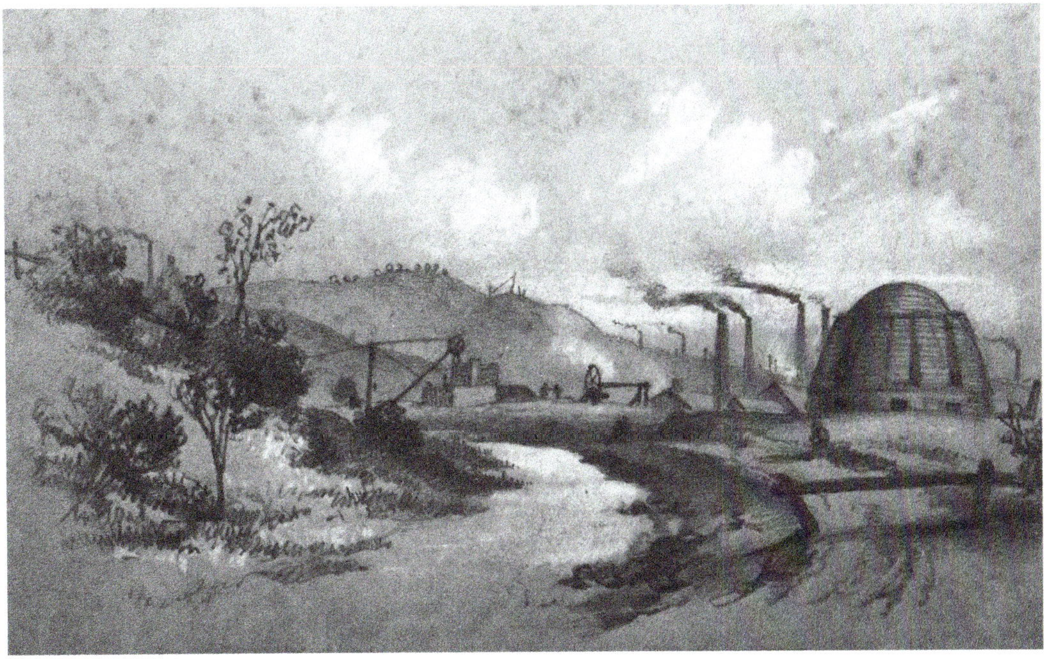

Snedshill

The Shropshire Canal carried coal and ironstone to Snedshill ironworks, originally owned by John Wilkinson and later by the Lilleshall Company in the nineteenth century. The ironworks are depicted in this undated sketch (above). At Snedshill, there was a 279-yard tunnel; the remains of a shorter one, which took the canal under the Holyhead Road, were still visible (below) until the construction of the Eastern Primary Road (Queensway) in the 1970s.

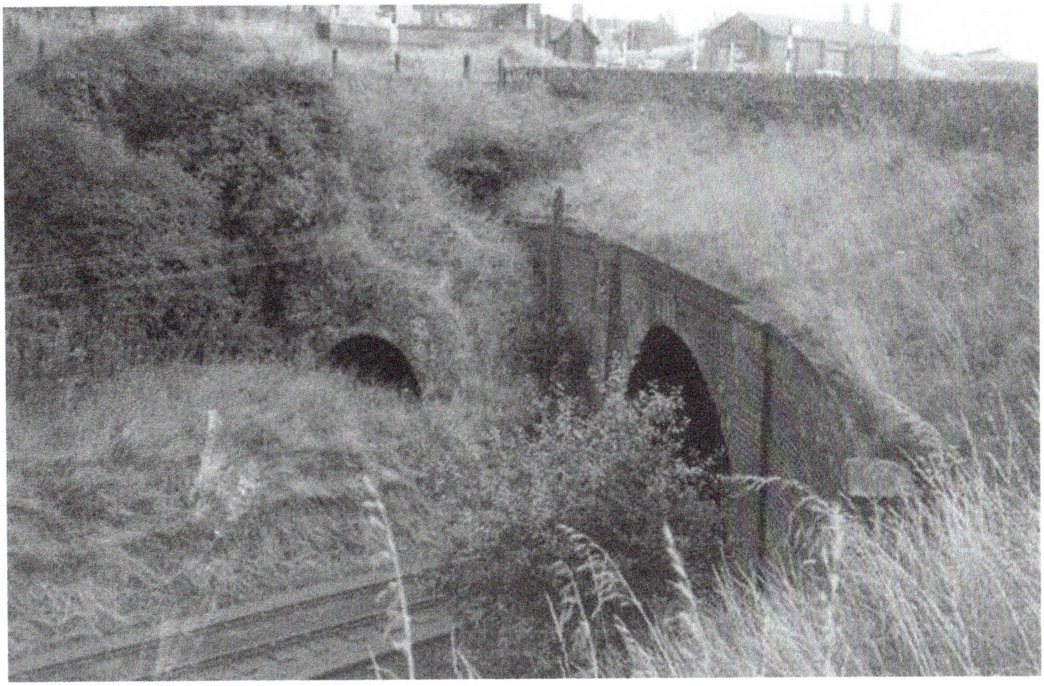

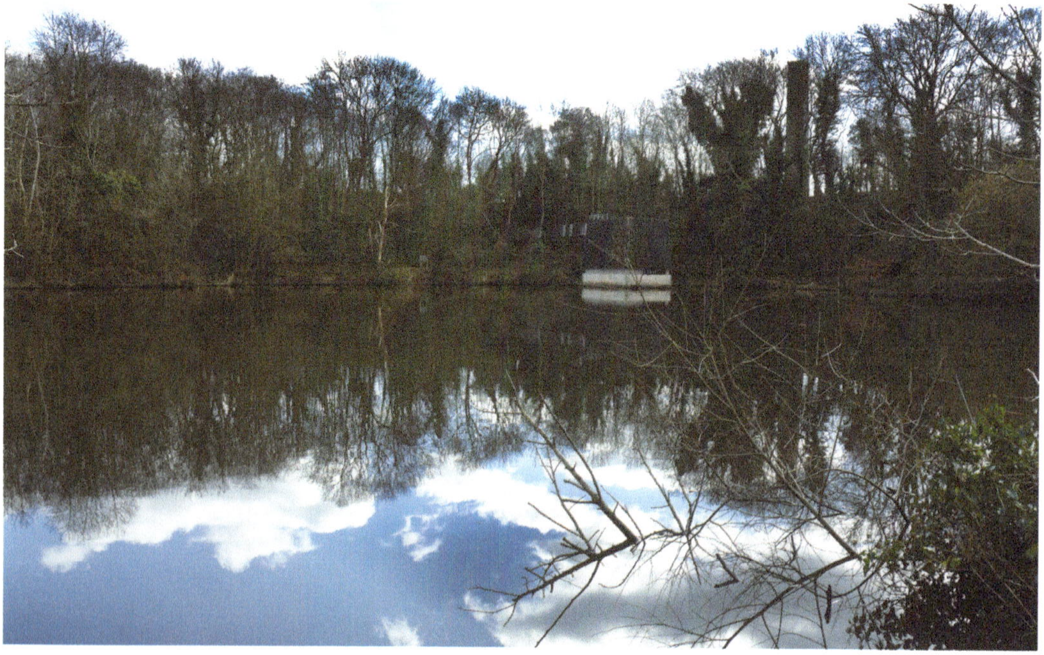

Reservoirs

There were two reservoirs at the summit level of the canal. The larger Randlay Pool (above), fed by the Randlay Brook and by the small Withy Pool, in fact lay some 20 feet below the level of the canal and required a steam engine to pump water into it. A half-mile further south, on the other side of the canal, was Hinkshay Pool. Originally supplied with water from local mines, this was some 20 feet above the level of the canal; the photograph below shows the retaining dam, with the reservoir on the right and an overflow pool and section of canal at the lower level.

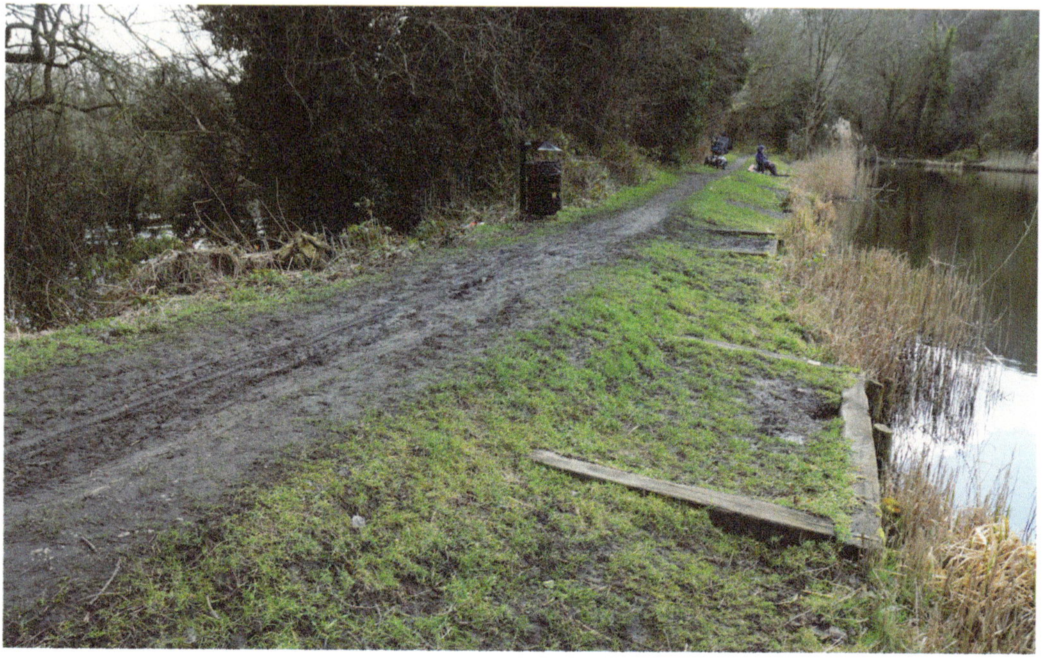

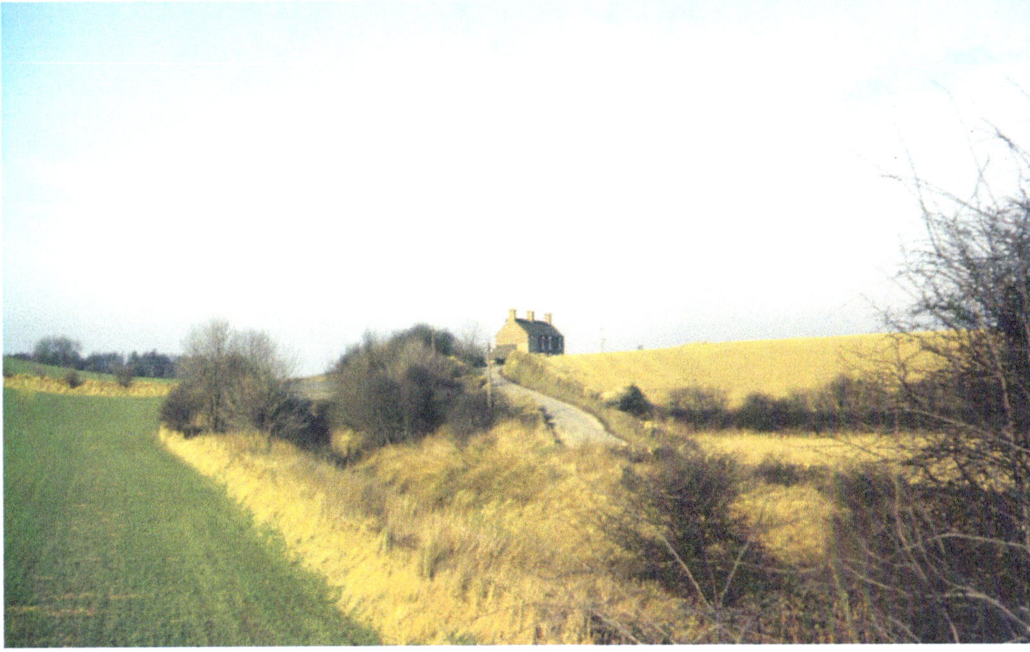

Southall Bank

The 281-yard canal tunnel south of Stirchley was made into a cutting for the Coalport Branch railway in 1860; this can be seen, crossed by a bridge, in the 1960s view (above). The cottages on the horizon are still known as Tunnel Row. Immediately south of the tunnel, the canal divided – the main line (eastern branch) heading for Coalport and the western branch for Coalbrookdale. The remains of the bridge that carried Stirchley (now Aqueduct) Lane over the eastern branch at this point can still be found in the undergrowth (below).

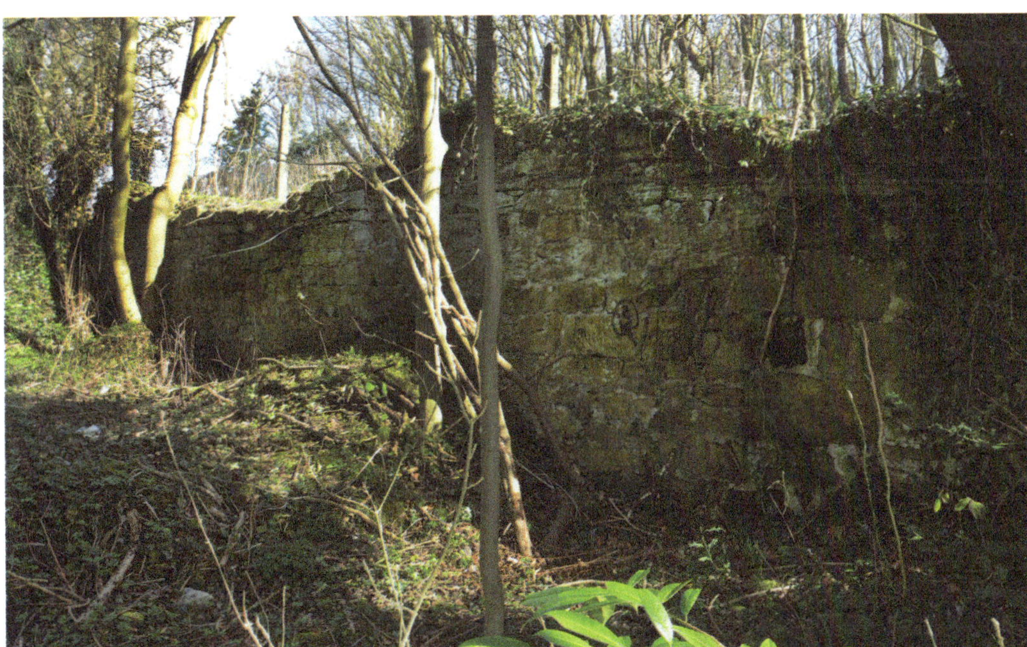

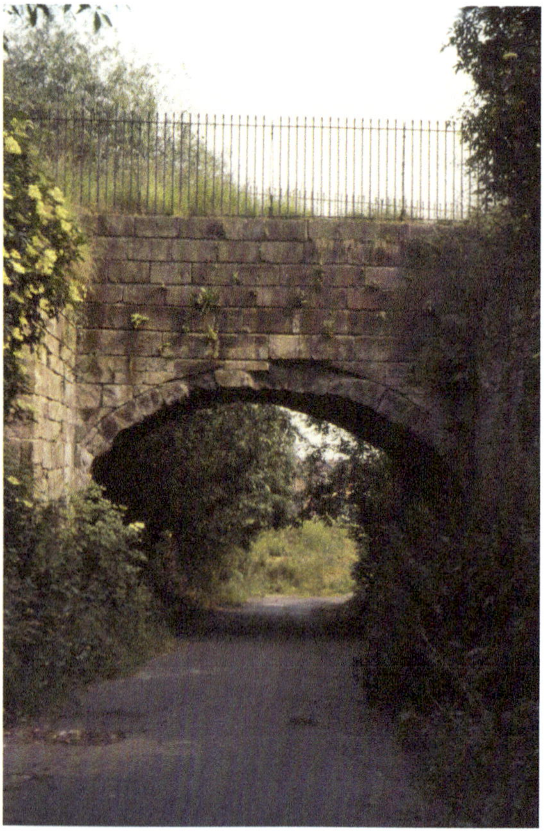

Aqueduct

To carry the Coalbrookdale branch of the Shropshire Canal over the Madeley turnpike road, a single-arch stone aqueduct was built (above). The settlement that grew up around the canal took its name from this aqueduct. When the canal closed, the aqueduct was used as a footbridge by local residents; this was the upgraded path in 2001 (below).

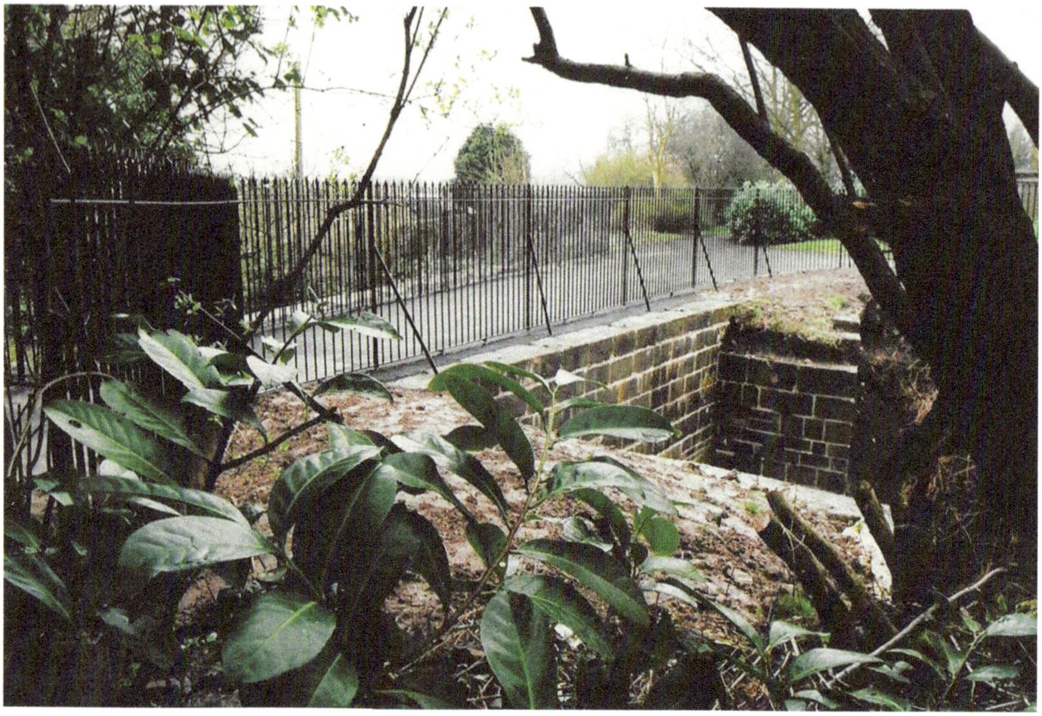

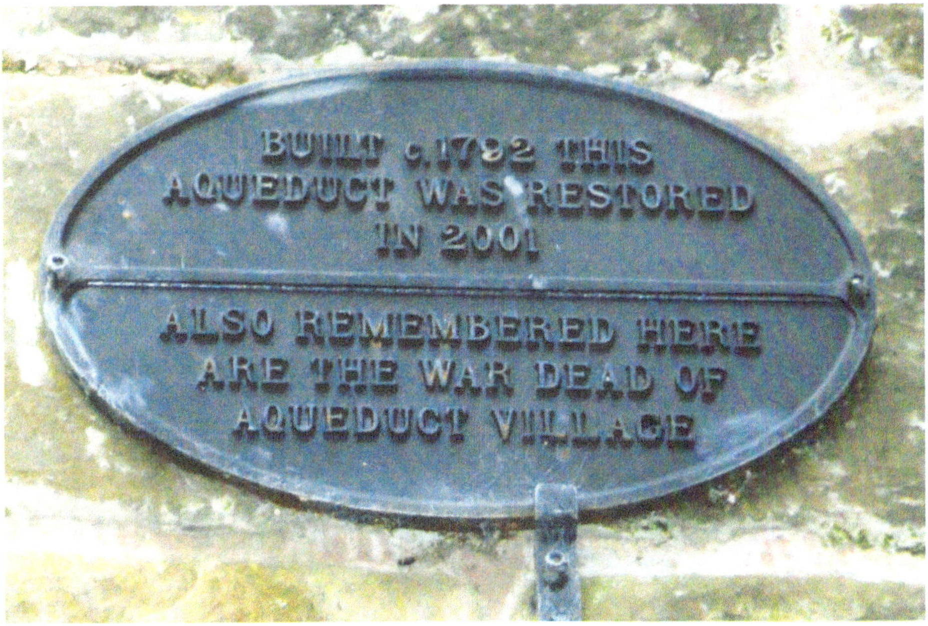

War Memorial

The aqueduct still stands, but over the years it suffered damage from road traffic (prior to the road being bypassed at the beginning of the Second World War) and disturbance caused by the laying of electricity cables. Some repair work was undertaken as a millennium project, and the commemorative plaque affixed to the aqueduct (above) now also acts as the village's war memorial (the original in the closed local church having been removed to St Michael's church, Madeley). The present state of the aqueduct can be seen in the bottom view.

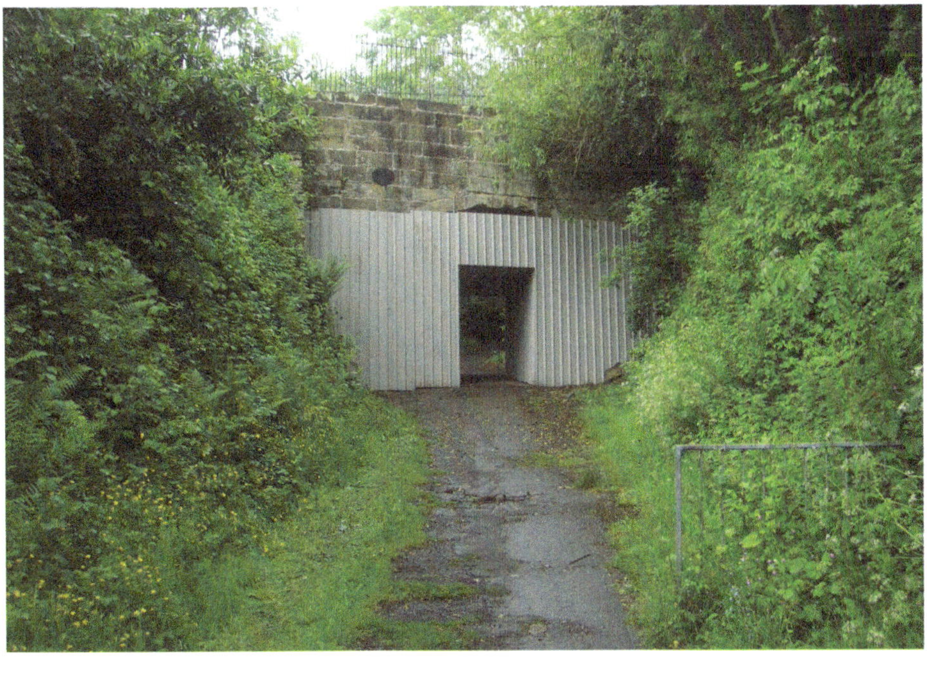

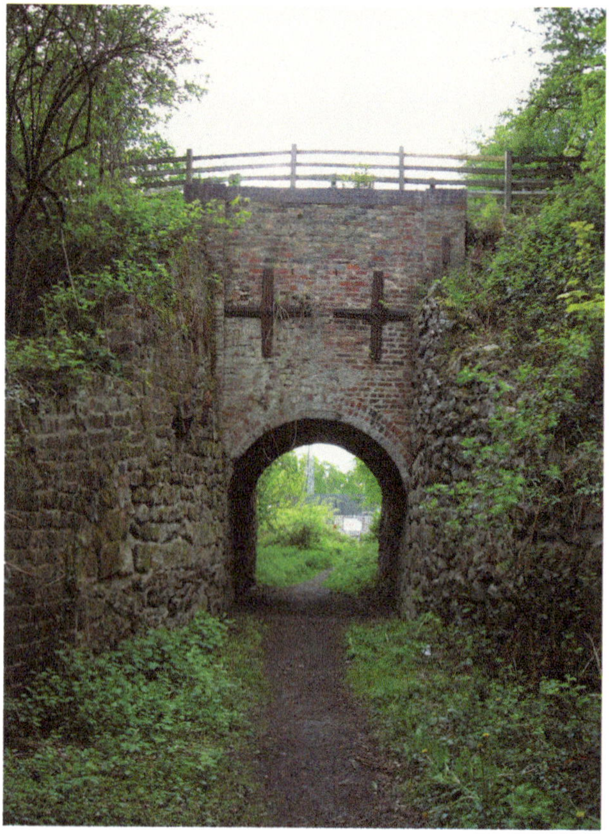

Bridges

Few of the bridges that carried roads and tramways over the Coalbrookdale branch of the canal survive, but two can still be seen. At Little Dawley, beyond a section of canal still in water, a tramway overbridge has been restored (left), and the remains of the bridge that carried Crackshall Lane over the canal just before its terminus are still evident (below).

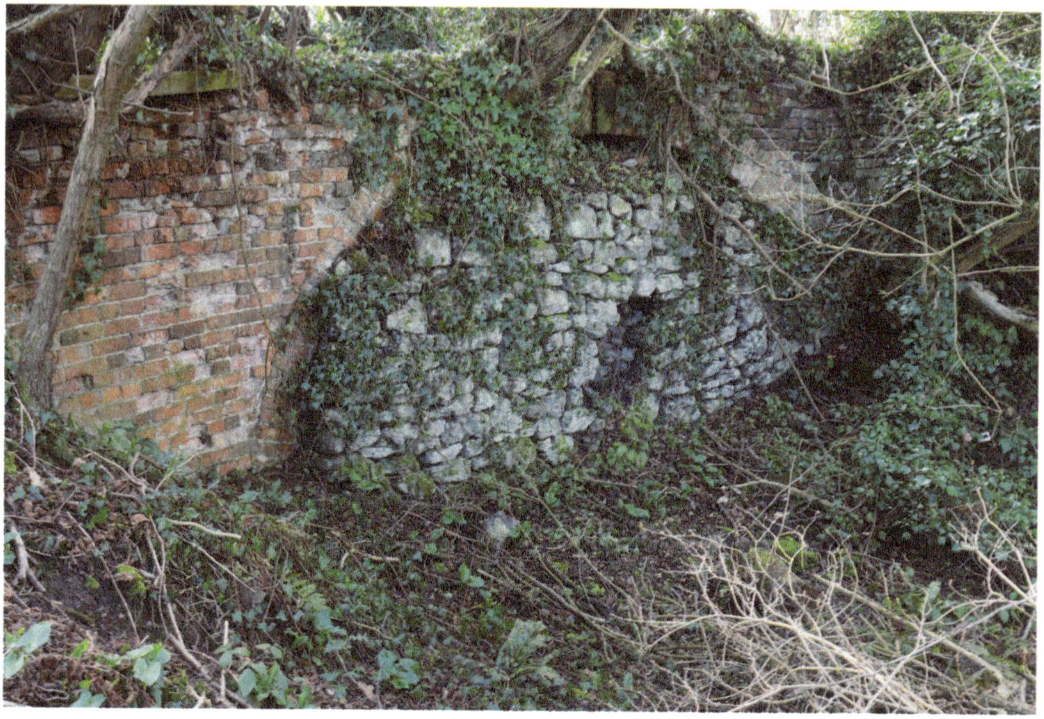

Brierly Hill Terminus, Coalbrookdale

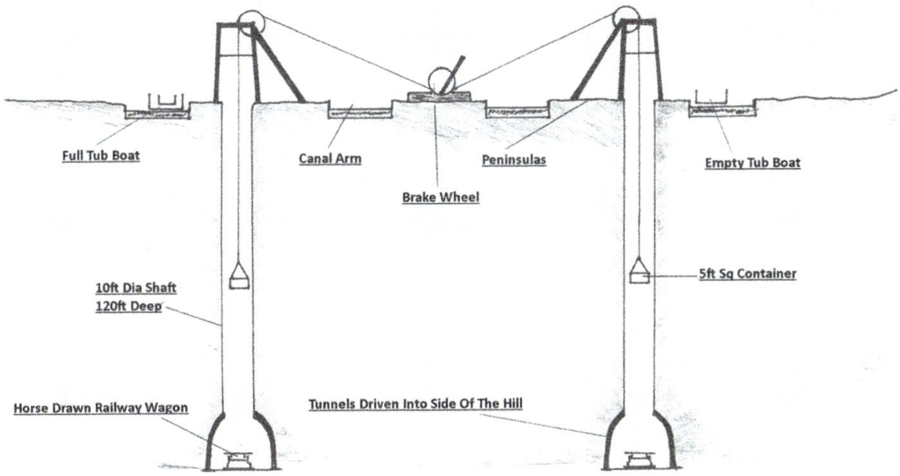

Tunnel-And-Shafts System

The original plan for the Coalbrookdale branch to reach the Severn was abandoned, and the canal terminated high above Coalbrookdale ironworks at Brierly Hill. Here, Reynolds devised a system (above) whereby raw materials were lowered down a shaft to an underground railway that carried them to the works or the river. Iron goods were lifted to the canal up the adjacent shaft. Within two years, the system was replaced by a tramway incline. The approach of the canal bed to what became known as 'The Old Wynd' can still be seen in this modern photograph (below).

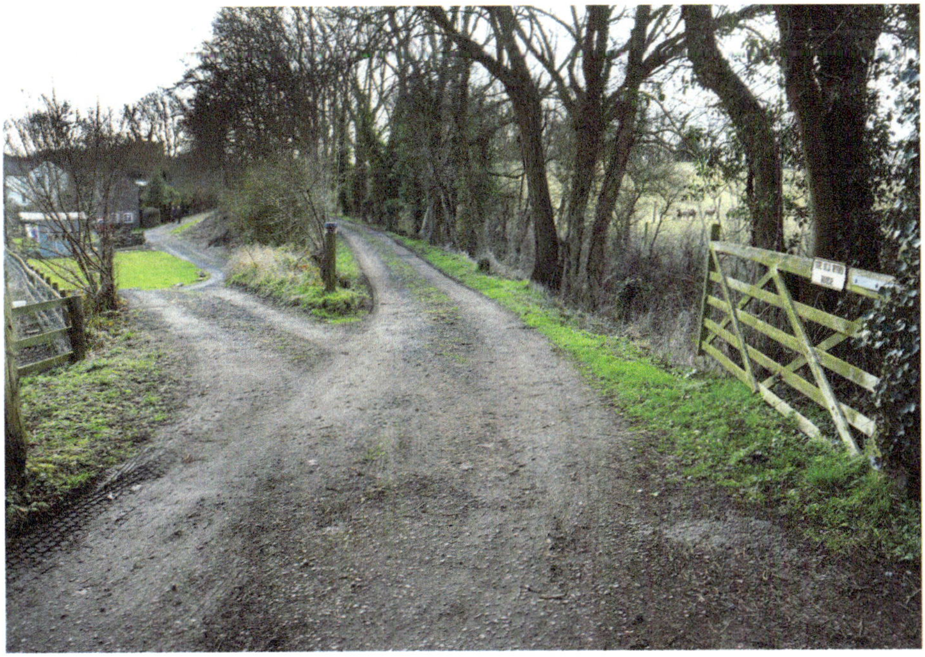

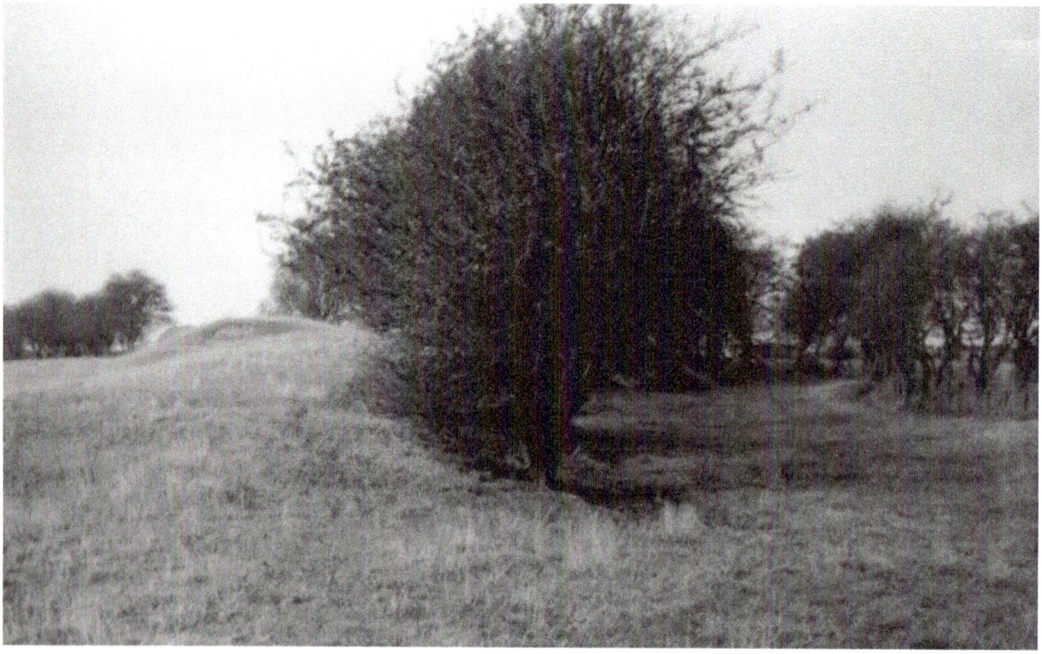

Windmill Inclined Plane

On the main line of the Shropshire Canal, east of Southall Bank, the canal dropped 126 feet down the 600-yard Windmill inclined plane. The remains of the top of the incline (above) were in evidence until the 1960s, but were demolished when the Brookside estate was developed. The shell of the tower of the nearby late seventeenth-century windmill, after which the inclined plane was named, still survives (below), and the small quarry that provided the stone for the top of the incline is now a grassy dell among the houses.

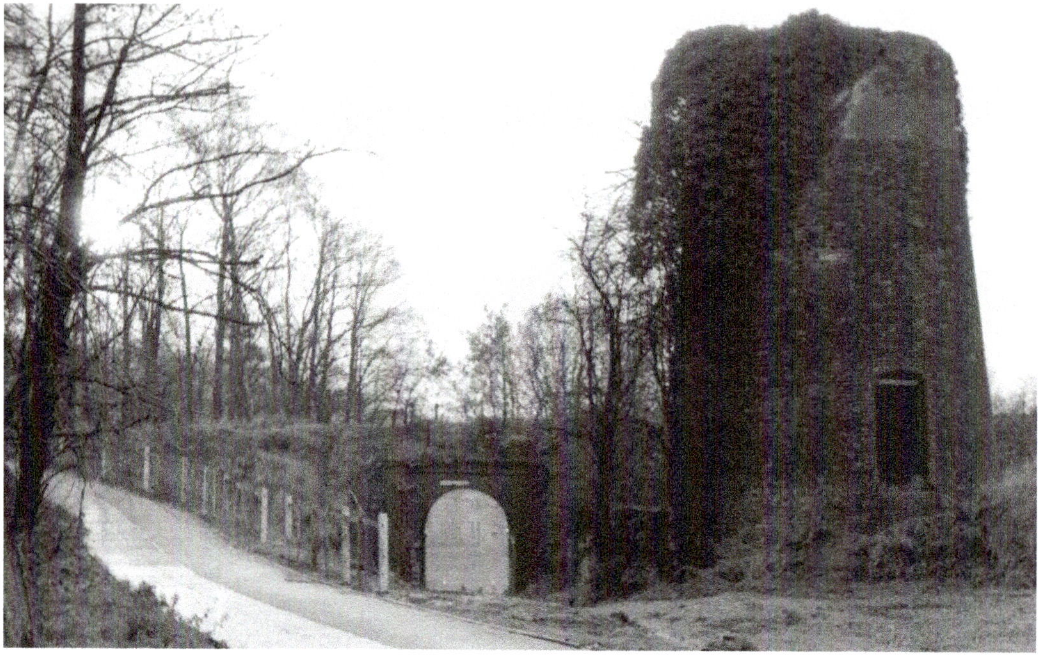

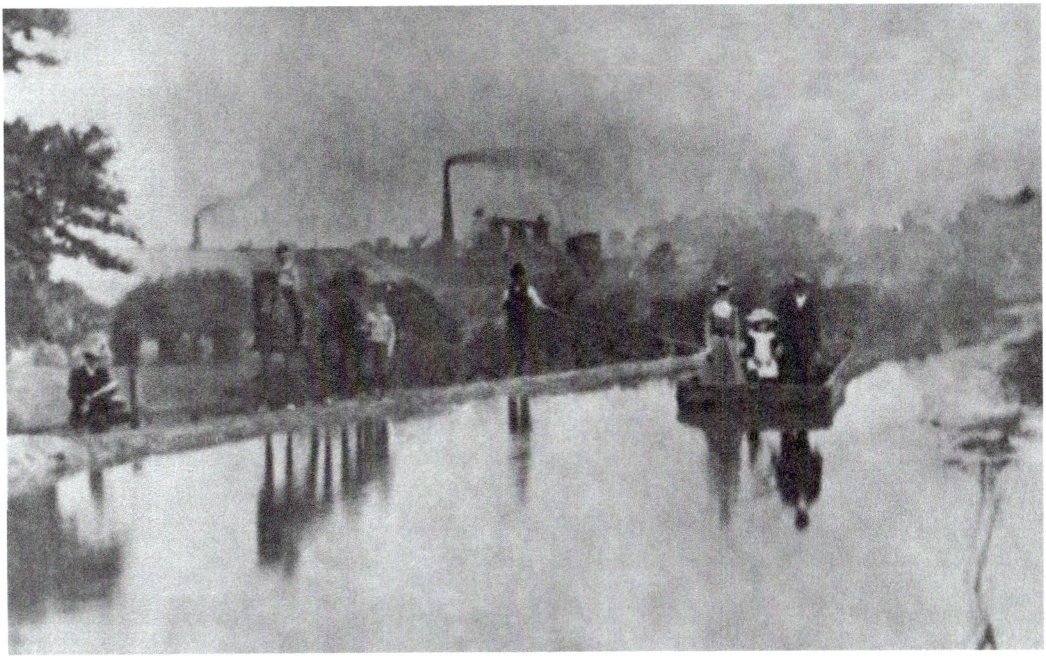

Tweedale Basin

The closure of the greater part of the Shropshire Canal in 1858 left only the 2-mile section between the bottom of the Windmill inclined plane and Coalport still in use. Coal and ironstone from the Madeley Wood Company's pits at Halesfield and Kemberton was carried by tramway to Tweedale Basin and by canal to the company's furnaces and brickworks at Blists Hill. Occasionally, tub boats provided 'treats', as shown at Tweedale Basin (above); at the same spot some were abandoned (below) when the canal finally closed in 1912.

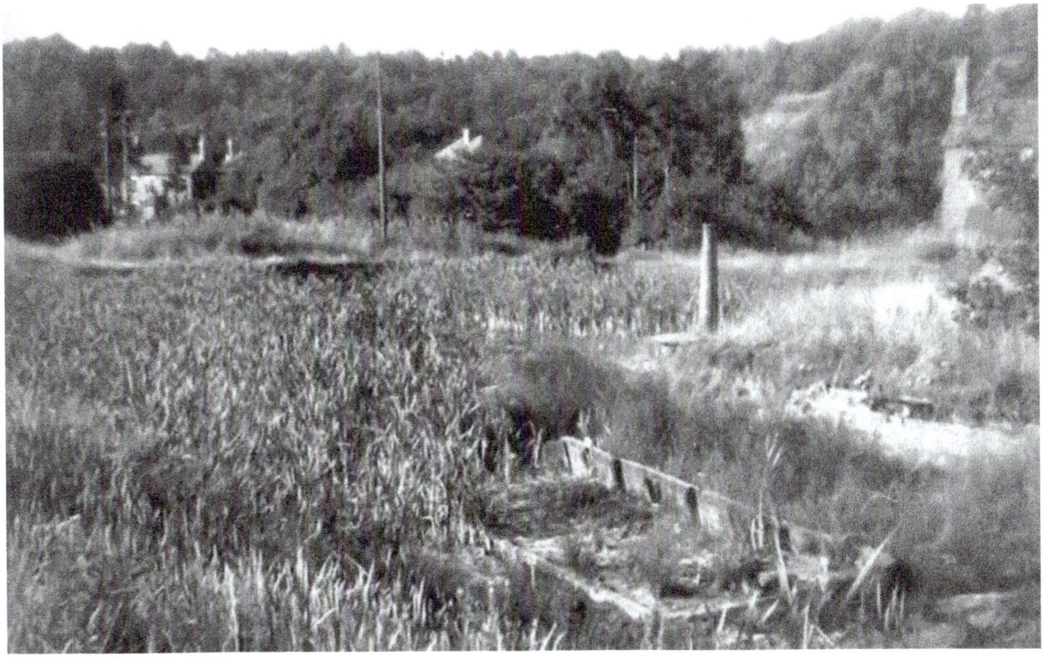

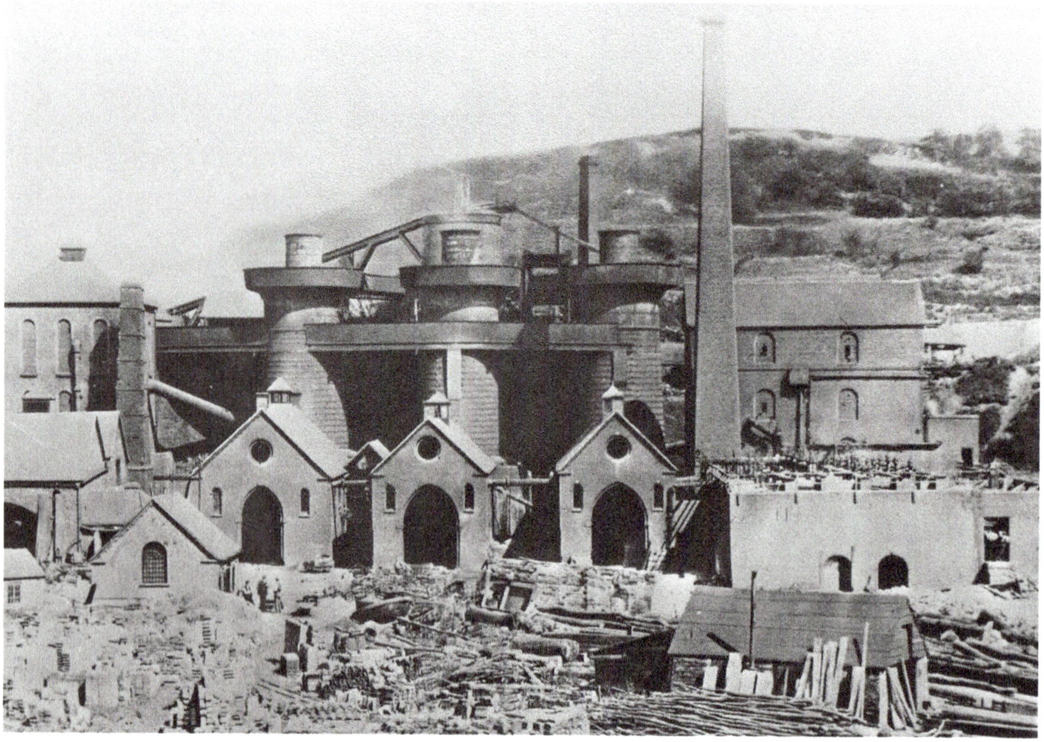

Blists Hill

The Madeley Wood Company's furnaces here (above) were supplied by the canal with coal and ironstone until they were blown out following a labour dispute in 1912. The site is now part of the IGMT Victorian Town, and some 400 yards of the canal have been restored (below).

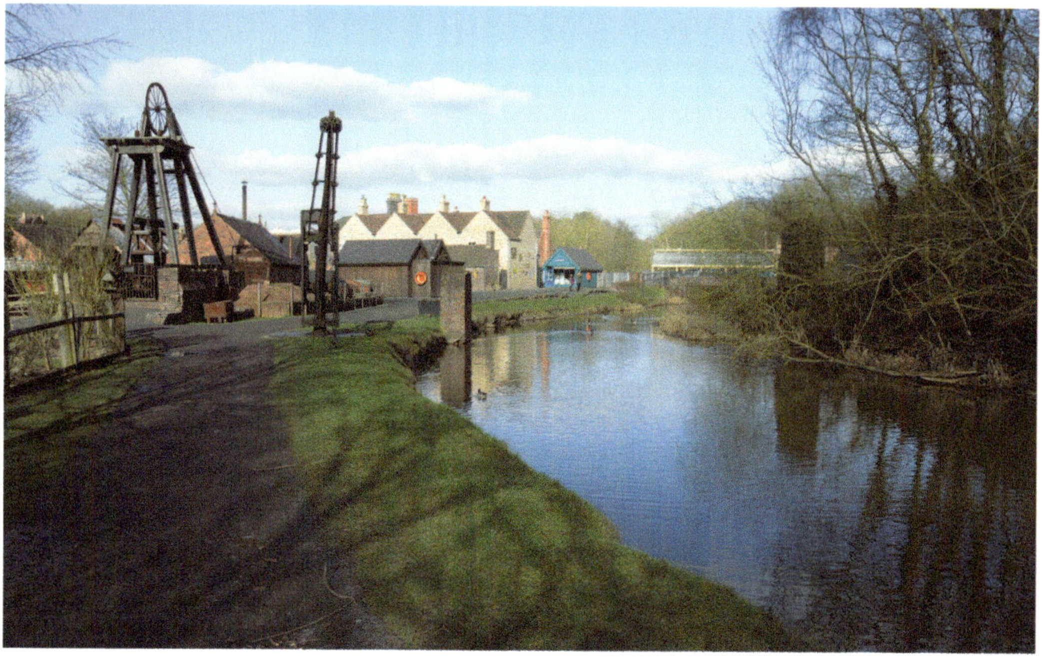

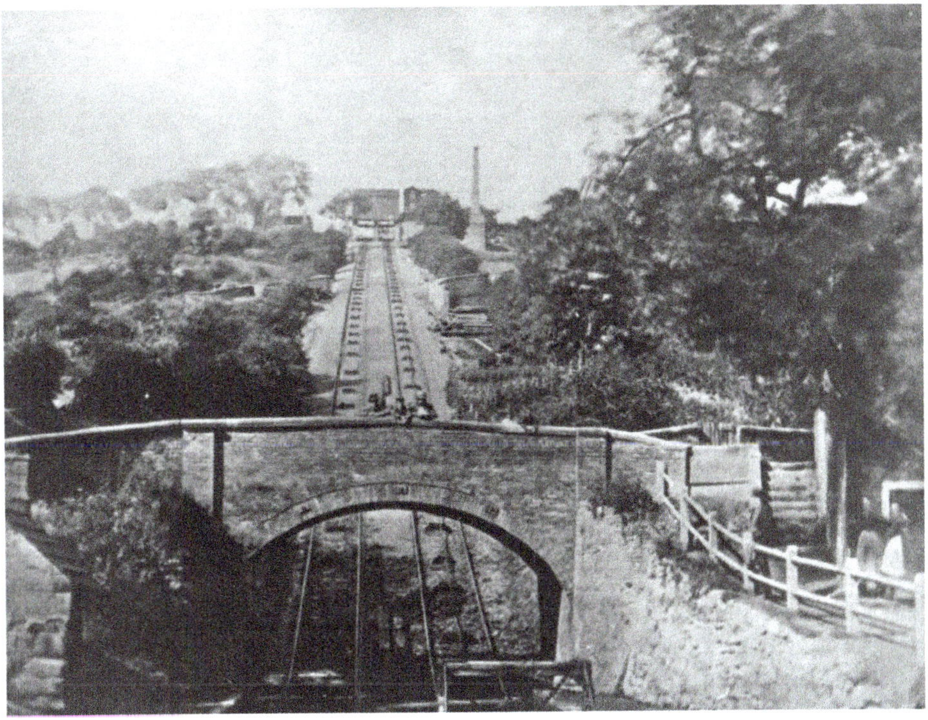

The Hay Inclined Plane

When the canal reached the edge of the Ironbridge Gorge, it had a drop of 207 feet, before running parallel with (and some 20 feet above) the river to Coalport bridge. The 350-yard-long incline is shown (above) at the time of its closure in the 1890s, and (right) after restoration by the IGMT in the 1970s.

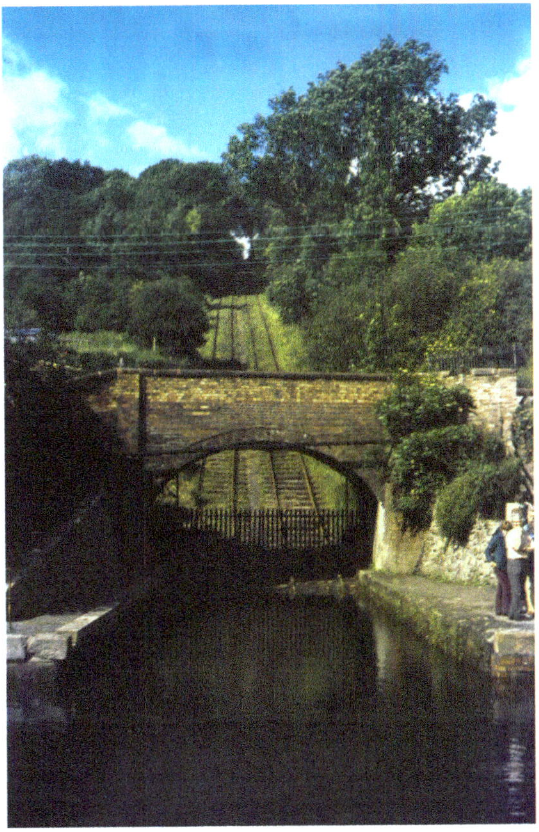

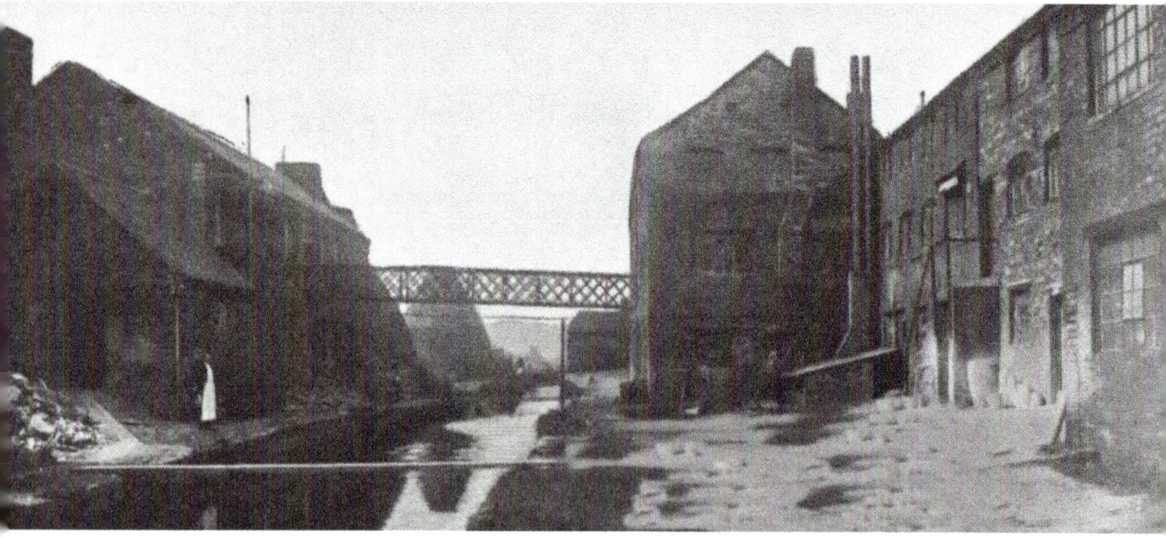

Coalport China Works

Coal from local pits was also conveyed by canal to Coalport China Works (above) until the closure of the Hay inclined plane. The section of canal from the bottom of the incline to the china works, now one of the IGMT museums, was restored in the 1970s (below).

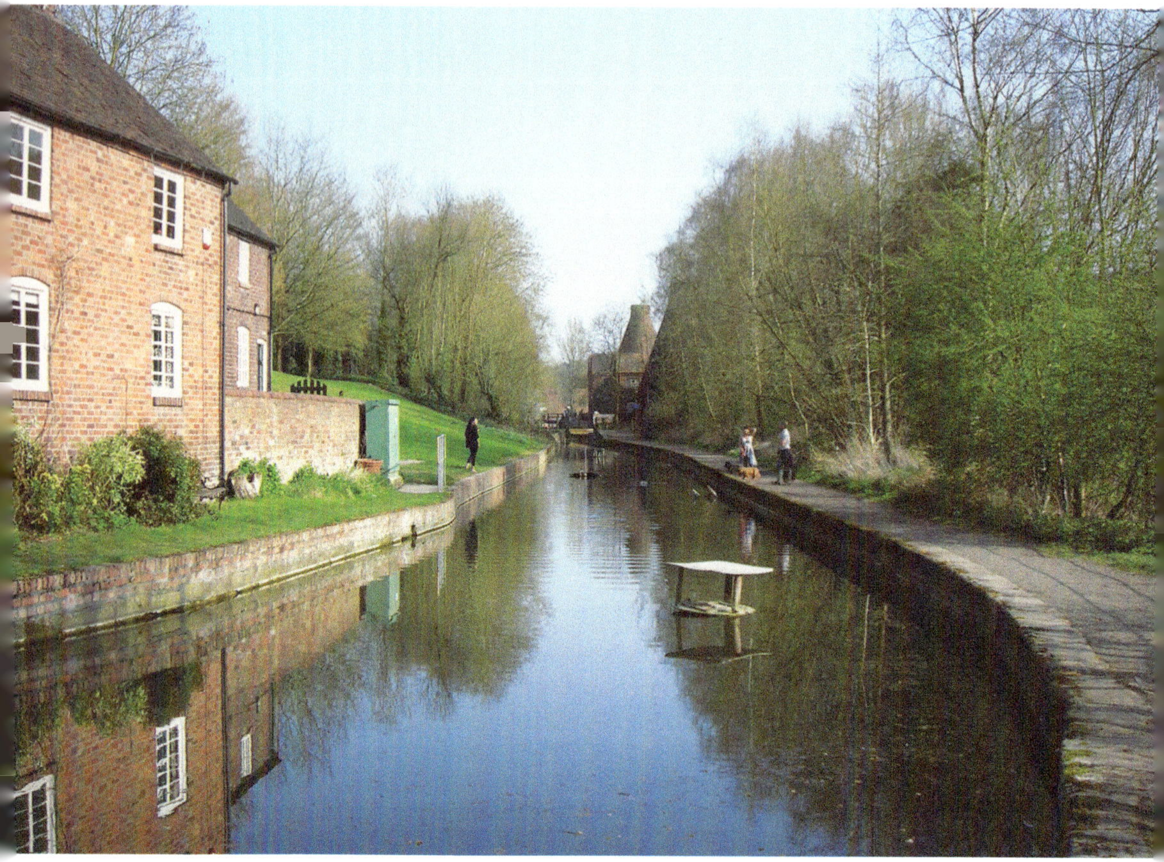

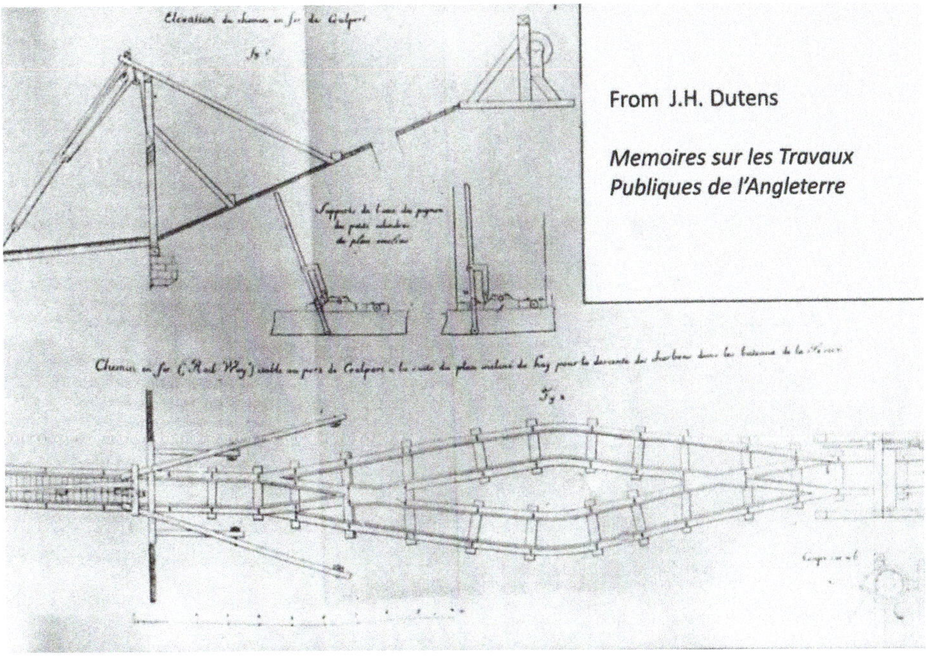

From J.H. Dutens

Memoires sur les Travaux Publiques de l'Angleterre

Transhipment At Coalport

At the end of the half-mile section of canal between the bottom of the inclined plane and Coalport Bridge, it was originally planned to lock down to the river. But this proved impractical and, instead, seven small inclines were used to transfer coal and pig iron from tub boats to vessels on the river – an arrangement shown in a drawing by a visiting French engineer in 1819 (above). The landscaped site today is shown below, with the line of trees marking the location of Reynolds' large warehouse.

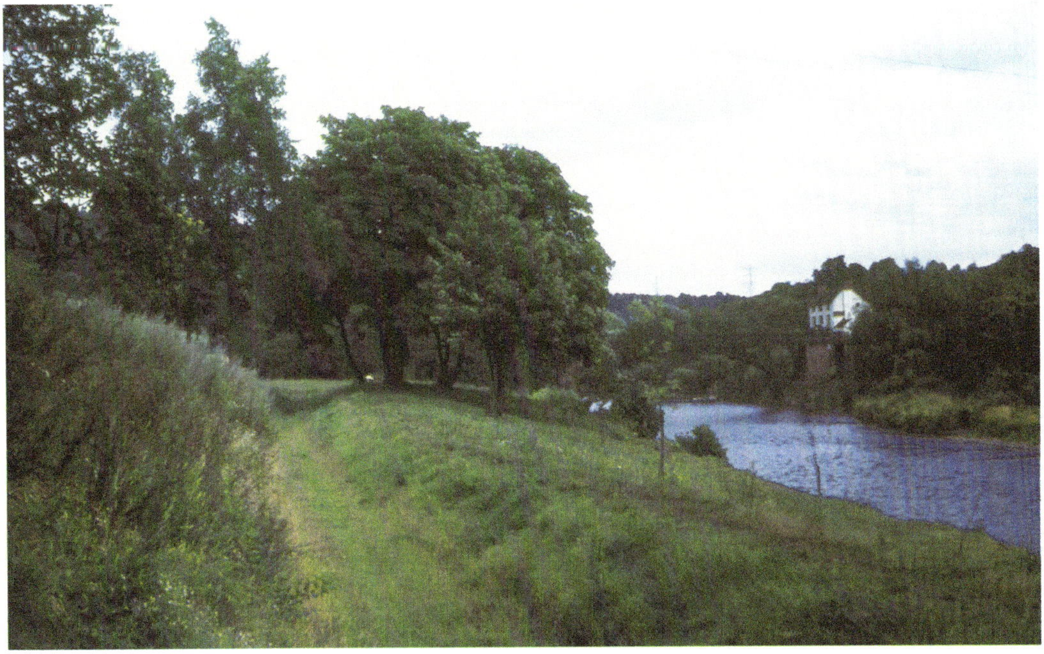

6
The Shrewsbury Canal

To carry coal from the East Shropshire mines to the county town and to wharves along its route, local industrialists, landowners and businessmen promoted the building of a canal from the existing Wombridge Canal to Shrewsbury. The 17-mile route was surveyed by George Young of Worcester in 1792, and the canal was constructed over the next four years. Josiah Clowes was appointed engineer, but on his death in early 1795 Thomas Telford completed the unfinished work. Telford, Surveyor of Public Works for Shropshire since 1787, had already been appointed assistant to William Jessop on the Ellesmere Canal.

The Shrewsbury Canal was a tub-boat canal whose main features were an inclined plane and large reservoir at Trench; a unique set of eleven guillotine locks between Trench and Eyton on the Weald Moors; aqueducts across the rivers Tern and Roden; and a tunnel at Berwick. Brought into use in stages, the canal was finally opened to Shrewsbury in February 1797. It had cost just under £65,000 to build and was modestly prosperous, with dividends rising slowly to reach £11 per £125 share in the years before 1835. However, the expected reduction in the cost of coal in Shrewsbury did not materialise!

In March 1797, Henry Williams was appointed Agent and General Superintendent of the Shrewsbury Canal. Williams had earlier been an assistant to William Reynolds; he was probably involved in the construction of the Ketley inclined plane and was the joint winner of a competition for the improved design for the inclined planes used on the Shropshire Canal and at Trench on the Shrewsbury Canal. Having already been appointed General Inspector and Surveyor of the Shropshire Canal, Henry Williams (below, inset) was set to play an important role in the affairs of the East Shropshire tub-boat system for the next forty years.

The fortunes of the Shrewsbury Canal improved when the Newport Branch of the B&LJC reached Wappenshall in 1835, and widening at certain points enabled the narrow boats off the national system to reach the county town.

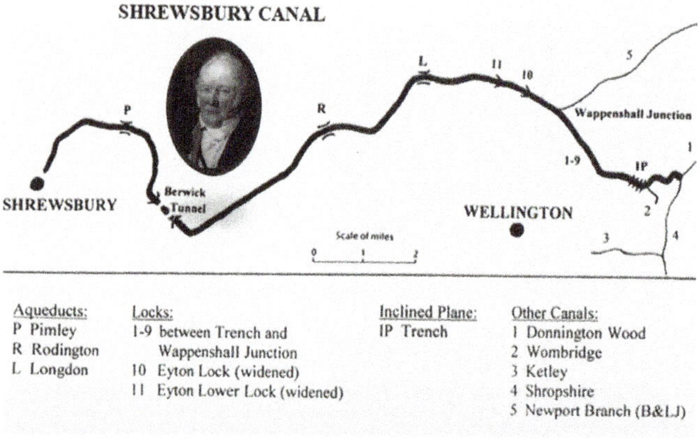

The Shrewsbury Canal.

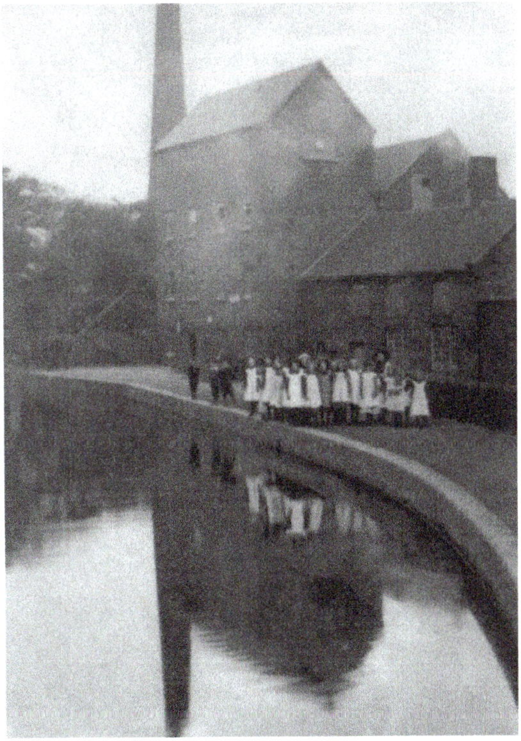

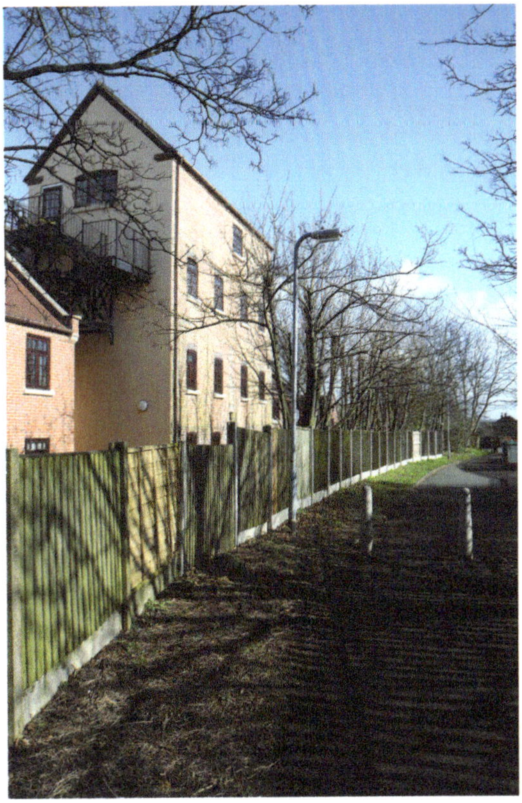

Bullock's Mill

On the easternmost section of the Shrewsbury Canal, originally part of the Wombridge Canal, was Bullock's Mill. Sometimes known as Donnington Wood Mill (although being in Wrockwardine Wood parish), the four-storey brick steam mill was built in 1818 and supplied with grain by canal until Trench inclined plane closed in 1921. The early twentieth-century photograph (above) shows a school party on the canal towpath in front of the mill, which, following its closure in the 1970s, was converted into apartments (below).

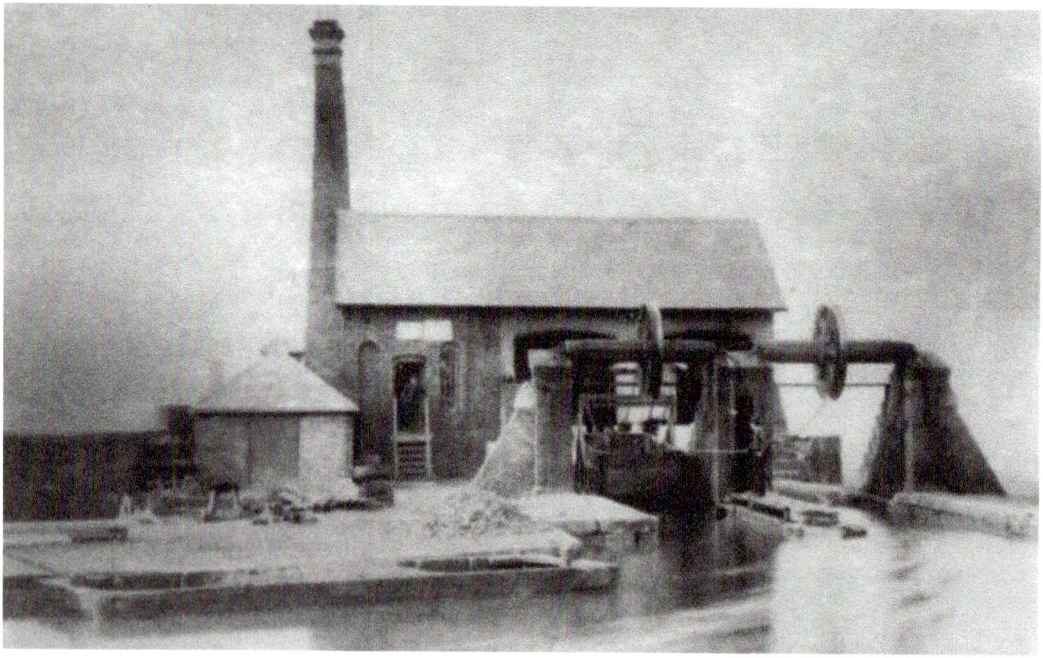

Trench Inclined Plane

Similar to the inclines on the Shropshire Canal, the 223-yard inclined plane at Trench descended 75 feet, with a gradient of about 1 in 9. It was the last canal incline to operate in the British Isles, closing in 1921.With most of the original heavy traffic passing down the plane, the steam engine at the top (above) was used mainly to haul ascending tub boats over the sill. One of the cradles used to carry the tub boats on the incline's two sets of rails can be seen below.

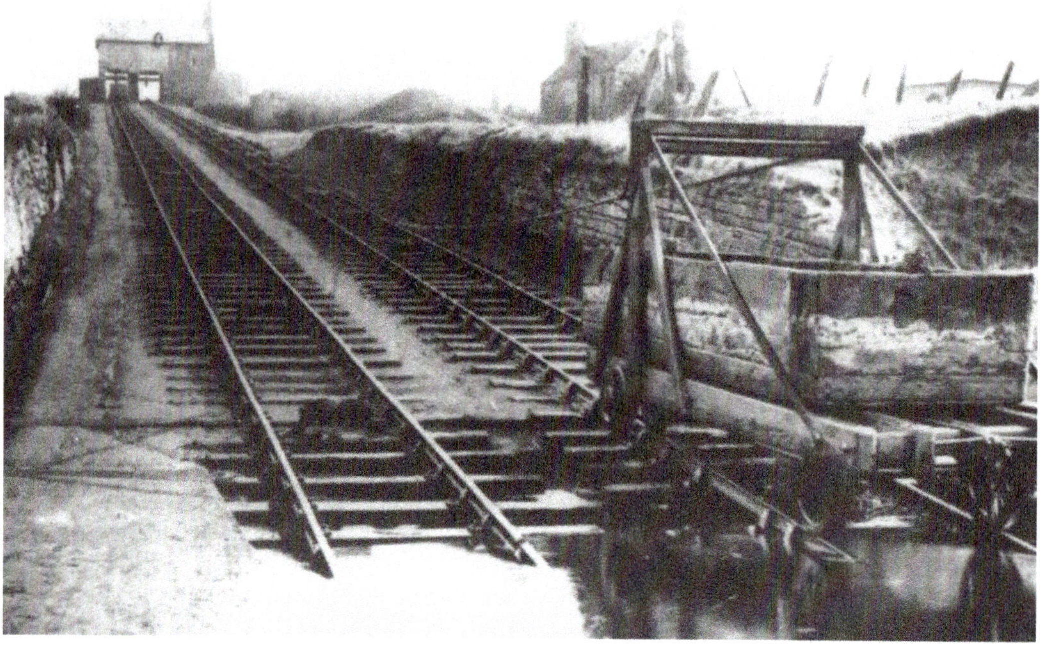

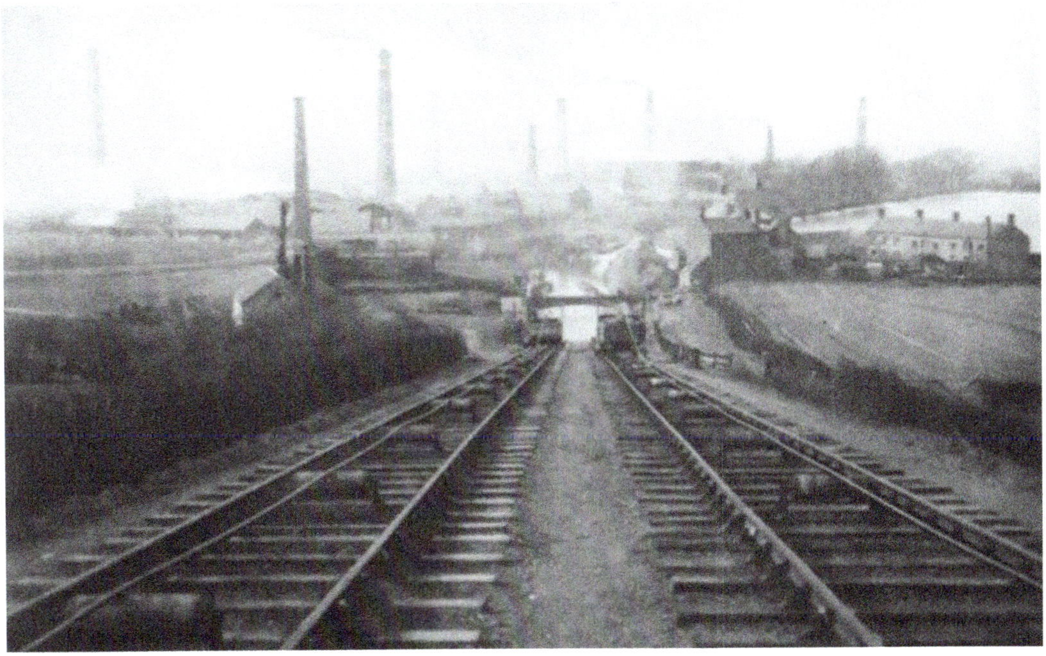

Inclined Plane And Reservoir

In the view looking down the incline (above), the Shrewsbury Canal's large reservoir can be seen on the right. Looking up the incline (below), the cast-iron trough crossing the rails near the bottom carries a feeder stream to the reservoir, which was behind the buildings on the left – the Shropshire Arms public house (also known as the Blue Pig) and cottages.

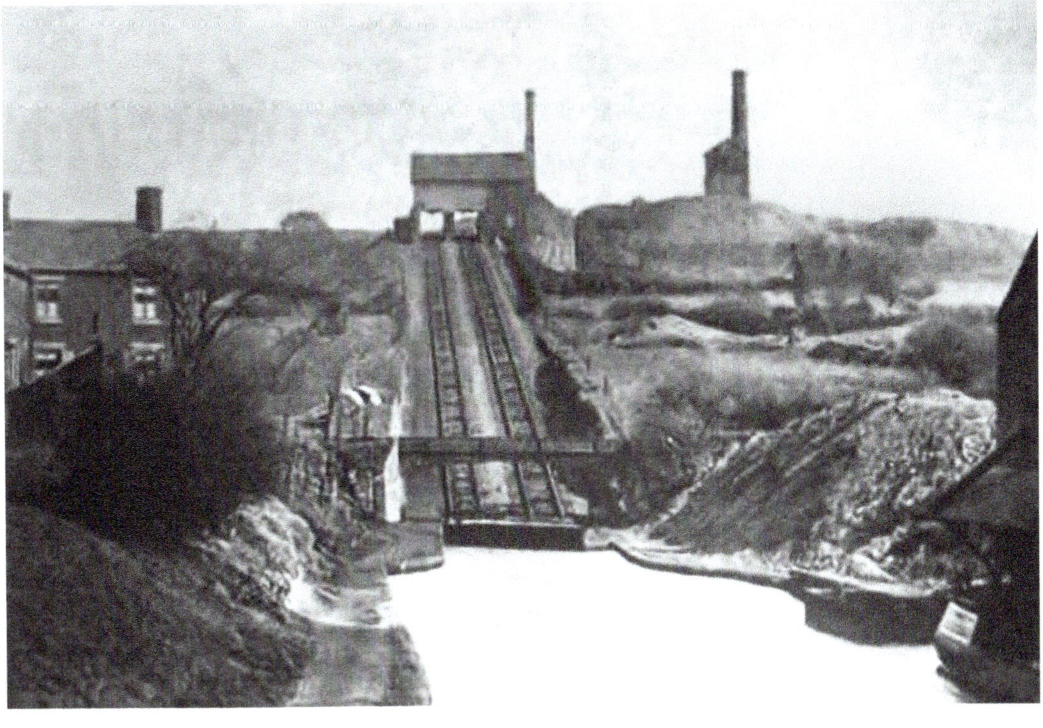

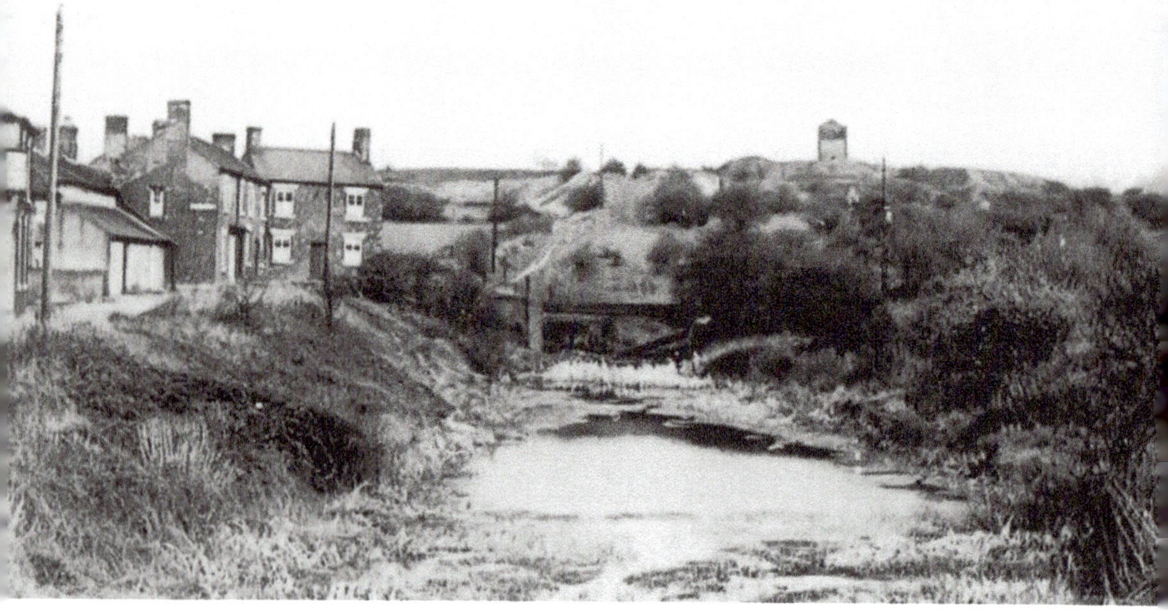

The Incline After Closure

The inclined plane at Trench closed in 1921 and, following the abandonment of the canal in 1944, the area took on the neglected look shown in the above photograph. In the 1970s, the incline was landscaped and the bed of the canal below was obliterated by the construction of the new Eastern Primary road (Queensway), but the Blue Pig survives (below).

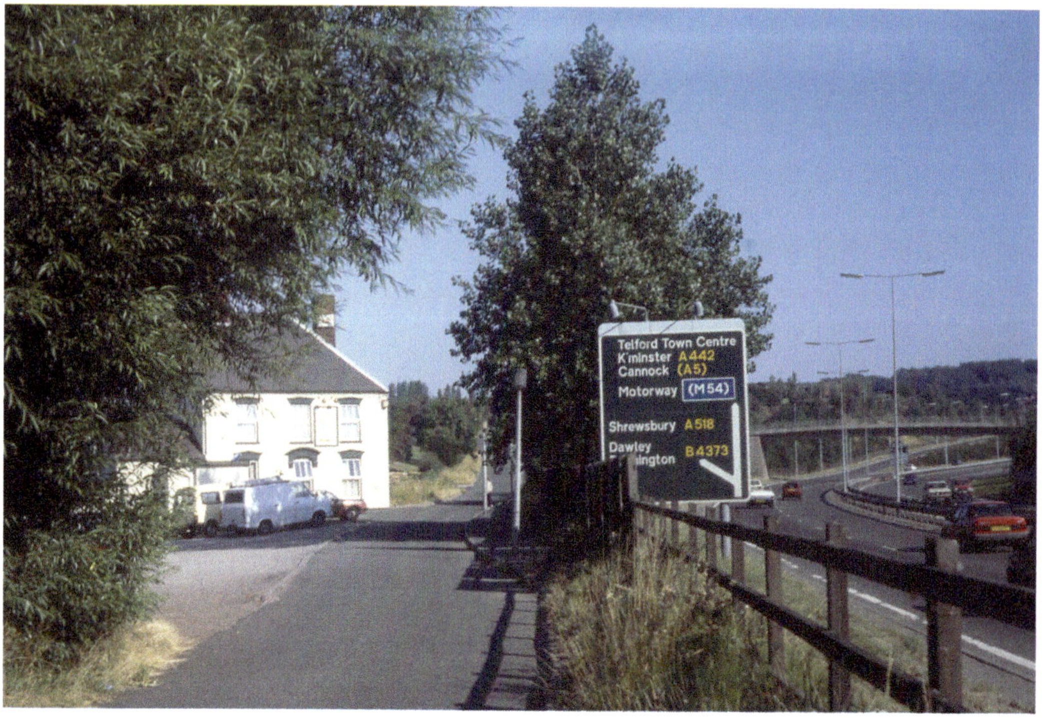

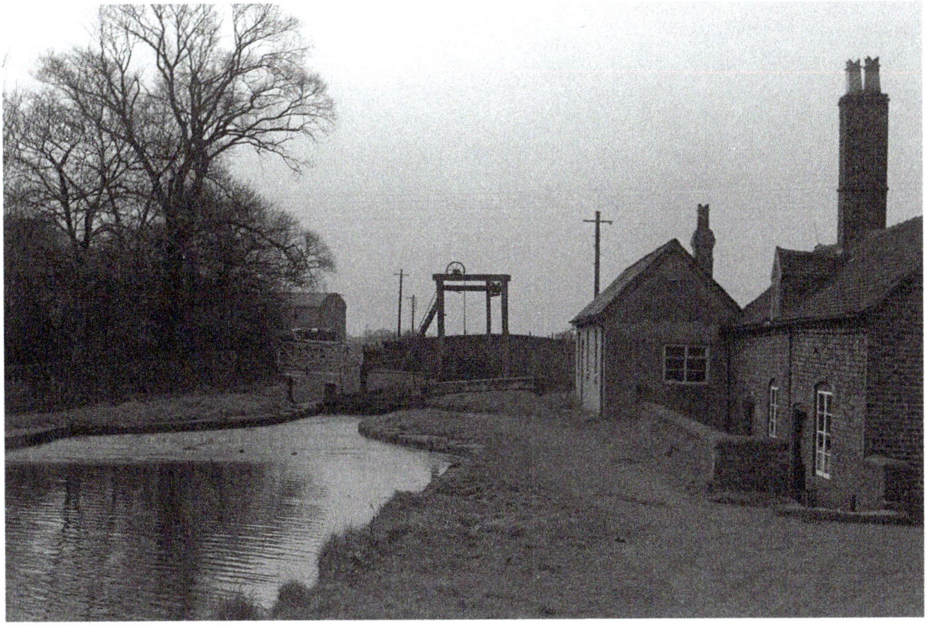

Trench Lock

The first of the eleven locks that took the Shrewsbury Canal 79 feet down to the level of the Weald Moors was at Trench. These locks, measuring 81 feet by 6 feet 7 inches, with a mitred top gate and a lifted 'guillotine' gate at the lower end, were designed to take up to four tub boats. Repairs to the locks and modifications to their lifting mechanism were undertaken in the early 1840s. The photographs show Trench lock some twenty years before the Queensway interchange was built, fittingly named Trench Lock Interchange.

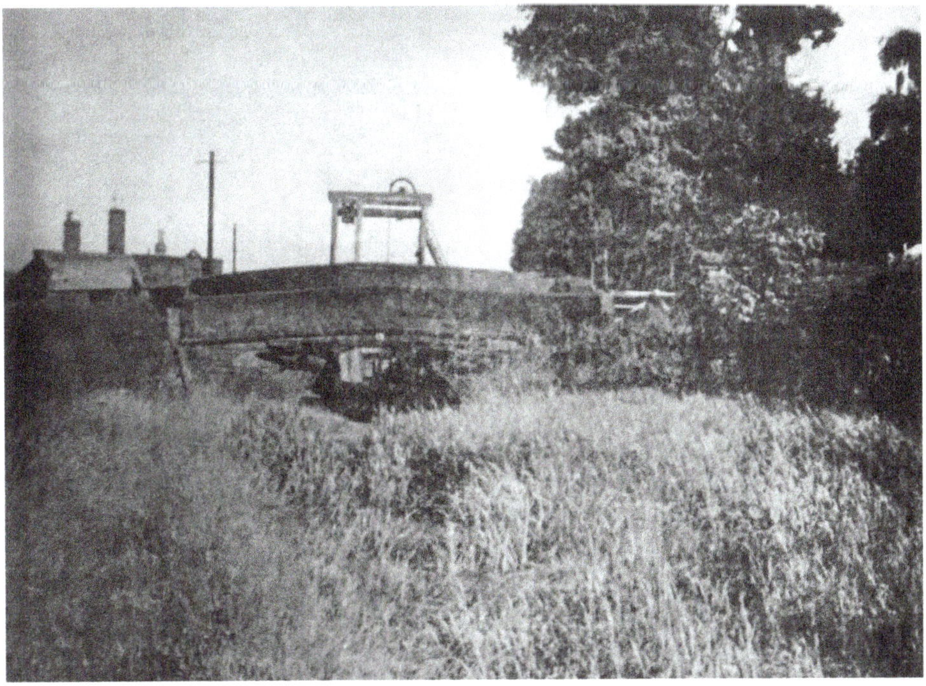

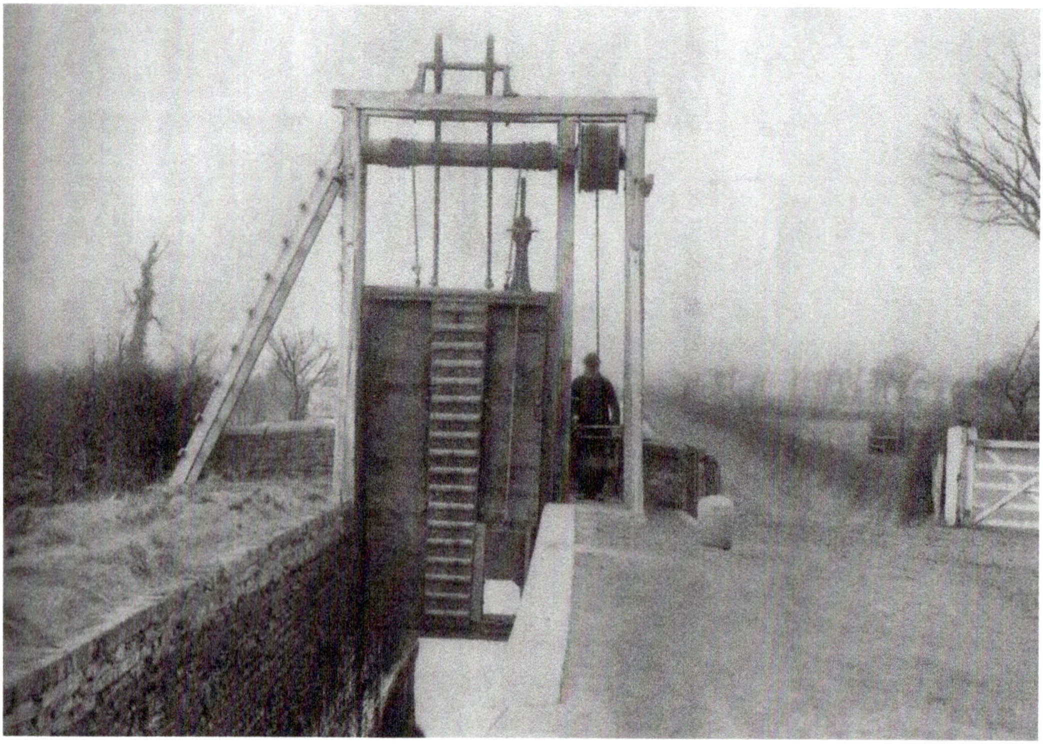

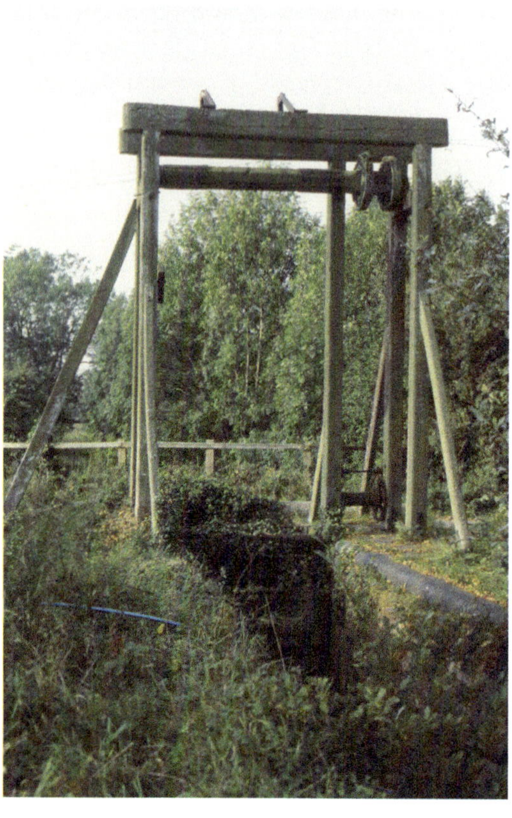

Hadley Park Lock

Hadley Park, the fourth in the series of eleven locks on the Shrewsbury Canal, is one of the two remaining examples with guillotine headgear still partly in place. The top photograph shows the lock soon after the canal was abandoned, and the recent view to the left indicates its present state.

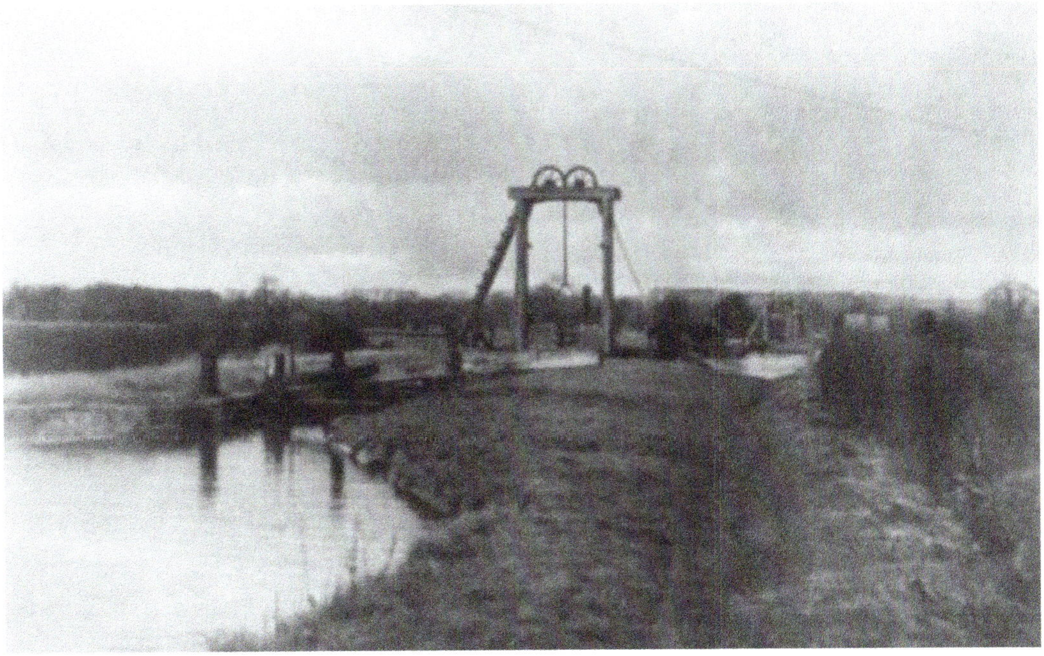

Other Guillotine Locks

Peaty (lock 5), Shucks (6) and Wheat Leasowes (7) are shown in this 1940s photograph (above), all of which are now demolished. When it was agreed to link the Shrewsbury Canal with the B&LJC by the Newport Branch, some bridges and the two Eyton locks were widened on the section between Wappenshall and Shrewsbury. However, on that part of the canal between Trench and Wappenshall, the nine locks and the bridges were not altered. The remaining chamber of the first lock at Eyton (lock 10), which was widened to 7 feet 4 inches, is shown below.

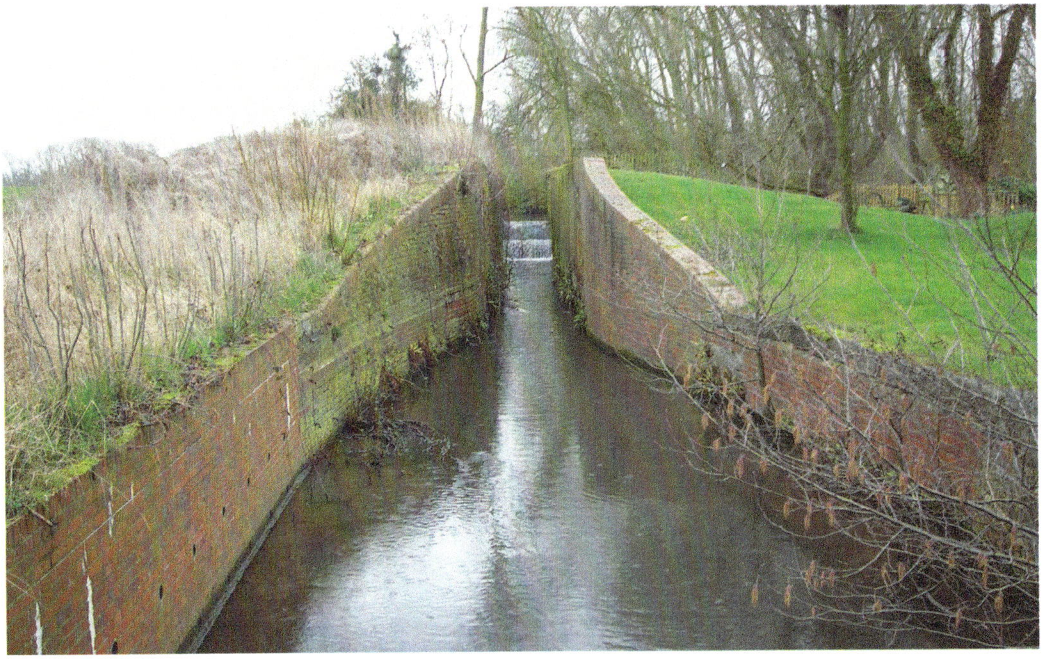

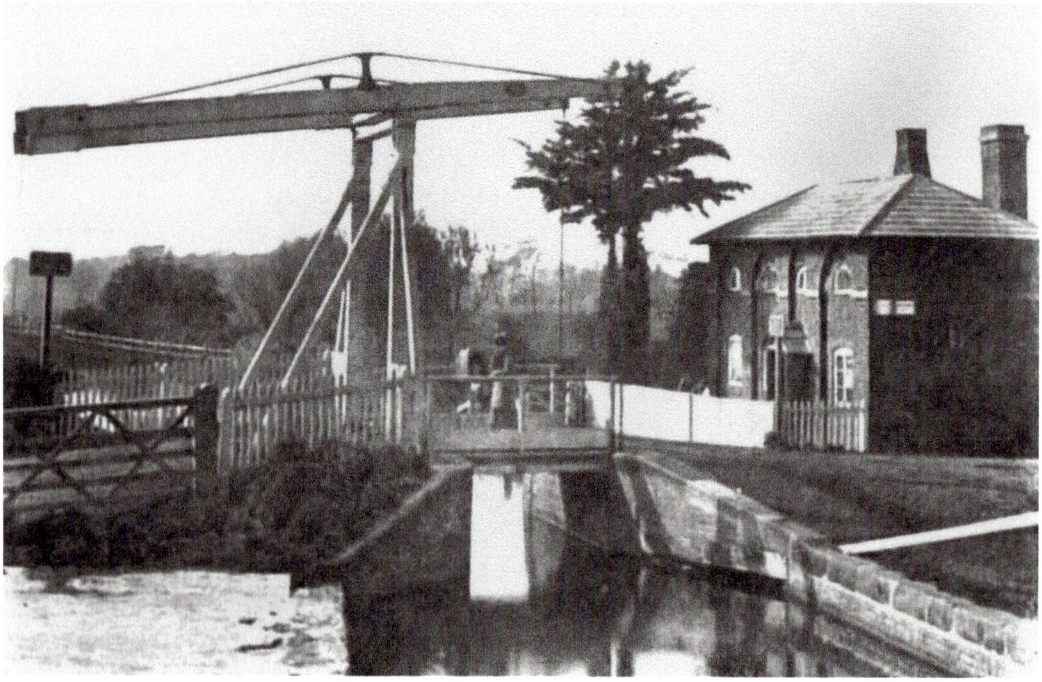

Eyton Upon The Weald Moors

Above: Originally, the road through the village crossed the canal below Eyton lock by a lifting bridge. *Below*: The bridge has gone and the road levelled at this point; the lock keeper's cottage has survived, but only one of its original windows remains.

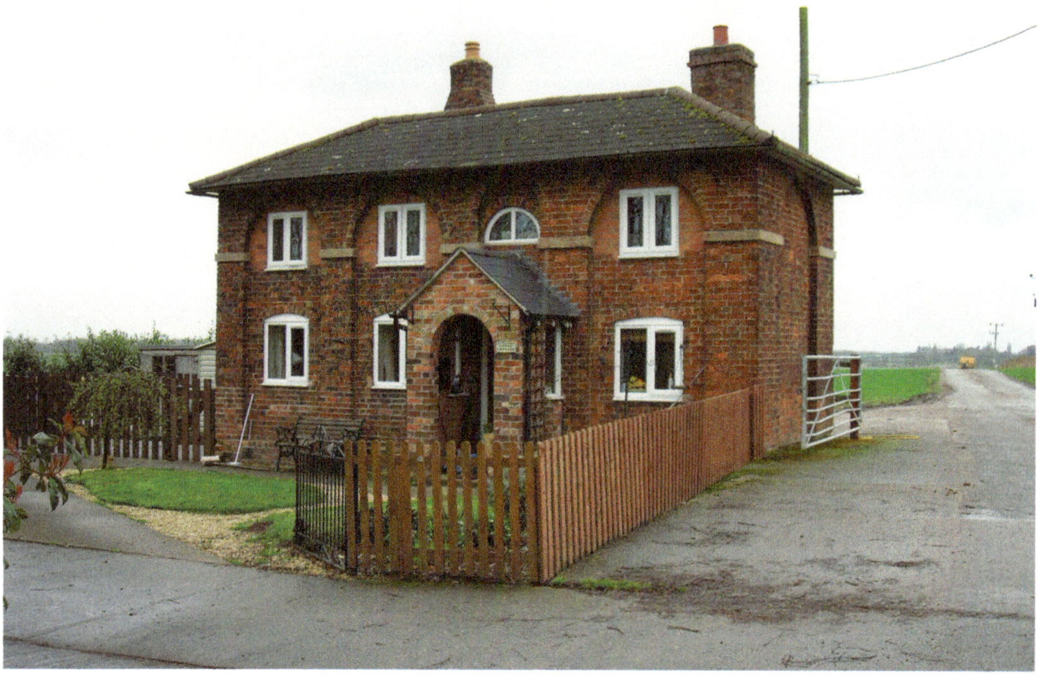

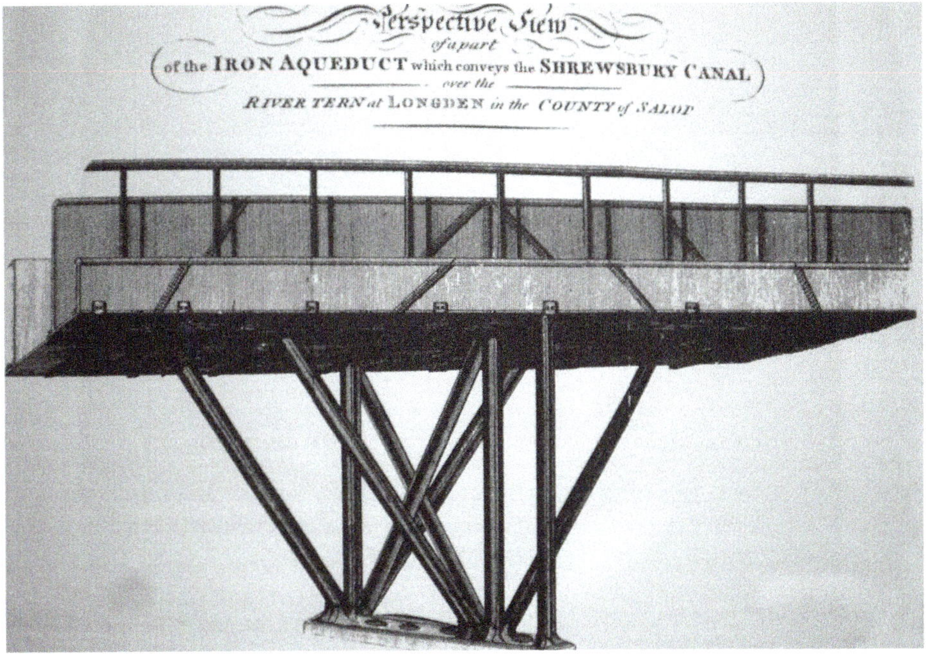

Longdon Aqueduct (1)

With the incline and locks completed by 1794, and Berwick Tunnel well under way, the newly appointed Telford's influence on the Shrewsbury Canal was in the completion of the aqueduct over the River Tern, which had been damaged by the floods of February 1795. Using Clowes' brick and masonry abutments, Telford designed a cast-iron trough on three slender cast-iron piers (above). The iron plates and cruciform-section piers (below) were cast at Reynolds' Ketley works.

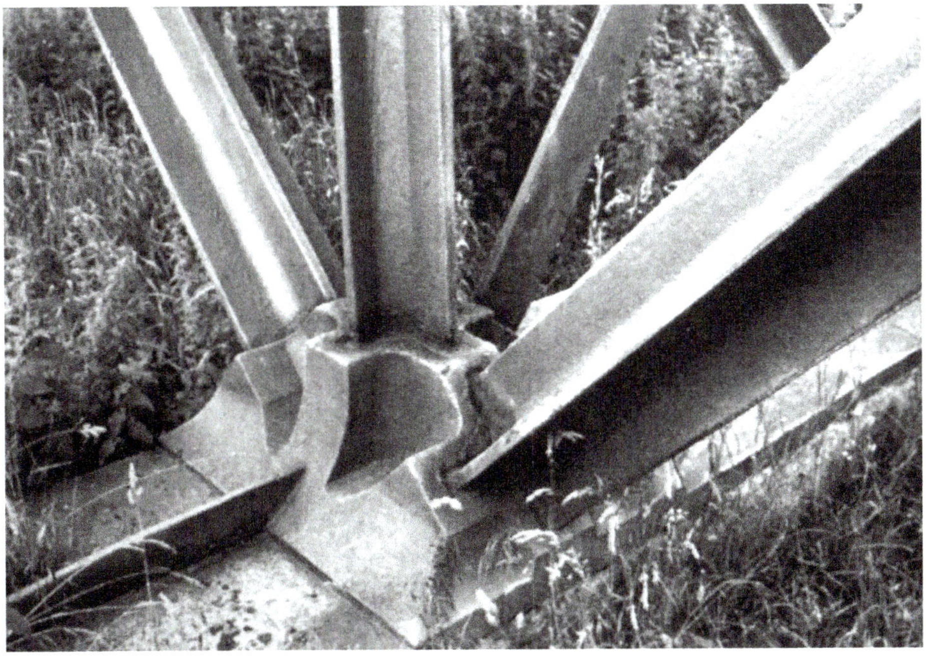

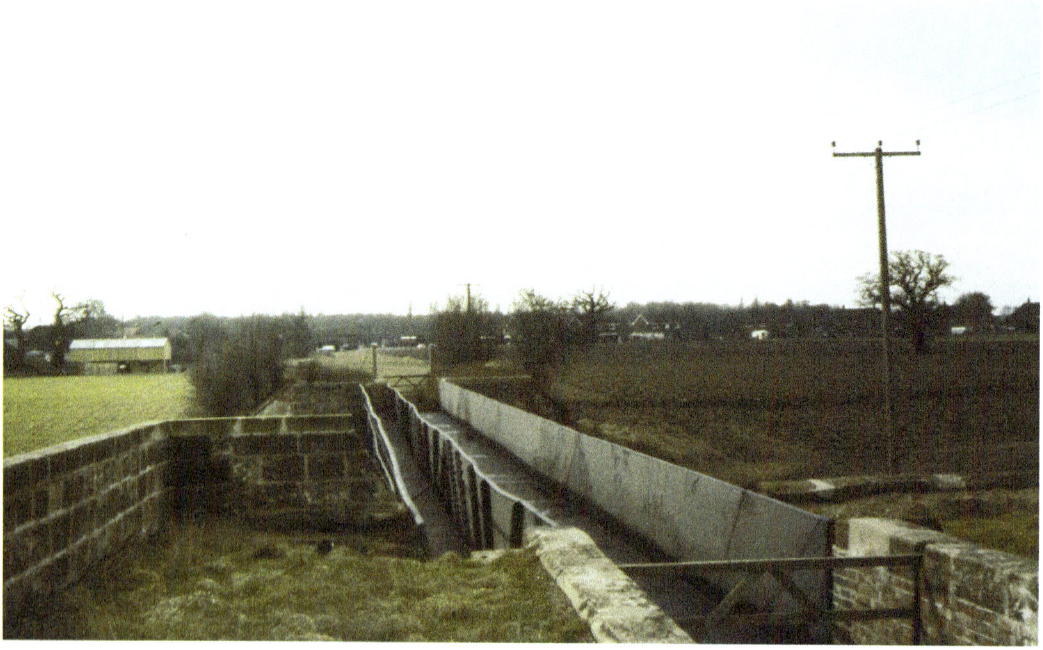

Longdon aqueduct (2)

The aqueduct's cast-iron trough (above), 7-feet 6-inches wide and 4-feet 6-inches deep, with a separate towpath running alongside, was 16 feet above and 62 yards across the river. Work on the aqueduct was completed by November 1796. Longdon was the first major cast-iron canal aqueduct to be built in this country (although a much smaller one on the Derby Canal was completed a month earlier), and it survives in splendid isolation (below).

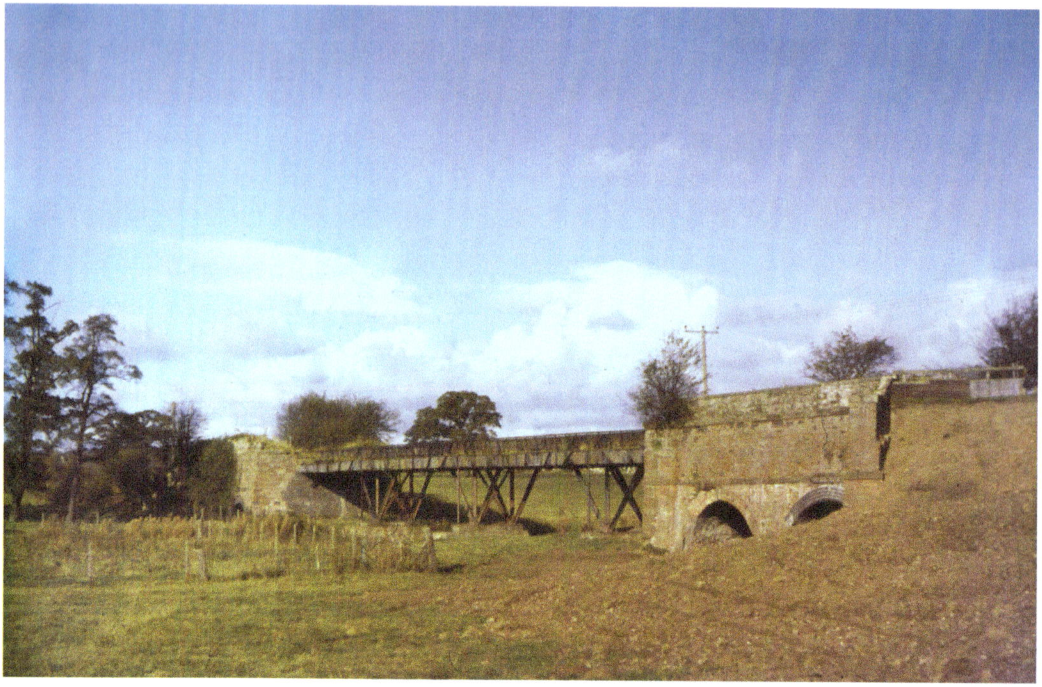

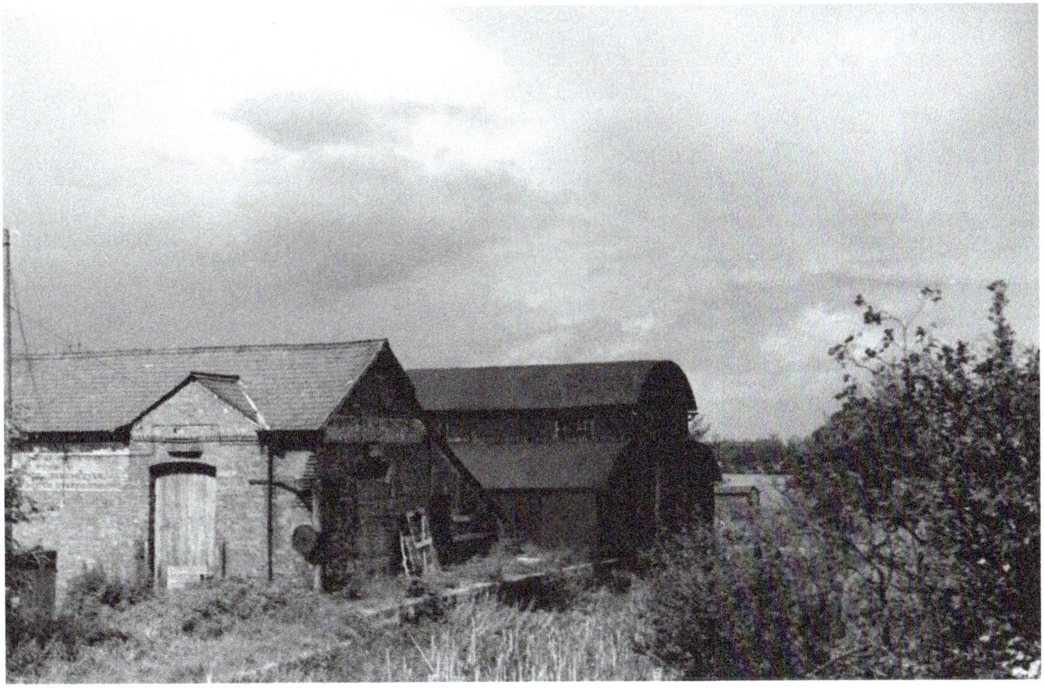

Longdon Wharf And Rodington Aqueduct

There were canal wharves at Long Lane, Longdon-on-Tern (above, twenty years after the canal was abandoned), Berwick and Uffington. The three-arch brick aqueduct, which carried the canal over the River Roden (below), was designed by Josiah Clowes. It was demolished in 1971.

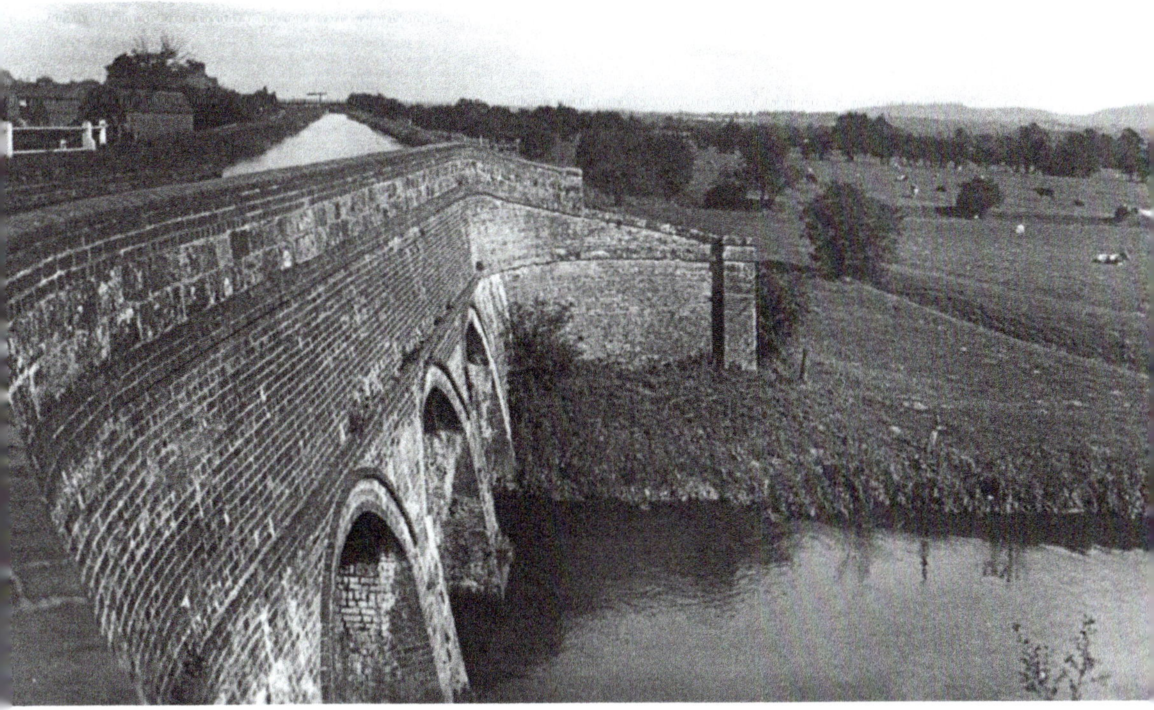

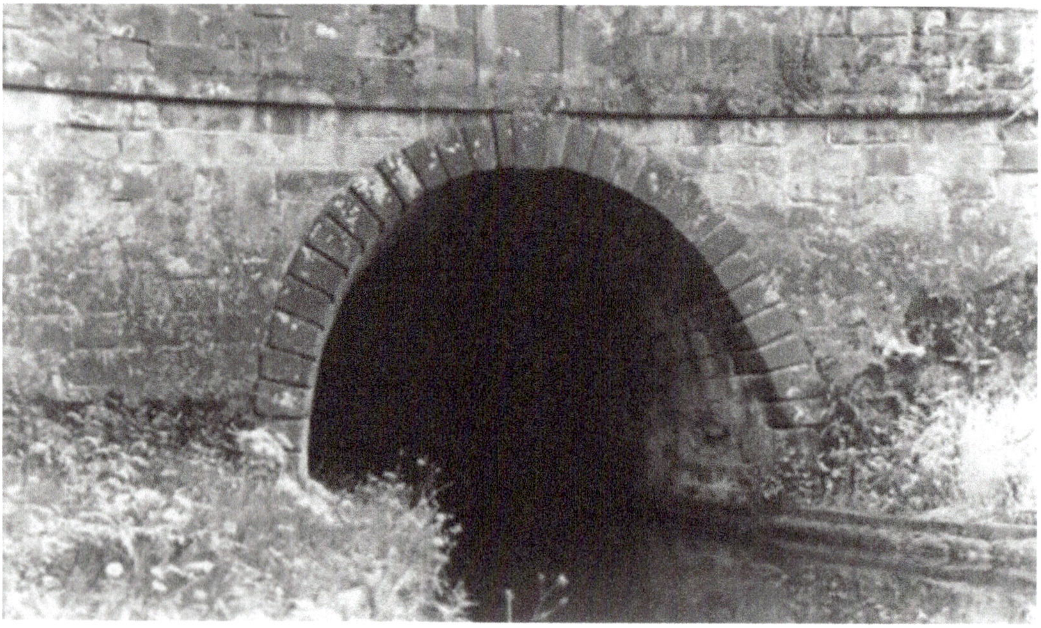

Berwick Tunnel

The canal swung south to avoid Haughmond Hill but still required a tunnel between Berwick and Preston. Berwick Tunnel (above) was 970 yards long and 10 feet wide, including a 3-foot-wide wooden towpath. When this was removed in 1819, 'legging' along the roof was required to get a boat through the tunnel. Vessels that reached the halfway point first had precedence over those coming the other way, but loaded boats heading towards Shrewsbury always had precedence over empty ones. Although the canal was abandoned in 1944, it was not until the 1960s that the two tunnel mouths were blocked up (below).

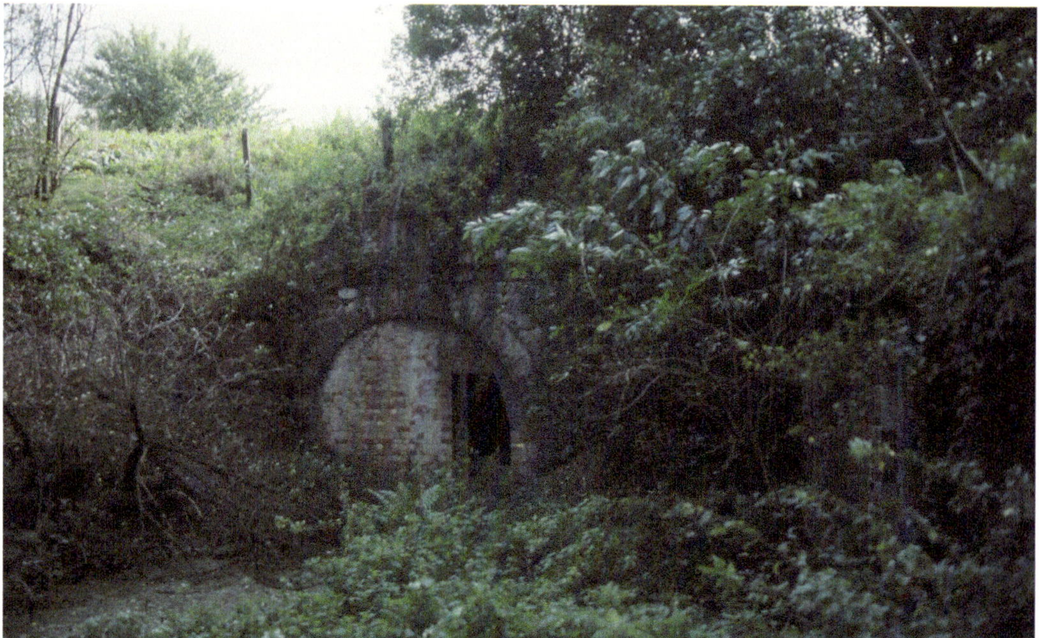

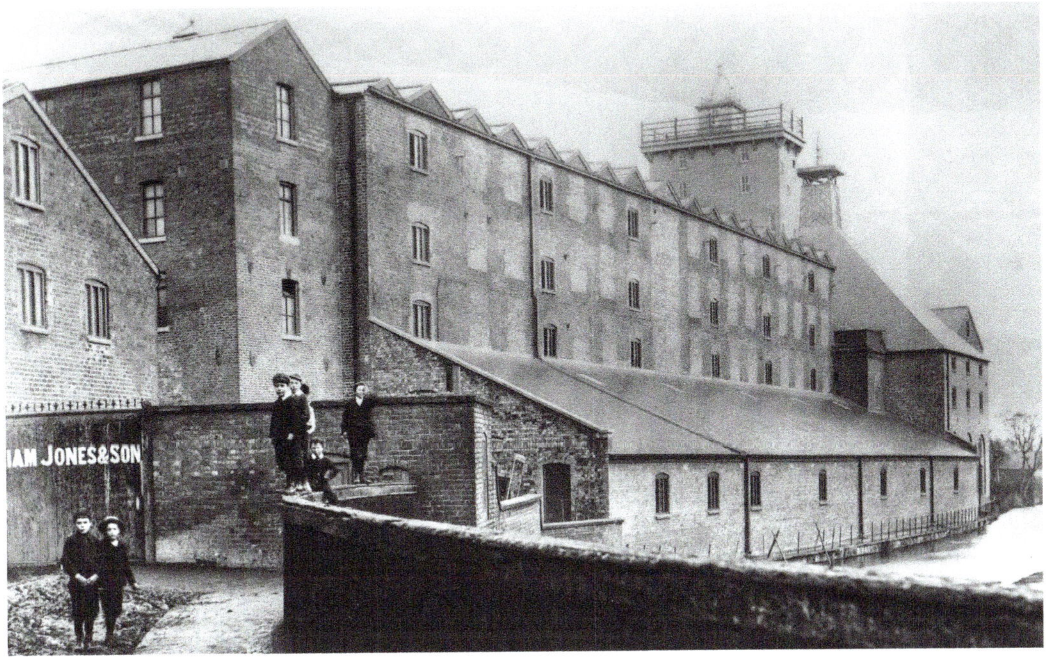

Shrewsbury

Above: The canal was opened to Shrewsbury in February 1797 and supplied coal to the town and to the newly built Flax Mill at Ditherington.

Below: Following the opening of the Newport Branch in 1835, through traffic to Shrewsbury from the national canal network increased and the Butter Market in Howard Street was built to handle the dairy produce brought in from the surrounding area, which was carried by canal from Shrewsbury.

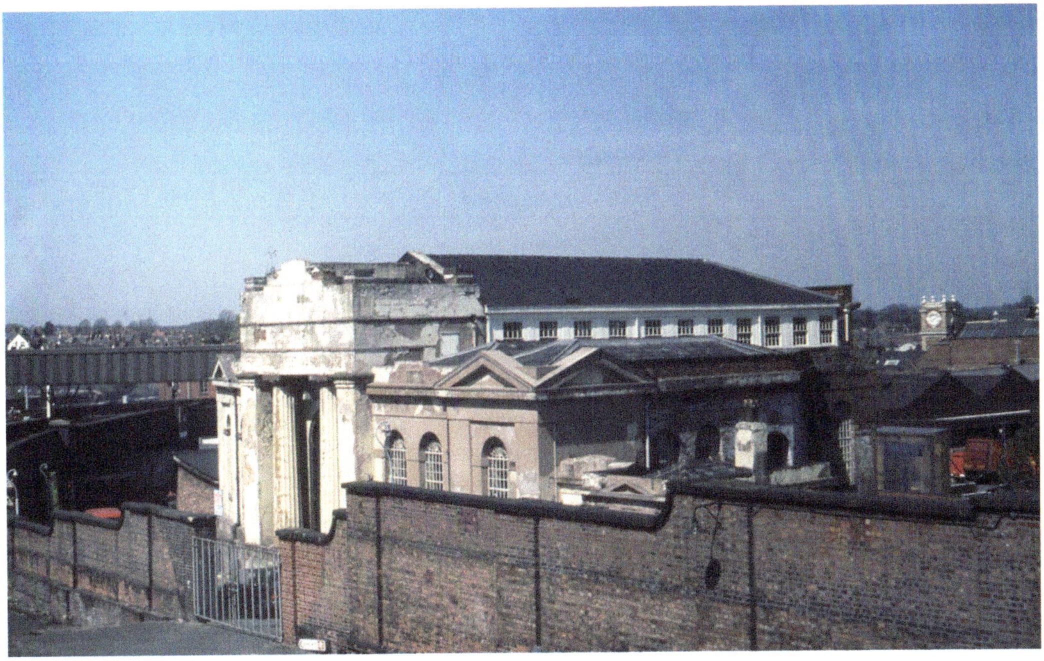

7
The Last Canal

The last canal built in Shropshire was opened at the beginning of the railway age. This was the branch canal that connected the main line of the new B&LJC at Norbury, via Newport, to the Shrewsbury Canal at Wappenshall, and finally linked the East Shropshire tub-boat system to the national narrow-boat canal network. The B&LJC was authorised by Parliament in 1826; for Thomas Telford, who was appointed engineer, this was to be his last canal project. The canal, including the branch, opened throughout in 1835 – a year after Telford's death.

The Newport Branch, built to the same dimensions and style of the main line, was just over 10 miles long. It had twenty-three locks descending westward, seventeen of which were in a flight near to Norbury Junction. There were two aqueducts, found at Forton and Kynnersley. A branch to Lubstree Wharf, near Donnington and serving the Lilleshall Company, was opened in 1844.

The junction between the tub-boat and narrow-boat systems at Wappenshall grew to be an important transhipment centre. In addition to handling goods being exported from the Coalfield area, it dealt with a wide range of imported consumer goods; the road to the wharf became one of the busiest in the area. The wharf's capacity was increased with the opening of a second warehouse in 1838, the ownership of which was retained by the Duke of Sutherland.

In 1846, the Shrewsbury Canal joined the Newport Branch as part of the newly formed Shropshire Union Railways & Canal Company, which itself was leased to the LNWR a year later. The opening of the Shropshire Union railway line from Shrewsbury, via Wellington, to Stafford in June 1849 had a direct impact on the two canals, and traffic declined in the late nineteenth and early twentieth centuries. The last trade on the canal was in the 1930s, and the entire East Shropshire system was officially abandoned in 1944.

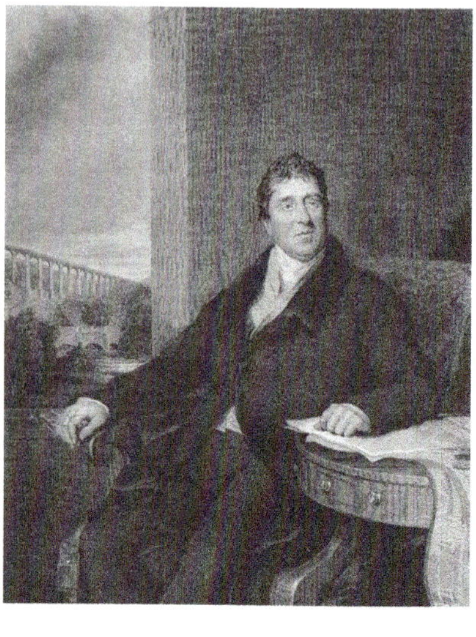

Thomas Telford (1757–1834), the first President of the Institution of Civil Engineers.

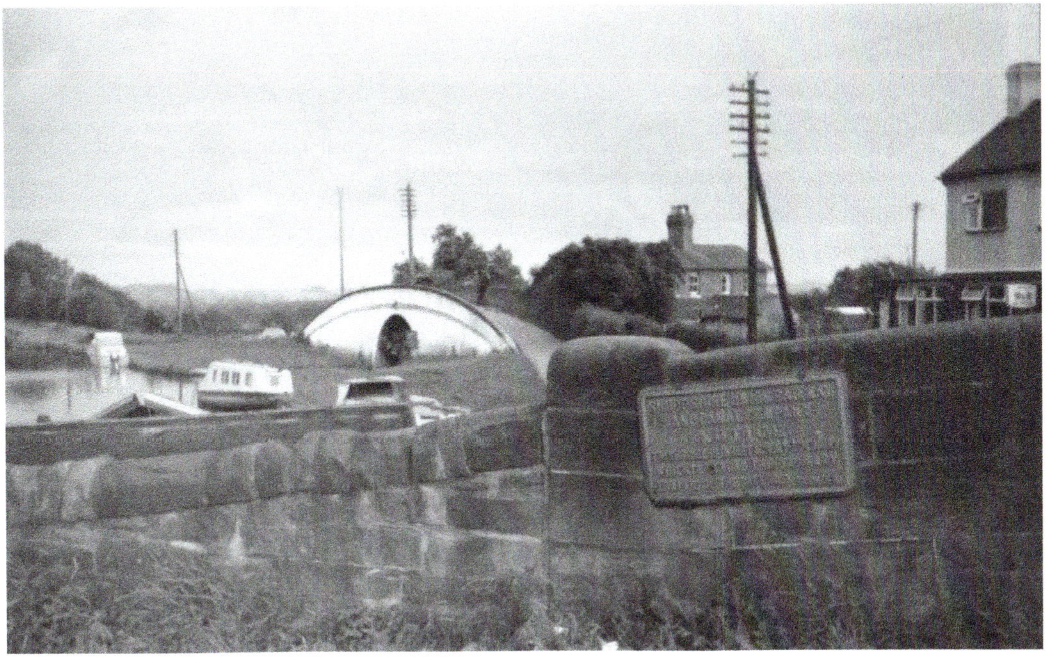

Norbury Junction

Above: The Newport Branch joined the main line of the BLJC near the small Staffordshire village of Norbury. Today, the yard and other facilities there serve the boats using the main line of the Shropshire Union Canal. (Note the misnamed bridge plate in the foreground.)

Below: The 1965 view westward from the towpath overbridge shows a short section of the Newport Branch used for moorings, with a dry dock beyond in what was the first lock. Remains of the canal can still be seen in the next four miles to Newport.

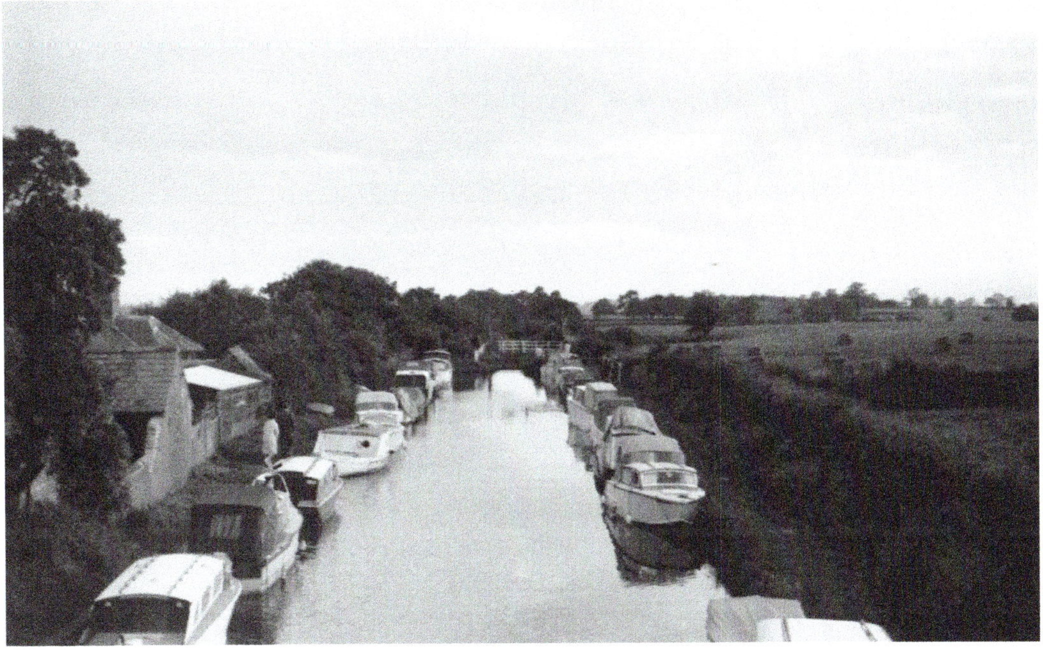

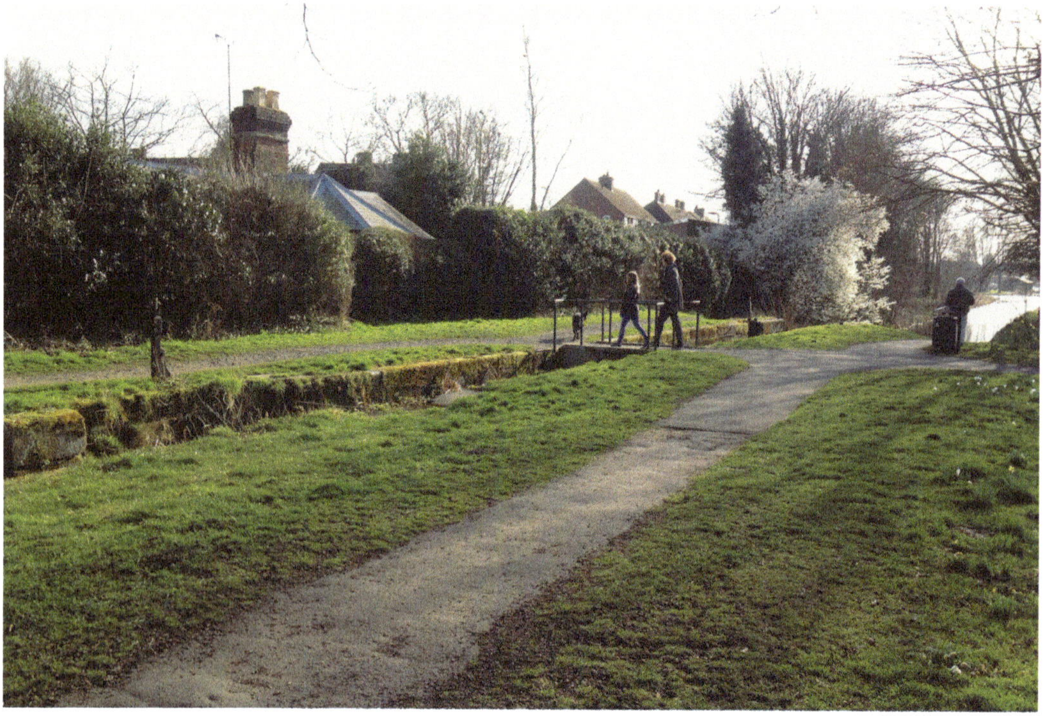

Newport

Above: On the approach to Newport, Haycock's Lock cottage has survived but is now half hidden by hedges.

Below: The section of canal through the town, shown in this early twentieth-century view, is still in water, but the former large warehouse has been removed to Blists Hill Victorian Town open-air museum and lock No. 20 has been dammed.

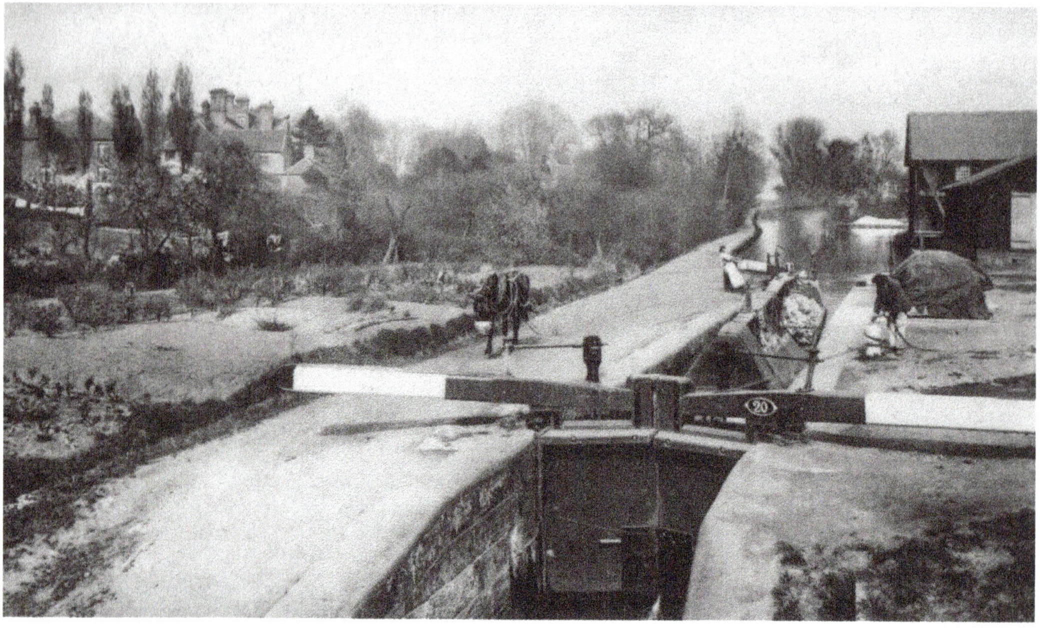

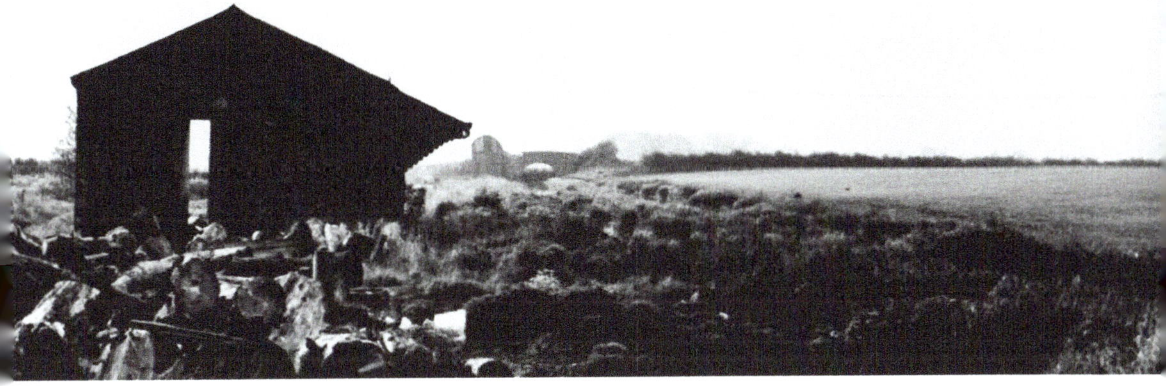

Humber Arm

In addition to Wappenshall Wharf, the Duke of Sutherland also owned Lubstree Wharf at the end of the short, ¾-mile section of the Newport Branch, known as the Humber Arm. This opened in 1844 and served the nearby mines and ironworks of the Lilleshall Company; it handled more traffic when a railway link from the wharf to the company's works was built in 1870. The remains of the rail-canal interchange building can be seen in these 1970s views, looking north (above) and south (below).

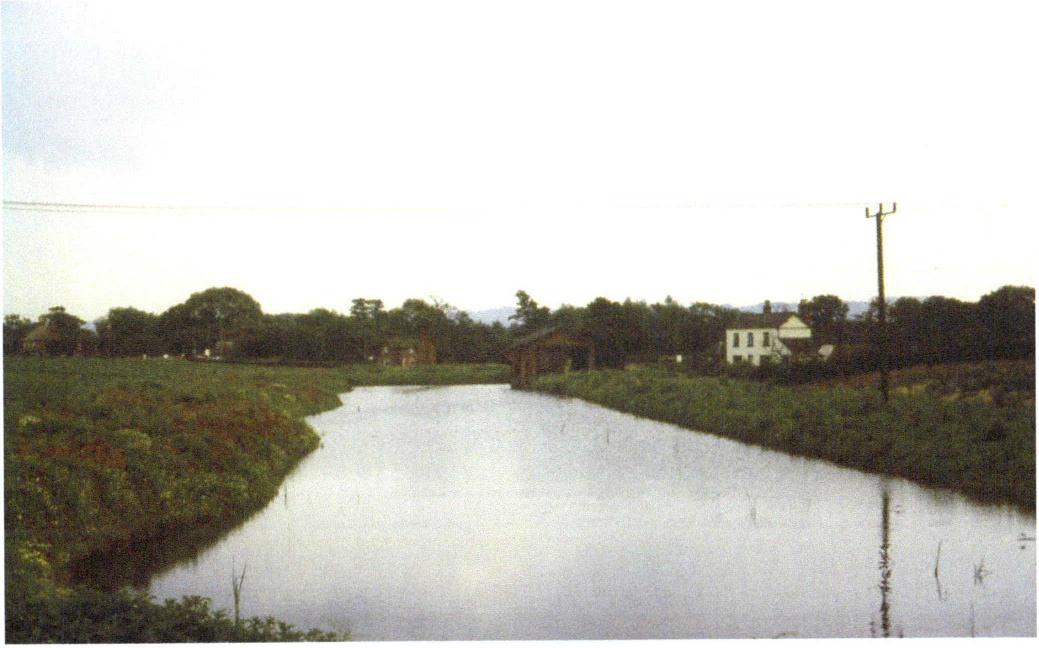

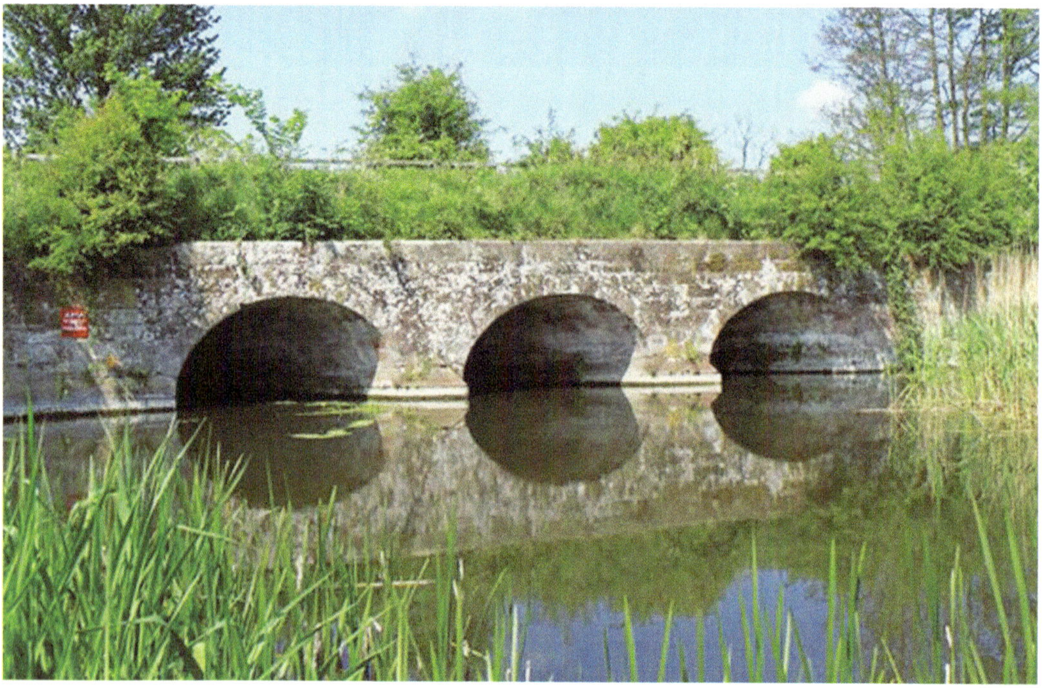

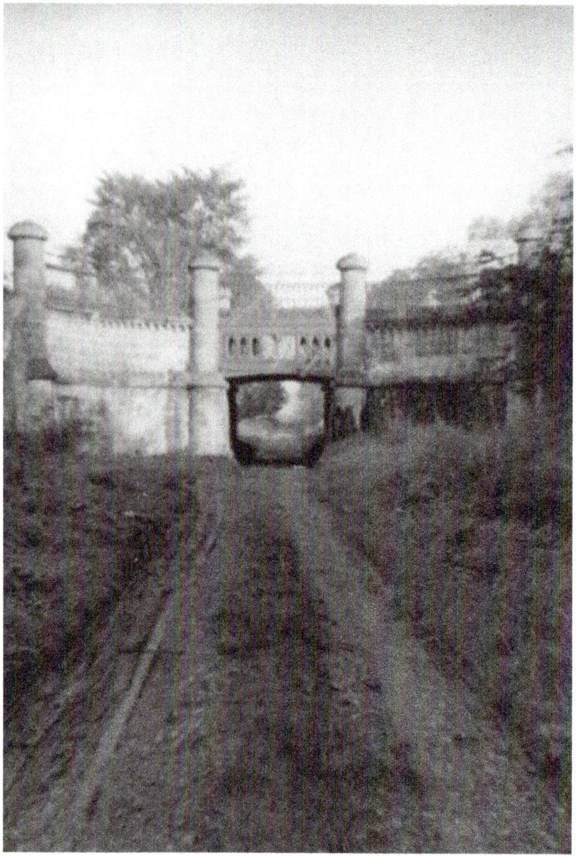

Aqueducts

Above: Between Norbury and Newport, the canal crossed the River Meese on the three-arch Forton Aqueduct, which is still intact.

Left: The ornate Kynnersley aqueduct carried the canal in a brick-lined trough enclosed in a cast-iron bridge over the Duke of Sutherland's drive linking Lilleshall with the village of Kynnersley. It was demolished in the mid-1960s.

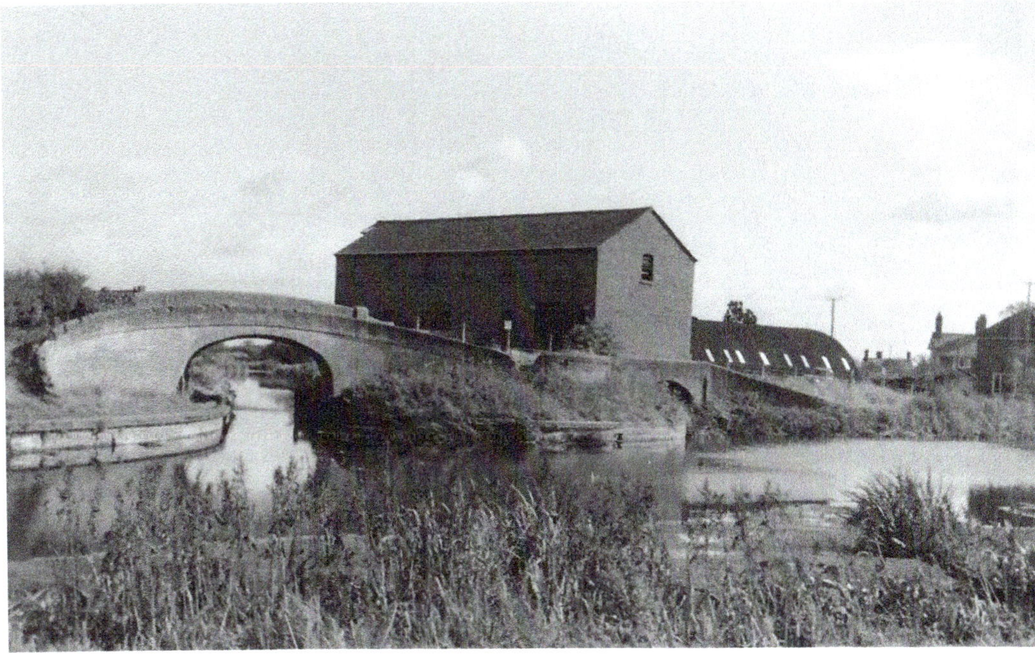

Wappenshall Junction

The transhipment and storage arrangements at Wappenshall can be seen in views of the junction in the 1960s, some twenty years after closure. Tub boats and specially built 6-foot 7-inch-wide narrow boats operated on the section of the Shrewsbury Canal to Trench (on the right of the above photograph), whereas conventional narrow boats worked through from the main line at Norbury to Wappenshall (below) and beyond to Shrewsbury.

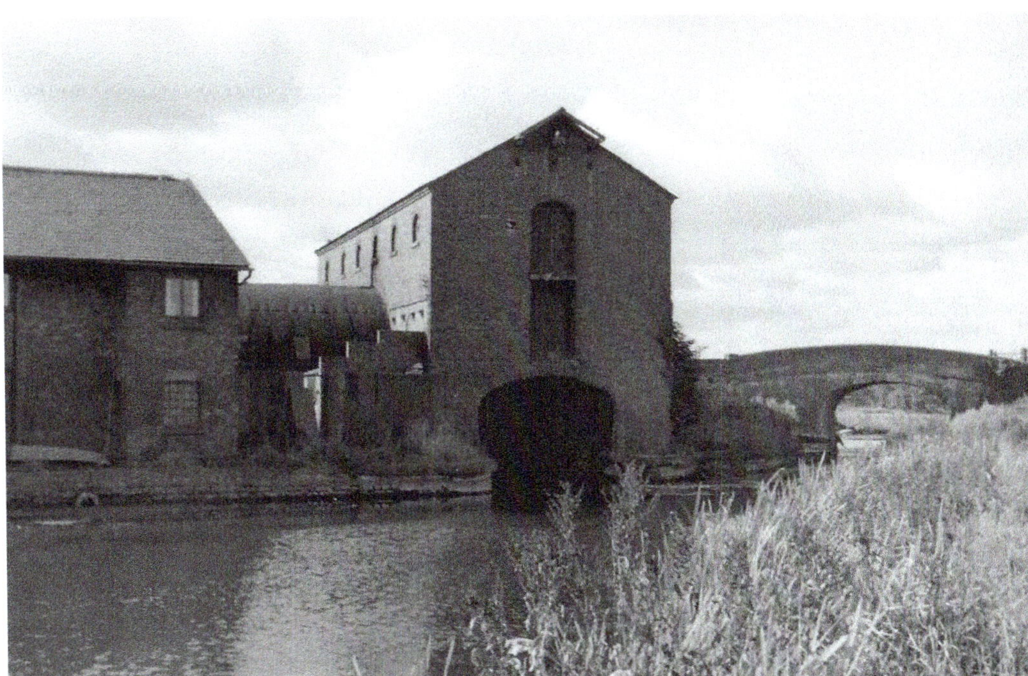

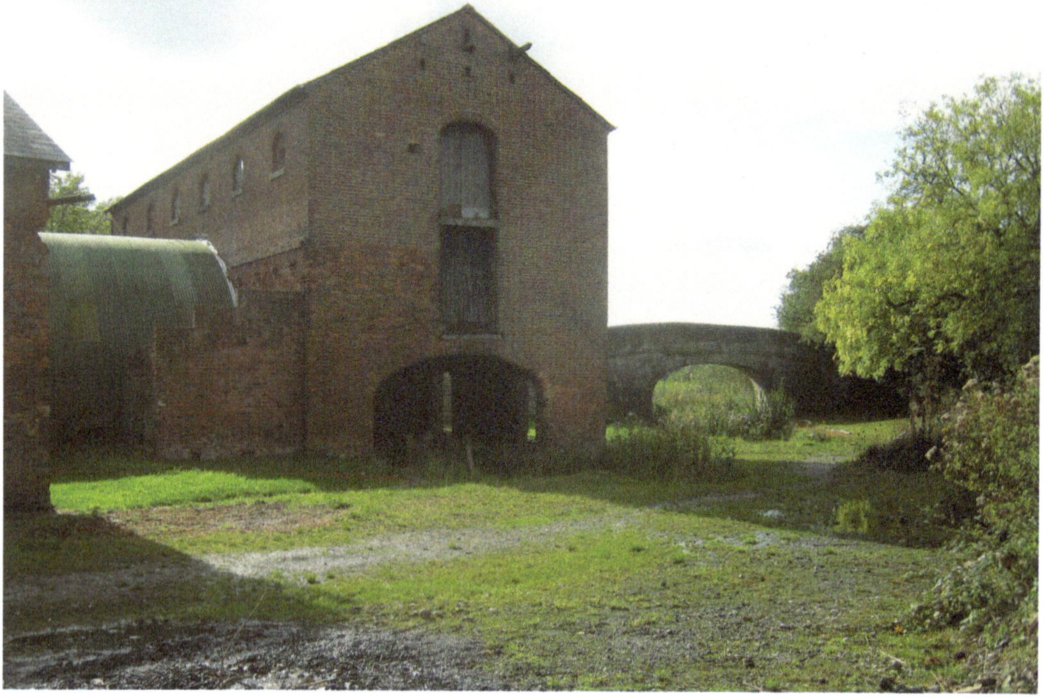

Today And Tomorrow

Following earlier attempts at restoration in the 1960s, the Shrewsbury & Newport Canals Trust was set up in 2000 to return the canals between Norbury Junction and Shrewsbury to navigation. With the assistance of Telford & Wrekin Council, the trust has acquired the warehouses at Wappenshall as it headquarters (above), and plans are in place to restore this site first (below).

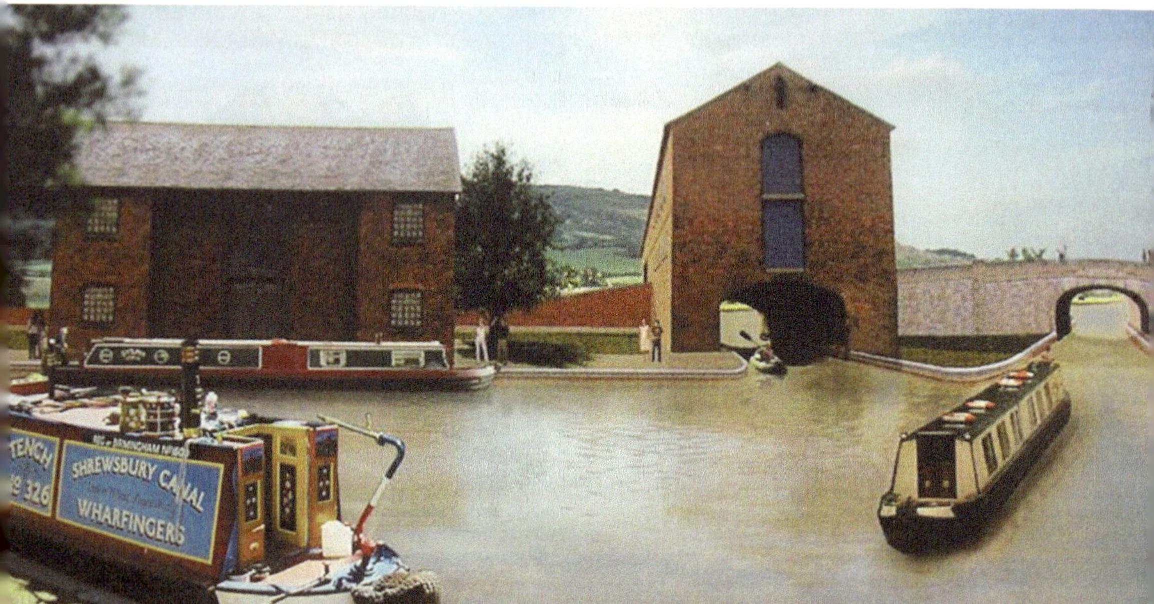